CORRUPTION

AND MARKET IN

CONTEMPORARY

CHINA

CORRUPTION

AND MARKET IN

CONTEMPORARY

CHINA

YAN SUN

CORNELL UNIVERSITY PRESS

Ithaca and London

First published 2004 by Cornell University Press
First printing, Cornell Paperbacks, 2004

Printed in the United States of America

Library of Congress Cataloging-in-Publication Data

Sun, Yan, 1959–
    Corruption and market in contemporary China / Yan Sun.
        p. cm.
    Includes bibliographical references and index.
    ISBN 0-8014-4284-2 (cloth : alk. paper) — ISBN 0-8014-8942-3 (pbk. :
alk. paper)
    1. Political corruption—China.   I. Title.
    JQ1509.5.C6S88 2004
    364.1′323′0951—dc22

                                                                        2004007180

Cornell University Press strives to use environmentally responsible suppliers
and materials to the fullest extent possible in the publishing of its books.
Such materials include vegetable-based, low-VOC inks and acid-free
papers that are recycled, totally chlorine-free, or partly composed of
nonwood fibers. For further information, visit our website at
www.cornellpress.cornell.edu.

Cloth printing   10 9 8 7 6 5 4 3 2 1
Paperback printing   10 9 8 7 6 5 4 3 2 1

For Ben, Kenny, and Gang
and
For my parents

CONTENTS

TABLES AND FIGURES

PREFACE

The Tiananmen Protests of 1989 first drew me to the issue of corruption. Traveling in several Chinese cities that summer, including Beijing, I learned firsthand that most public grievances were directed at the rise of official corruption since urban reforms in 1984. Foreign media talked a lot about a prodemocracy movement, but my observations and conversations left me in no doubt that corruption was the rallying point for the citizens. Two years later, I published my first professional article, "The Tiananmen Protests of 1989: The Key Issue of Corruption" in *Asian Survey*. At that time, "corruption" mainly referred to profiteering by the children of well-placed officials—buying low from the state plan and selling high in the market. This type of corruption subsided with the end of central planning in 1992.

I returned to China for another extended summer in 1995, and corruption was again the topic of the country. Beijing's deputy mayor committed suicide in the spring amid panic over investigations into his and his aides' abuses. The mayor, Chen Xitong, resigned over related scandals, and both he and his son were eventually convicted. A mere three years after the launch of full transition to the market, it seemed, corruption was returning with a vengeance. With corruption as a research topic in mind, I visited the library and bookstores of a local law school. There I encountered many books, textbooks, legal documents, and casebooks on corruption. I was fascinated by a rich reservoir of sources to which I could have such easy access. On the law school campus, I talked to some faculty members about the issue, among them the author of one of the casebooks that I would later use for this study. From there, my experience with the corruption and anticorruption realities of China grew into this book.

I have been frequently asked, by those unfamiliar with China as well as some of those who know the country, "Aren't you afraid of getting into trouble? Isn't it dangerous to look for and sneak out the materials?" Such questions are asked with particular earnestness when alleged cases of espionage capture the headlines. Yet the sources I use are not classified or sensitive material: they can be found in law schools, libraries, bookstores, and party offices, to which every Chinese can have access. The only time I ran into a little trouble had to do with Henry Wu, the so-called human rights activist based at the Hoover Institution. During the summer of 1995, Wu was arrested in China for sneaking into prisons and hospitals and fabricating evidence for his foreign-funded programs. His use of false identities and his covert activities were widely reported in the Chinese media. I began to worry a little, not about my own safety, but about whether the law school librarians who welcomed me every day would become apprehensive about the real nature of my research. Luckily those young women seemed apolitical and did not pay attention to that sort of news. Things went smoothly until one morning I went to the local branch of the CCP's Disciplinary Inspection Commission (DIC), the party's main instrument against corruption.

On learning of my research interests, two officials in the documents office were warm and supportive, allowing me to photocopy materials and purchase their publications. Encouraged by their openness and friendliness, I left my business card with them. Apparently they did not recollect Henry Wu's story at that particular moment. They sent me off warmly and promised to answer any further questions I might have. I headed off downtown for more bookstores. Returning to my parents' residence, I found the two DIC officials anxiously waiting for me. They wanted me to return all their materials to them, worrying that if something like the Henry Wu incident were to happen, they—not I—would be in serious trouble. In fact, they had arrived at my parents' place soon after I had left their office, even calling the DIC office on my parents' college campus to make sure there was nothing in my family's background that would produce a treacherous daughter.

It was apparent that they were concerned, not about any damage I might bring to China by exposing its dark side, but by damage I might do to their careers. Since this was the mid-1990s, when Chinese citizens no longer feared political repercussions, my parents asked if they, as local residents, could purchase the same materials. The answer was affirmative: if my parents then passed those materials to me, the matter was not their official responsibility, and so it did not concern them. Unflappable, my father went back to the DIC office a few days later and got the same materials from the same two individuals. I have been subscribing to the monthly digest published by that office ever since. This journal, titled *Dangfeng Lianzheng Wenzhai* before 1999 and *Dangfeng Lianzheng* thereafter, is my single most important source. For the record, I have never had any trouble carrying these and other materials in and out of China. They are openly published materials, and it is not unlawful to take them out of the country.

I have many colleagues and friends to thank for the development and maturation of the project. My chairwoman Patricia Rachal helped arrange time and latitude for me to carry out the research. My colleague Andrew Hacker gave me the idea that I should not use abstract theories and models but real stories to convey a concrete sense of what corruption is really like in China. He read various drafts during the course of my writing. My colleague Lenny Markovitz's unfailing faith kept me going, and I value all the intellectual and moral support he has given me along the way. Donald Zagoria, my colleague from another CUNY campus, has been a reliable source of advice and encouragement since we finally met in the spring of 2003. My chairwoman at CUNY Graduate Center, Ruth O'Brien, gave me advice on the politics and mechanics of publishing, and offered moral support. Alvin So, at Hong Kong University of Science and Technology, and James Tang, at Hong Kong University, provided generous support while in Hong Kong. He Gaochao, formerly at Hong Kong University of Science and Technology, offered fruitful discussions and insightful comments.

I am deeply indebted to Minxin Pei, who offered generous advice and encouragement whenever I needed it. I am equally grateful to a few of his former colleagues at Princeton University, especially Lynn White III and Gil Rozman, who both attended a seminar where I presented a very early version of this project. Professor White provided many helpful comments on my manuscript, and his suggestions were indispensable in my revision of the introductory chapter. I also benefited from comments from members of the Modern China Seminar at the East Asian Institute, Columbia University, where I presented an early version of chapter 2. Andrew Nathan and Tom Bernstein at EAI provided challenging insights, inspiration, and gracious advice over the course of my manuscript preparation. In particular, Professor Bernstein's suggestion regarding state capacities, along with Elizabeth Remick's concerning disincentives, resulted in chapter 6 here. Professor Remick's comments also helped me to think more clearly about the relationship between corruption and the economic reform process. Kellee Tsai's comments helped me to sharpen the analytical framework of the book as well as to strengthen the organization and presentation of the introductory chapter.

A special word of thanks is reserved for Roger Haydon, my editor at Cornell University Press. Roger appreciated the importance of the topic from the beginning and has remained enthusiastic about the manuscript throughout the strenuous process of reviews, revisions, and editorial work. I have benefited greatly from his interest, enthusiasm, efficiency, and great editorial skills.

To all of the aforementioned people, I express my deep gratitude: they deserve whatever credit this book may get, whereas I own its faults and errors.

For research support, I thank the Research Foundation of the City University of New York for three research grants for the project; a Presidential Research Award from CUNY Queens College; and a faculty research mentoring fellowship from the college. Jianming Yang and Wai Yan Ng, along with several other students involved in the mentoring fellowship, provided research assistance. I also express appreciation to the University Seminars at Columbia University for their help in publishing this book. Material in this work was presented at the University Seminar on Modern China.

To Ben, Kenny, and Gang I am grateful for their putting up with my hours in front of the computer. My children almost think being a professor is a cool profession, since I get to sit so much in front of the screen while they are allocated only limited amounts of computer time.

A final word about translation matters. Since I use such an abundance of Chinese sources, I give the titles of Chinese articles in English. Only Chinese book titles appear in both Pinyin and English translation. Nor are Chinese articles referenced in the bibliography. Though many of the articles come from the monthly digest, *Dangfeng Lianzheng Wenzhai,* they were originally published in a wide range of national and regional periodicals. Space does not allow me to identify the original publication in which each first appeared. Rather, a list of periodicals from which the articles were digested is provided in Appendix 2, along with English translation.

The Chinese currency values frequently cited in this book should be understood in the context of not only the exchange rate but also the average income and purchase power parity. China's official exchange rate prior to 1994 was $1 to Y5.75 and still lower in the early 1980s, but the black market rate could go as high as $1 to Y10–12 in the early 1990s. The *yuan* has been pegged to the dollar at $1 to Y8.28 since 1994, and the black market for the dollar has also subsided since. When converted to the dollar, a bribe of Y10,000 may not look extraordinary at first—about $1250. But given that the annual income averages between Y8,000–Y16,000 ($1,000–$2,000) in urban China, the bribe then amounts to the entire annual salary of an average Chinese. Added to the factor of purchase power parity, Y10,000 feels more like $10,000 in actual value in the Chinese context.

YAN SUN

New York City and Barrington, Rhode Island

ABBREVIATIONS

ICMB	Industry and Commerce Management Bureaus
CCPDIC	Chinese Communist Party Discipline Inspection Commission
DIC	Discipline Inspection Commission
DFLZ	*Dangfeng Lianzheng* (Party Ethics and Government Integrity)
DFLZWZ	*Dangfeng Lianzheng Wenzhai* (Digest of Party Ethics and Government Integrity
RMRB	*Renmin Ribao* (People's Daily)
PC	People's Congress
PCC	Political Consultative Conference
PPC	Provincial People's Congress
PPCC	Provincial Political Consultative Conference
SEZ	Special Economic Zone
SOE	State-owned enterprise
TVE	Township and village enterprise

CORRUPTION

AND MARKET IN

CONTEMPORARY

CHINA

INTRODUCTION

The Transition to the Market and Corruption

"For thFe past several years, wealthy Chinese officials, businessmen, bookies and gangsters have been cutting a golden path to the casinos of Las Vegas, losing vast sums of money, much of it not theirs. Their exploits combine capitalist-style excesses of the rich and famous with post-Communist sleaze, and Vegas's glitter with China's ancient fascination with gaming, while reflecting China's mind-boggling corruption and its record-breaking economic growth."[1] On first look, most readers would find it hard to believe that this *Washington Post* report, dated March 26, 2002, was talking about mainland China. There, in a land that Westerners still frequently refer to as a Communist country, gambling houses of the world have opened offices to attract and serve big clients. As the *Post* report continued, "Starting several years ago, the MGM Grand, Harrah's, the Venetian, Caesars Palace and the Stratosphere, among others, opened offices in China or began dispatching representatives to China to organize groups of high-stakes gamblers. Casinos from South Korea, the Philippines, Australia and North Korea have followed suit." Fast becoming the gambling world's leading source of growth, "high rollers from China and the amount they are willing to gamble have captured the imaginations of Vegas's gambling industry." Many of those "fat cats" are gov-

[1] John Pomfret, "China's High Rollers Find a Seat at Table—in Vegas—Wealthy Aren't Afraid to Blow Millions, Especially When the Money Isn't Theirs," *Washington Post,* March 26, 2002.

ernment officials and CEOs of state firms who have embezzled public funds and taken huge bribes, or business people who have acquired huge wealth through smuggling, tax evasion, or other dubious activities.

Like other former socialist economies that have undergone monumental transition, post-Mao China has experienced unprecedented levels of corruption. Almost every public opinion survey since the late 1980s has shown corruption to be the top concern among the general public. It was this very issue, rather than democratization per se, that contributed to the widespread social roots of the Tiananmen protest movement of 1989. More than a decade later, corruption has not been tamed by greater economic liberalization. Rather, it has grown routine and more severe in character, scope, and scale. In Chinese popular perceptions, there were more honest officials than dishonest ones in the first decade of reform (1980s), but the reverse may hold true in the second. One folk saying vividly illustrates how the public views the problem: "If the Party executes every official for corruption, it will overdo a little; but if the Party executes every other official for corruption, it cannot go wrong." Bribe taking has become such an accustomed practice that in one poor county, the party secretary received repeated death threats for rejecting Y600,000 in bribes during his tenure from 1999 to 2001. He had to be promoted to a different location against his will.[2] In another region with officially impoverished counties, a delegation of the UN Food and Agriculture Organization arrived for a local conference on development. On seeing rows of imported luxury cars at the conference site, they reputedly asked, "Are you really poor?"[3] The outbreak of SARS in the spring of 2003 inspired scathing political humor that again underscored the extent of cadre abuse: "Lavish dining and wining, the Party cannot cure it, SARS did it. Public funded sightseeing, the Party cannot cure it, SARS did it. A sea of documents and meetings, the Party cannot cure it, SARS did it. Deceiving those above and cheating those below, the Party cannot cure it, SARS did it. Frequenting prostitutes, the Party cannot cure it, SARS did it!" The evolution and character of cadre abuse under China's market reforms since 1978 is the subject of this book.

The meaning of corruption is a complex and contested one. Some conceptions emphasize "public office" and "legalistic" criteria, defining corruption as deviation from the duties of the public office and the confines of the law. Yet such criteria suffer from problems of identifying clear roles and rules, while leaving little room for the richness and subtlety of cultural and social settings. Other conceptions emphasize "public interest" and "public opinion" factors, defining corruption as deviation from public interests and public

[2] Wu Xiaofeng and Jiang Niao, "Repeated Threats against a County Party Secretary Who Declined Y600,000 in Bribes," DFLZ 8 (2001): 38–40.
[3] "The Hot Waves of Automobiles," DFLZWZ 7 (1994): 9–10.

opinions. But such definitions suffer from imprecision and political maneuverability. For societies in transition, in particular, corruption is often a politically contested or unresolved concept, further complicating the matter.[4] In the Chinese context, those who favor effective enforcement and market efficiency prefer a narrow definition, limiting it to the core element of "abuse of the public office."[5] Those who favor tough enforcement and party discipline, on the other hand, endorse a broad concept, one covering not only public office but also public interest and public opinion factors.[6] Even different regions have different conceptions of corruption, depending on local policy conditions and experience. As one Chinese folk saying dramatizes: "A model worker in Guangdong may be a criminal in Shanghai, a chair of meetings in Hainan may be a bearer of handcuffs in Beijing."

For my purpose here, I use a definition that corresponds with what the Chinese disciplinary and legal authorities define as corruption. That is, corruption is the "abuse of public power (*gonggong quanli*) by occupants of public office (*gongzhi renyuan*) in the state and party apparatus for private interests."[7] This is essentially a public-office-centered, narrow conception of corruption. The rich meanings and manifestations of Chinese corruption will become clear as the dramatic story of the post-Mao years unfolds.

THE TRANSITION TO THE MARKET AND CHINA

The case of China is of great importance to theories of economic liberalization and political corruption. As in other former socialist economies, corruption is frequently cited in China as the leading barrier to a genuine

[4] Michael Johnston, "The Search for Definitions: The Vitality of Politics and the Issue of Corruption," *International Social Science Journal* 149 (Summer 1996): 321–335; Robin Theobald, *Corruption, Development, and Underdevelopment* (Durham: Duke University Press, 1990): ch. 1; and John Gardiner, "Defining Corruption," in A. J. Heidenheimer and Michael Johnston, *Political Corruption: Concepts and Contexts* (New Brunswick, N.J.: Transaction Publishers, 2000): 25–40. For Chinese conceptions, see Yan Sun, "The Politics of Conceptualizing Corruption in Reform China," *Crime, Law and Social Change* 35 (April 2001): 245–270.

[5] E.g., Wang Huning, *Fan fubai—Zhongguo de Shiyan* (Combating Corruption—the Chinese Experiment) (Beijing: Sanhuan Chubanshe, 1993): 30–31; Liu Mingbo, *Lianzheng Sixiang yu Lilun* (Theories of and Reflections on Honest Administration) (Beijing: Renmin Chubanshe, 1994): 358–361. For a summary of Chinese discussions, see Mu Ye, "A Summary Account of Public Discussions on the Corruption Issue," *Lilun Xuexi Yuekan* 2 (February 1994): 52–53; and Yi Dong, "A Summary of Studies on Corruption and Bureaucratic Negligence among Public Officeholders," *Zhengzhi yu Fa* 2 (February 1994): 61–64.

[6] Office of Public Promulgation and Education, the Discipline Inspection Committee of the Chinese Communist Party, ed., *Fanfu Changlian Jianghua* (Topics on Fighting Corruption and Promoting Honest Administration) (Beijing: Zhonggong Zhongyang Dangxiao Chubanshe, 1994), passim.

[7] The Discipline Inspection Committee, Supervisory Office, and Marxism-Leninism Research Office of Beijing University, eds., *Fanfubai Zongheng Tan* (Essays on Combating Corruption) (Beijing: Beijing Daxue Chubanshe, 1994): 122.

transition to the market and a major source of public discontent. Yet China is unusual in that it has not adopted the big bang model of comprehensive, systemic transformation. Its gradualism and economic primacy run contrary to the conventional wisdom of those Western advisers who see partial reform as implausible.[8] Yet despite its half reforms and rampant corruption, China has experienced unprecedented levels of economic growth for more than two decades. The Chinese case thus poses many theoretical paradoxes. If conventional liberalism holds democracy and transparency as key to reducing corruption, why have more thoroughly reformed postsocialist societies not fared better regarding the level of corruption, especially Russia, other former Soviet republics, and the Balkan states? If prevailing indictments of corruption hold the problem responsible for undermining economic growth and development, why has not the Chinese economy been seriously hindered? At the same time, if revisionist theories view corruption as contributing to economic efficiency, why have not the other postsocialist economies fared as well as the Chinese? By defying conventional theories, the Chinese case forces a reexamination of conventional theories and a search for new answers.

REFORM AND CORRUPTION: STRONG LINKAGES

Generally corruption is likely to occur under two sets of circumstances. One is the presence of *opportunity,* such as the extensive role of the government as a regulator, allocator, producer, and employer; the weakening of institutional and legal sanctions; and the prevalence of regulatory loopholes and legal ambiguities. The other is the presence of *motivation,* such as confusion over changing values; weakness of moral sanctions; relative impoverishment; and a lack of alternative access to self-enrichment. Both conditions have been present in postsocialist economies. But is the reform context a key structural and motivational cause of surging corruption in recent times?

Several studies on post-Communist transition confirm strong causal linkages between economic reform and corruption, unintended as they may be by policy designers. These studies show that differences in the model of reform and the strength of the state have led to divergent opportunities and incentives during transitions from socialism. Reform models are important determinants of levels of corruption because they help shape the kind and

---

[8] Cited in Peter Nolan, *China's Rise and Russia's Fall* (New York: St. Martin's Press, 1995): ch. 4; and Nolan, *State and Market in the Chinese Economy: Essays on Controversial Issues* (London: Macmillan, 1992): 218. See also Steven Goldstein, "China in Transition: The Political Foundations of Incremental Reform," *The China Quarterly* 144 (Dec. 1995): 1106.

scope of self-seeking opportunities and incentives for officials and social groups.[9] The structure of government institutions and political processes are also important determinants because weak governments that cannot control their agencies experience high levels of corruption.[10]

Some area specialists of post-Soviet politics thus point to the nature of transition as a key cause of the type and level of recent corruption. According to Steven Solnick, a key reason for Russia's "insider privatization" of Soviet-era state assets was the defection of local and enterprise officials when hierarchical authority broke down and ministerial superiors could no longer stop them from claiming property already under their control. Why did China's central authority retain control over local officials even when the latter increasingly gained the resources to defect during economic and fiscal reforms? Solnick emphasizes the incentives that Chinese reforms have created, such as local governments' roles as shareholders and as tax authority, for preserving hierarchical links. Since local officials rely on their position in the bureaucracy to preserve their "quasi-ownership rights," they faced strong incentives to keep their state and party position and accepted whatever discipline necessary to retain it.[11] This explanation is plausible for much of the 1980s and early 1990s. Michael McFaul has shown that the easy access enjoyed by new nomenclature managers to Russia's new political system have allowed them to lobby for favorable property rights shares, tax exemptions, and industrial subsidies. These benefits in turn became powerful incentives to engage in predatory behavior and resist competitive productive behavior.[12] This explanation points to the special vulnerability of Russia's new system to corruption.

Other students of post-Communist transition identify the failure of state building as the central reason for derailed transition to market democracy, especially in post-Soviet Russia.[13] Here the new government's lack of attention to the role of the state in the transitional process, coupled with the weakness of the state more generally, has resulted in a dearth of key legal and

[9] Yan Sun, "Reform, State, and Post-Communist Corruption: Is Corruption Less Destructive in China than in Russia?" *Comparative Politics* 32:1 (Oct. 1999): 1–20.

[10] Andei Shleifer and Robert W. Vishny, "Corruption," *Quarterly Journal of Economics* 108:3 (1993): 599–617.

[11] Steven Solnick, "The Breakdown of Hierarchies in the Soviet Union and China," *World Politics* 48:2 (January 1996): esp. 232–33.

[12] Michael McFaul, "State Power, Institutional Change, and the Politics of Privatization in Russia," *World Politics* 47:2 (1995): 210–43; and McFaul, "The Allocation of Property Rights in Russia," *Communist and Post-Communist Studies* 29:3 (1996): 287–308.

[13] See a review of studies on the Russian transition by Cynthia Roberts and Thomas Sherlock, "Bringing the State Back In—Explanations of the Derailed Transition to Democracy," *Comparative Politics* 31:4 (July 1999): 477–97.

regulatory institutions critical for free enterprise and unfettered competition. All this has left the state incapable of enforcing contracts; defending property rights, investors, and consumers; or regulating banks, commodity exchanges, and stock markets.[14] Some attribute the failure of state building to the political strategy of Russia's reform elite.[15] Others blame the elite's neoliberal ideology, which led the government to neglect state building while placing undue faith in the "invisible hand."[16] Still others find that Russian leaders lost control over much of the process in the postcollapse context.[17] The failure of market-supporting institutions to emerge spontaneously, in contrast to what the post-Soviet government assumed, has nourished fertile soil for predatory behavior. The result is pervasive lawlessness, corruption, and rent seeking in post-Soviet Russia.[18] The problem also persists in other former Soviet republics and to a lesser extent in East-Central European economies.

State building is the process by which state capacity is created, enhanced, or restored, capacity being the ability of the state to govern effectively.[19] Particularly pertinent are three dimensions of state capacity essential to an effective and legitimate state.[20] The institutional dimension includes national political institutions and their capacity to make and enforce political and economic rules. The legitimacy of these rules, especially among the elite and the degree of state autonomy from pressure groups, are important parts of this dimension.[21] Institutions also shape the environment in which markets form and operate—the legal structure to settle property rights and ensure fair competition in the marketplace.[22] Poor institutional infrastructure and poor

---

[14] McFaul, "State Power," 210–43; McFaul, "The Allocation," 287–308; and Federico Varese, "The Transition to the Market and Corruption in Post-socialist Russia," *Political Studies* 45:3 (1997): 579–96.

[15] E.g., Adam Przworski, *Democracy and Market: Political and Economic Reforms in Eastern Europe and Latin America* (New York: Cambridge University Press, 1991): 165ff; and Peter Rutland, "Has Democracy Failed Russia?" *National Interest* (Winter 1994–95): 3–12.

[16] Peter Stavraski, *State Building in Post-Soviet Russia: The Chicago Boys and the Decline of Administrative Capacity* (Washington, D.C.: Kennan Institute, 1993).

[17] Roberts and Sherlock, "Bringing the State Back," 478.

[18] Commission on Security and Cooperation in Europe, *Briefing on Crime and Corruption in Russia* (Washington, D.C.: The Commission, 1994); CSIS Task Force Report, *Russian Organized Crime and Corruption, Putin's Challenge* (Washington D.C.: Center for Strategic Studies, 2000); and Victor Sergeyev, *The Wild East: Crime and Lawlessness in Post-Communist Russia* (Armonk, N.Y.: M. E. Sharpe, 1998).

[19] This paragraph is based on the synthesis by Roberts and Sherlock, "Bringing the State Back," 480–81.

[20] Merilee Grindle, *Challenging the State: Crisis and Innovation in Latin America and Africa* (Cambridge: Cambridge University Press, 1996).

[21] Theda Skocpol, "Bringing the State Back In: Strategies of Analysis in Current Research," in Peter Evans, Dietrich Rueschemeyer, and Theda Skocpol, eds., *Bringing the State Back In* (New York: Cambridge University Press, 1985): 3–37.

[22] Douglas North, *Structure and Change in Economic History* (New York: W. W. Norton, 1981); and North, *Institutions, International Change, and Economic Performance* (Cambridge: Cambridge University Press, 1990).

governance tilt weak states to lawlessness and inefficiency. The political dimension of state building comprises linkages between state and society and their effects on state capacity. Cooperative links and strong civil societies contribute to the state's effectiveness.[23] Weak links and polarized intraelite conflicts, as in post-Soviet Russia, motivate politicians to favor the exchange of state resources for political support rather than devote political capital and resources to build state capacity. Moreover, when organized social supports are weak and private interests are concentrated, those political exchange relationships are likely to cluster at the level of political and economic elites, which will likely encourage the emergence of an economic oligarchy. The administrative dimension of state building, finally, entails the state's ability to provide essential public goods, such as law and order, and market infrastructure. Their successful provision and delivery depend on the extractive capacities of the state, and the compliance, organizational coherence, and professional competence of its bureaucracies.

An effective state should exhibit significant capacities in all three dimensions of state capacity. Poorly institutionalized states possess less capacity, though not necessarily equivalent deficits in every dimension.[24] At one end, the new Russian state is profoundly weak in all dimensions of capacity. Systemic collapse and economic crisis deprived it of the time and stability to build basic institutions. Sharp intraelite conflicts and weak links with society draw political elite's attention to political survival and advancement rather than basic state building. Elite focus on purchasing political support, in turn, has undermined markets and popular support, as governing elites are inclined to tolerate patronage, rent seeking, and corruption. The result is a combination of bureaucratic capitalism—where political and administrative elites have the power to control market behavior and rewards—and oligarchic capitalism, where an interlocking group of wealthy businessmen monopolize access to policymakers and national resources while restricting domestic and international competition.[25] But political exchange relationships do not stop at the top. If the oligarchy of crony capitalists have benefited from a takeover of the major assets of the Soviet economy and from preferential state policies, the rest of the economy has been dominated and plagued by organized crime, the latter having thrived on the corruption of lower-level officials and law enforcement agents.

[23] Robert Putnam with Robert Leonardi and Raffaella Y. Nanetti, *Making Democracy Work: Civic Traditions in Modern Italy* (Princeton, N.J.: Princeton University Press, 1993): 176.

[24] Robert and Sherlock, "Bringing in the State Back," 481; and Solnick, "The Breakdown," 209–38.

[25] Roberts and Sherlock, "Bringing the State Back," 485–86; and Joseph R. Blasi, Maya Kroumova, and Douglas Kruse, *Kremlin Capitalism: Privatizing the Russian Economy* (Ithaca: Cornell University Press, 1997).

The weakening of state institutions and capacities is also blamed for worsening corruption in reform-era China. Most notably, the so-called New Left
scholars in China (or the Liberal Left as they call themselves) fault the government's blind faith in the market, especially after 1992, for the erosion of
state authority and loss of control over local agencies and agents.[26] Many not
in the New Right camp concur on strong links between institutional decline
and rising corruption. Xueliang Ding, a prominent sociologist, asks, Why
have property transformations in China, a regime characterized by political
continuity rather than systemic change, displayed similarities with illicit privatization in other postsocialist societies? Differentiating between the state as
a formal organization and its bureaucrats as individual interest groups, he argues that the latter can exist in both relatively strong states with regime continuity and in relatively weak states with discontinuous regimes. He admits
that what differentiates China from the others is the relative strength of the
Chinese state:

> Regime continuity in China helps to sustain a relatively high level of
> administrative strength and organizational discipline within the state
> apparatus than in Russia. . . . This may explain in large measure why
> private capture of state property in China . . . has been less audacious
> and wild than in Russia. The Chinese state . . . is still capable of pro-
> viding some services . . . as the guardian of public property, while the
> more fragile government in Russia seems to have given public officials,
> bankers, managers, and the mafia almost a free hand in dividing up the
> nation's wealth.[27]

Other studies of Chinese corruption readily recognize the institutional and
policy factors as key structural causes. But many deal with early reform periods.[28] A few recent studies have linked worsened corruption, such as increasing abuse in state enterprise reforms,[29] managerial corruption and

---

[26] See a summary discussion in Lu Zhoulai, "An Economic Analysis of Corruption," *Tian Ya* 3
(May 2000): 31–37; and Joseph Fewsmith, *China since Tiananmen* (New York: Cambridge University
Press, 2001). See also Wang Shaoguang and Hu Angang, *Report on the State of the Nation: Strengthen-
ing the Leading Role of the Central Government during the Transition to the Market Economy* (New Haven:
Yale University Press, 1993).

[27] Xueliang Ding, "The Illicit Asset Stripping of Chinese State Firms," *The China Journal* 43 (2000):
26; and "Who Gets What, How?" *Problems of Post-Communism* (May–June 1999): 39, 40.

[28] The most notable are Xiaobo Lu, *Cadre and Corruption: the Institutional Involution of the Chinese
Communist Party* (Palo Alto, Calif.: Stanford University Press, 2000); and Julia Kwong, *The Political
Economy of Corruption in China* (Armonk, N.Y.: M. E. Sharpe, 1997).

[29] Xueliang Ding, "The Illicit Asset Stripping," 1–28; "Who Gets What?" 32–41; "Informal Pri-
vatization through Internationalization: The Rise of Nomenklature Capitalism in China's Offshore
Business," *British Journal of Political Science* 30 (Part 1) (2000): 121–46; and "Systemic Irregularity and
Spontaneous Property Transformation In the Chinese Financial System," *The China Quarterly* 163
(September 2000): 655–76.

labor protests,[30] and changing forms of corruption,[31] to post-1992 reforms.

None of these studies, however, is comprehensive or conclusive about the
nature of the interaction between market transition, changing institutions,
and corruption. None has examined corruption across China's reform periods with different incentive structures and outcomes. None has examined
corruption across China's diverse localities with different reform experiences
and developmental trajectories. None has examined corruption at both the
macro, systemic level and the micro, individual level. None has examined the
changing disincentives against, rather than just incentives for, post-Mao corruption. Finally, none has linked the patterns and impact of corruption with
the different categories of corruption.

REFORM AND CORRUPTION: WEAK LINKAGES

In a departure from prevailing emphases on the structural inducements of
economic liberalization, one recent analysis rejects a direct linkage between
China's market transition and rising corruption. In his book *Cadre and Corruption,* Xiaobo Lu argues that surging corruption in contemporary China is
not a malaise of a transitional society. The advent of market and liberalizing
reforms are not its fundamental causes. Nor is it the imperfect market that
dictates the behavior of officials with redistributive power. Instead, Lu proposes an explanatory thesis of "organizational involution." He refers to the
evolving incapacity of the Communist party as an organization to maintain
committed, coherent, and deployable cadre over the fifty years since the party
came to power. This involution results from the organization's failures to
adapt itself to a changing environment after 1949, or to be transformed by
rationalization and bureaucratization that characterize a Weberian image of
modern bureaucracy. Its members have adjusted to the postrevolution regu-
larization of a revolutionary movement not through revolutionary ideologies or modern institutions and practices, but through reinforced and
elaborated traditional modes of operation. In other words, informal practices
and neotraditional modes remain sustained within the regime structures. In
fact, they continue to dominate. As such, the regime embarked on an invo-

[30] Feng Chen, "Subsistence Crisis, Managerial Corruption and Labor Protests in China," *The
China Journal* 44 (July 2000): 41–63.
[31] Gong Ting, "Jumping into the Sea: Cadre Entrepreneurs in China," *Problems of Post-Communism*
(July–August 1996): 26–33; Gong, "Forms and Characteristics of Corruption in the 1990s: Change
with Continuity," *Communist and Post-Communist Studies* 30:3 (1997): 277–88; and Gong, "Dangerous Collusion: Corruption as Collective Venture in Contemporary China," *Communist and Post-Communist Studies* 35:1 (2002): 85–105.

lutionary path, or becomes indefinitely patrimonial. Corruption is explained as part of the larger deviant behavior among the party's units and ranks under such organizational involution. And reform-era corruption is explained in the context of the ruling party's organizational involution as the root cause of cadre corruption consistently throughout PRC history.[32]

Among policy and academic circles within China, a neoliberal school of thought also emphasizes China's political arrangements as the root of contemporary corruption. Its moderate version emphasizes the excesses of government power. The noted economist Wu Jinglian frequently faults the "intervention and destruction of economic activities by bureaucratic power." Xin Xiangyang of the People's University fervidly condemns the excess and abuse of government power in a book titled *A New Theory of Government,* blaming it for corruption and all other major problems of Chinese society.[33] In a more radical version, blame falls on state power itself. Advocates on the New Right (or neoliberals) fault government power itself, rather than just the ways its power is distributed and supervised, as the ultimate source of corruption. They repeat the axiom that "power corrupts and absolute power corrupts absolutely." The reduction of corruption, they claim, demands reducing public power itself. That is, to let the market take over what the government does in the economy, especially, to privatize state-owned enterprises (SOEs), protect property rights, promote nonstate enterprises, and let the market work its magic.[34]

These interpretations raise several problems. First, neither the "organizational involution" thesis nor the "absolute power" proposition explains the changing forms and mechanisms of reform-era corruption. The involution thesis elucidates the state's inability to rationalize and regularize its bureaucracy, but does not answer whether there would have been such a dramatic surge of corruption without economic liberalization. The absolute power thesis does not explain why reform-era corruption has actually grown, even while the state has retreated steadily, and sometimes dramatically, from the economy. Second, neither perspective can explain why former socialist economies elsewhere, with their comprehensive break from previous political and economic systems, have experienced levels and forms of corruption similar to and sometimes worse than China's. The mechanisms and processes

[32] Xiaobo Lu, *Cadre and Corruption;* Lu, "From Rank-Seeking to Rent-Seeking: Changing Administrative Ethos and Corruption in Reform China," *Crime, Law, and Social Change* 32:4 (1999): 347–70; and Lu "Booty Socialism, Bureau-prenuers, and the State in Transition: Organizational Corruption in China," *Comparative Politics* 32:3 (2000): 273–95.
[33] Xin Xiangyang, *Xin Zhengfu lun* (A New Theory of Government) (Beijing: Gongren Chubanshe, 1994): especially ch. 7 on corruption.
[34] These authors are critiqued in Lu, "An Economic Analysis," 31–37, 43.

of the market transition, then, still provide a powerful common denominator for understanding corruption during the transition from socialism.

CORRUPTION AND REFORM: NEGATIVE EFFECTS

Prevailing literatures suggest that corruption should exert negative effects on transitional economies. One major theoretical repertoire here came from economics in the 1970s and early 1980s, in the theory of rents. According to economists Krueger, Bhagwati, Buchanan, and others, rents are created whenever governmental action interferes with markets to keep prices either above or below competitive levels, resulting in artificially contrived privileges. The fight for such privileges leads to rent seeking, in which scare resources are spent to capture rents created by government action. Since these expenditures produce no value from a social point of view, they are considered as dissipation of resources.[35] Rent seeking is particularly costly to growth, moreover, because rent-seeking activities are subject to naturally increasing returns. Rent seeking is self-sustaining in that an increase in rent-seeking activity may make rent seeking more attractive relative to productive activity. Further, rent seeking may impede innovative activities the most and hence sharply reduce the rate of economic growth. This is because innovators need government-sponsored goods, such as permits, licenses, and import quotas, much more than established producers.[36] Empirically oriented studies since the 1980s reaffirm that corruption is never a better alternative to honest public policy and that in the long run, it distorts and retards development.[37]

Since the 1990s, various global forces have turned the international discourse definitely against corruption. Negative international reaction to corruption has followed a rising flux of scandals and growing evidence of public

[35] Anne Krueger, "The Political Economy of a Rent Seeking Society," *American Economic Review* 64 (1974): 291–303; Jadish N. Bhagwati, ed., *Illegal Transactions in International Trade* (Amsterdam and New York: North-Holland-American Elsevier, 1974); and J. M. Buchanan, "Rent Seeking and Profit Seeking," in Buchanan et al., eds., *Toward a Theory of the Rent-Seeking Society* (College Station: Texas A & M University Press, 1981): 8–11; Robert D. Tollison, "Rent Seeking: A Survey," *KYKLOS* 35 (1982): 575–602; and Robert D. Tollison and Gordon Tullock eds., *The Political Economy of Rent Seeking* (Boston: Kluwer Academic, 1988).

[36] Kevin Murphy, Andrei Shleifer, and Robert Vishny, "Why Is Rent-Seeking so Costly to Growth?" *American Economic Review* 83:2 (May 1993): 409–14.

[37] David Gould, *The Effects of Corruption on Administrative Performance* (Washington, D.C.: World Bank, 1983); Richard Hodder-Williams, *An Introduction to the Politics of Tropical Africa* (London: Allen & Unwin, 1985): 17; A. Riding, *Mexico: Inside the Volcano* (London: I. B. Tauris, 1987); Robert Klitgaard, *Controlling Corruption* (Berkeley: University of California Press, 1988); Peter Ward, ed., *Corruption, Development, and Inequality* (New York: Routledge, 1989).

disgust with corrupt officials and institutions in many countries. The end of the Cold War has freed patron states from tolerating corrupt clients so as to keep them in the Western camp. The global economy and the spread of emerging markets have led American companies to press for international antibribery reforms, as the (American) Corrupt Practices Act of 1977 restricts them in competition with European firms that can deduct foreign bribes from domestic taxes. In 1996, the IMF and the World Bank for the first time declared corruption the "enemy of development" and made "tackling corruption" a priority for borrowing countries.[38] On December 16, 1996, the United Nations adopted a resolution against commercial bribery, calling on member states to make such bribery a crime and to end tax deductions for enterprise bribe expenses. Needless to say, the East Asian financial crisis has heightened attention to the role of corruption in fostering crony capitalism.

The growing indictment of corruption is joined by a revival of scholarly attention to the effects of corruption on growth. From economists of the IMF and the World Bank to long-term students of corruption, critics offer scathing indictments of corruption's harm on growth and development. Instead of efficiency, corruption favors not the most efficient but the most connected and unscrupulous, and creates entry barriers for those without connections. Often favors are sought not for productive activities but inefficient subsidies, monopoly benefits, or regulatory oversight. Bribes invite misallocation of resources by indulging wasteful and low-quality projects. The expectation of "speed money" encourages purposeful red tape. Instead of investment, corruption diverts funds from development. Given the secretive nature of corrupt payments, they are more likely to be privately consumed, diverted into illicit activities or foreign bank accounts. This capital flight is a cost on a nation's growth. Even centralized corruption is distortionary. Because it is necessary to keep corruption secret and avoid detection, officials may induce investment and transactions in the direction of lower-detection activities, favoring wasteful rather than efficient projects. Instead of growth, corruption adversely affects it. As a tax on *ex post* profits, it deters the entry of new players, products, and technology that require an initial fixed-cost investment. Corruption encourages rent seeking rather than entrepreneurial activities, since the latter is likely to be less profitable than the former. Smallest businesses are most vulnerable to costly corruption. In the final analysis, it is impossible to confine corruption to relatively beneficial areas, as corruption tends to feed on itself.[39] As for empirical evidence, Mauro has used

[38] Paul Lewis, "A World Fed Up with Bribes," *New York Times,* November 28, 1996.
[39] Pranab Bardhan, "Corruption and Growth: A Review of Issues," *Journal of Economic Literature* 35 (September 1997): 1320–46; Kimberly Elliot, *Corruption and the Global Economy* (Washington, D.C.: Institute for International Economics, 1997); Daniel Kaufmann, "Corruption: The Facts," *Foreign Pol-*

the Business International index to estimate the effects of corruption on the average ratio of total and private investment to GDP for the period between 1960 and 1985 for a cross-section of sixty-seven countries. He finds corruption to lower investment, thereby reducing growth.[40] Kaufman and Shang-Jin Wei find that effective red tape and bribery are positively correlated across firms.[41]

While these insights offer plausible explanations for thwarted growth in some transitional economies, they do not explain the Chinese paradox of high growth and high corruption. It is still relevant to look at theories that espouse corruption's functional roles.

CORRUPTION AND REFORM: FUNCTIONAL EFFECTS

Revisionist views of corruption, dating back to the heyday of the modernization theory, emphasize utilitarian consequences of behavior and corruption's role in overcoming structural barriers to development in modernizing societies. The revisionist literature offers three major perspectives. The efficiency one views government policies as so imperfect that corruption may bring about better economic policies, since the private sector can get around cumbersome regulations, and corrupt money tends to flow to investment rather than consumption.[42] The functionalist-integration perspective highlights the role that corruption can play to integrate social forces into the economic process, from which they may otherwise be excluded and politically and socially alienated.[43] The historical perspective emphasizes the characteristics and developmental stage of the socioeconomic institutions of a developing country, on which the causes and effects of corruption can be fairly assessed.[44]

icy 107 (Summer 1997): 114–31; and Rose-Ackerman, *Corruption and Government: Causes, Consequences, and Reform* (Cambridge: Cambridge University Press, 1999).

[40] Paolo Mauro, "Corruption and Growth," *Quarterly Journal of Economics* 109 (August 1995): 681–712.

[41] Daniel Kaufman and Shangjin Wei, "Does 'Grease Money' Speed up the Wheels of Commerce?" NBER Working Paper No. 7093 (April 1999): 1–16.

[42] David H. Bayley, "The Effects of Corruption in a Developing Nation," *Western Political Quarterly* 19 (1966): 719–23; N. H. Leff, "Economic Development through Bureaucratic Corruption," *American Behavioral Scientist* 8:3 (1964): 8–14; Colin Leys, "What Is the Problem about Corruption?" *Journal of Modern African Studies* 3 (1965): 215–30; Jose Abueva, "The Contribution of Nepotism, Spoils, and Graft to Political Development," *East-West Center Review* 3 (1966): 45–54; and James Scott, "An Essay on the Political Functions of Corruption," *Asian Studies* 5 (1967): 501–23.

[43] Samuel Huntington, *Political Order in Changing Societies* (New Haven: Yale University, 1967): 59–64.

[44] Gabriel Ben-Dor, "Corruption, Institutionalization, and Political Development: the Revisionist Theses Revisited," *Comparative Political Studies* 7:1 (1974): 63–83; Joseph S. Nye, "Corruption and Political Development: A Cost-Benefit Analysis," *American Political Science Review* 61 (1967): 417–27;

A more state-oriented view challenges the rent-seeking literature on its ideological bias because of its objection to government activity in the economy. Obsessed with the market as the most efficient mechanism, the rent theory ignores the role of states in economic transformation, a role that can sometimes restrain as well as stimulate social waste. The rent-seeking literature also fails to give attention to the politics and political processes of government-business relationships. In assuming pure markets, it does not acknowledge that a bureaucracy is inevitably needed to provide basic services to society, even if at a minimal level, and "rent havens" will always exist. In assuming that rents are always allocated by competitive processes, it misses the point that the allocation of rents inevitably involves the role of politics (or various affective ties) and hence rents will not always be allocated by market processes.[45] Further, the theory fails to differentiate between beneficiaries of rents in the state and those outside the state. The former may constitute the more productive bureaucratic capitalism while the latter, the more predatory booty capitalism. Finally, distinction may be made between competition for generalizable policy benefits (lobbying) and that for particularistic privileges (bribery).[46] Different structures of corruption may entail different efficiency effects. Decentralized structures tend to produce independent monopoly in the corruption process, encouraging fragmented rent seeking and a greater degree of dissipation of rents. Centralized structures, on the other hand, tend to produce joint monopoly, leading to a lesser degree of rent seeking, relatively less dissipation, and potentially less detrimental outcomes from the standpoint of development.[47]

Still others, whom we may call neorevisionists, contend that corruption can vary in character and impact from one setting to another. Paul Hutchcroft proposes several sets of such variability. First, corruption can be more or less calculable/predictable depending on the strength of formal authority relative to informal networks and the coincidence of authority and power. The greater this strength and coincidence, the more predictable the forms of corruption are and the less costly their effects. Second, the allocation of rents can be distinguished between "rent seeking" and "rent deployment." The lat-

John Waterbury, "Endemic and Planned Corruption in a Monarchial Regime," *World Politics* 25 (1973): 533–55; John Waterbury, "Corruption, Political Stability, and Development: Comparative Evidence from Egypt and Morocco," *Government and Opposition* 11 (1976): 426–45.

[45] Margaret Levi, *Of Rule and Revenue* (Berkeley: University of California Press, 1988): 24; Peter Evans, *Embedded Autonomy: State and Industrial Transformation* (Princeton, N.J.: Princeton University Press, 1995): 24–25.

[46] Paul Hutchcroft, "The Politics of Privilege: Assessing the Impact of Rents, Corruption, and Clientelism on Third World Development," *Political Studies* 45 (1997): esp. 641–42.

[47] Shleifer and Vishny, "Corruption," 599.

ter, referring to the deployment of rents from above to groups exerting little efforts, promotes less dissipation of resources than rent seeking and thus has the potential for less detrimental outcomes for development. Third, corruption can encourage or discourage market competition by helping to either circumvent policies that obstruct markets or to obstruct the efficient functioning of markets. Finally, whether gains from corruption will be invested depend on the motivations of rent allocators and recipients, the capacity of the state to promote developmental goals, and the security of the investment environment.[48]

Others draw attention to the varying processes of corruption. Tracking the locus of rents, Andrew Wedeman differentiates between rent scrapping, where rents accrue to the state office, and dividend collecting, where rents accrue to the private sector (bribers). The latter set of rents, thus, is a share of private profits. The more unproductive and secretive nature of rent-seeking activities, in turn, are more likely to threaten the security of private capital, leading to capital flight and consumption. By contrast, better business environments and growth rates, more likely in profit-sharing arrangements, tend to encourage the usage of corrupt gains for productive activities.[49] With reference to transitional economies, one scholar explicitly argues for a relativist approach: "Those who think corruption hurts growth compare corruption to a well-working free market. In contrast, those who see corruption's benefits compare it to a poorly functioning market or no market at all—that is, a pretransition economy." If a key goal of transitional economies is the development of a vibrant nonstate economy, then corruption has its utility in privatizing state assets and encouraging new start-ups.[50]

In the Asian context, scholars of East and Southeast Asian development have long observed the variation of corruption's impact on local development. They note the combination of high growth and limited corruption in capitalist East Asian states, but high growth and high corruption in Southeast Asian states such as Thailand and Indonesia. They also observe low growth and high corruption in other Southeast Asian states, notably the Philippines.[51] According to Robert Wade, the shortest answer to why the abuse of

[48] Paul Hutchcroft, "The Politics of Privilege: Rents and Corruption in Asia," in Arnold J. Heidenheimer and Michael Johnston, eds., *Political Corruption*: 489–513.

[49] Andrew Wedeman, "Looters, Rent-scrappers, and Dividend-Collectors: Corruption and Growth in Zaire, South Korea, and the Philippines," *Journal of Developing Areas* 31 (Summer 1997): 457–478.

[50] Scott Kennedy, "Comrade's Dilemma: Corruption and Growth in Transitional Economies," *Problems of Post-Communism* 44:2 (March–April 1997), 31.

[51] See contributions in Andrew MacIntyre, ed., *Business and Government in Industrializing Asia* (St. Leonards, Australia: Allen and Unwin, 1994).

public power is limited in East Asia is that the region's states are relatively
"hard." The position of a state in relation to its society can be thought of as
varying along a continuum from decentralized and constrained by social
groups ("soft") to centralized and relatively insulated from society ("hard").
Because hard states have the capacity to resist private demands, they are able
to exert control over the direction of the society and economy.[52] Along somewhat similar lines, Hutchcroft differentiates among several broad types of capitalist systems, on the basis of the relative strengths of the state versus business
interests and the variation among state apparatuses. Of particular interest here
are two major types of rent capitalism (systems in which rent-seeking behavior dominates): the patrimonial administrative state and bureaucratic capitalism, exemplified by Thailand and Indonesia, and the patrimonial oligarchic
state and booty capitalism, as exemplified by the Philippines.[53]

In the patrimonial administrative state, the bureaucratic elite is the major
beneficiary of patrimonial largess and exercises power over a weak business
class. Government service provides the greatest opportunities for combining
high income with security, prestige, and power. Because the major beneficiary of rent extraction is based in the administrative apparatus of the state,
this form of rent capitalism can be characterized as bureaucratic capitalism.[54]
By contrast, in the patrimonial oligarchic state, access to the state remains
the major avenue to private accumulation, but the dominant social force has
an economic base largely independent of the state apparatus. As typical of
patrimonial polities, there is weak separation between official and private
spheres; but unlike the patrimonial administrative state, the influence of ex-
trabureaucratic forces swamps that of the bureaucracy. The type of rent capitalism resulting in this oligarchic state reflects the relative weakness of the
state apparatus vis-à-vis business interests. In contrast to bureaucratic capitalism, the principal direction of rent extraction is reversed: a powerful oligarchic business class extracts privilege from a largely incoherent bureaucracy.
It is, thus, booty capitalism.[55]

The bureaucratic capitalism of Southeast Asia was once regarded as not
having gotten in the way of economic development, and may have in fact
contributed to the close collaboration between business and the state. Even
after crony capitalism became a major target of blame during the region's fi-

[52] Robert Wade, *Governing the Market* (Princeton, N.J.: Princeton University, 1990): 333–42.
[53] Paul Hutchcroft, "Booty Capitalism in the Philippines," in MacIntyre, ed., *Business and Government,* 221; and Hutchcroft, *Booty Capitalism: the Politics of Banking in the Philippines* (Ithaca: Cornell
University Press, 1998).
[54] See the Thai case in F. W. Riggs, *Thailand: the Modernization of a Bureaucratic Polity* (Honolulu:
East-West Center Press, 1966): 250–51.
[55] Hutchcroft, "Booty Capitalism," 226–32.

nancial crisis in the late 1990s, there is no consensus that this form of capitalism caused the crisis. Some analysts hold economic liberalization and the global financial market as more responsible, while others find levels of corruption not unusual in affected countries before the crisis.[56] Moreover, despite the disgrace of "crony capitalism," recent works on patron-client networks, rent-seeking activities, and ethnic business networks still affirm their tempering effects on corruption in Southeast Asia, the region most affected by the currency crisis of 1997.[57] Looking at the rent-seeking process historically, Khan and Jomo find "net social benefits" in the informal clientelism of the region, declaring that "not only was there no simple correlation between the extent of rent seeking and long-run economic performance, there was little correlation between the intensity of rent seeking and the country's vulnerability to the financial crisis of 1997."[58] Some see developmental advantages in the national and international reach of Asian ethnic business networks, in comparison with corruption in other developing societies.[59]

Of relevance is the structural similarities of the Chinese case. With the survival of its basic political institutions and bureaucrats, the continuance of what Lu characterizes as organizational involution of a patrimonial administrative state, and a growing market economy where the major beneficiary of rent extraction is based in the administrative apparatus of the state, the Chinese system exhibits many features of the patrimonial state and bureaucratic capitalism. New business elites appear even weaker vis-à-vis the state than their East Asian counterpart, willing to be subordinate to the state and reluctant to exert activism.[60] By contrast, Russia's postsocialist system, with its weak political institutions, new powerful economic oligarchies, and the latter's easy access to the state exhibits many features of the oligarchic state and booty capitalism. In short, the strength of the state makes a difference as to variations in the impact of corruption.

But does the Chinese case fit into all the "favorable" settings that produce functional corruption? Existing studies show a complex picture. Writing on

[56] Beatrice Weder, *Model, Myth, or Miracle: Reassessing the Role of Governments in the East Asian Experience* (New York: United Nations University Press, 1999).
[57] Mushtaq H. Khan, "Patron-Client Networks and the Economic Effects of Corruption in Asia," in Heidenheimer and Johnston, eds., *Political Corruption* (2002): 467–88; and Alice Sindzingre, "A Comparative Analysis of African and East Asian Corruption," in ibid.: 441–62.
[58] Mushtaq H. Khan and K. S. Jomo, eds., *Rents, Rent-Seeking, and Economic Development: Theory and Evidence from Asia* (Cambridge: Cambridge University Press, 2000): 4. I thank Kellee Tsai for bringing this point to my attention.
[59] Sindzingre, "A Comparative Analysis," 441–62.
[60] Margaret Pearson, *China's New Business Elite: The Political Consequences of Economic Reform* (Berkeley: University of California Press, 1997): ch.6.

China's early reform period, one economist finds the role of bureaucratic corruption amounting to "creating a corps of entrepreneurial market-makers"
who "gather information about trade opportunities and act as go-between
in actual exchanges."[61] After 1992, when cadres set up businesses no longer
tied to government institutions or incumbent officials, Ting Gong sees a positive role change for government cadre, transforming from bureaucratic to
business elite. The process exerts a subversive effect on the long established
principle of bureaucratic hierarchy.[62] Other studies observe corruption's
destabilizing effects, blaming it for the outbreak of the Tiananmen protests.[63]
Ding Xueliang links corruption to the growing covert transfer of state properties by firm managers in the 1990s, while Chen Feng links it to labor unrest.[64] My own paper comparing corruption in postreform China and Russia
deals with some complexities of the issue but has in many ways been overtaken by empirical developments.[65]

The role of corruption is also a hotly contested issue within China. On
one side, local and grass-roots officials, libertarian economists, and neoliberal
intellectuals play down the negative effects of corruption. Local cadres frown
on anticorruption efforts on three grounds. First, such efforts interfere with
"reform and opening." If officials and enterprises are preoccupied with rooting out corruption, they would be more cautious about encouraging new
practices and would have to place economic development secondary to honest administration. Second, corruption may be conducive to developing the
market by acting as a "lubricant," helping to "loosen up" the administrative
command system on one hand and "facilitate" commercial exchanges on the
other. Third, corruption is a necessary trade-off and as such, it is an inevitable
part of the reform process. The logic here is that just as increased efficiency
necessarily interferes with equality, so does the market necessarily erode traditional, noncommercial mores and stimulate speculative urges.[66] Finally,
corruption is believed to contribute to efficiency by forcing state organs and
their functionaries to improve service, allowing the private sector more access to government decisions, and enhancing market coordination.[67]

[61] Barbara N. Sands, "Decentralizing an Economy: The Role of Bureaucratic Corruption in
China's Economic Reforms," *Public Choice* 65 (1990): 89.
[62] Gong, "Jumping into the Sea," 26–33.
[63] Clemens S. Ostergaard and Christina Petersen, "Official Profiteering and the Tiananmen Square
Demonstrations in China," *Corruption and Reform* 6 (1991): 81–107; and Yan Sun, "The Chinese
Protests of 1989: The Issue of Corruption," *Asian Survey* 3:8 (1991): 762–82.
[64] Ding, "Who Gets What?"; "The Illicit Asset Stripping;" and "Informal Privatization"; and Chen
Feng, "Subsistence Crisis," 41–63.
[65] Yan Sun, "Reform, State and Corruption," 1–20.
[66] Cited in Zhou Jingrong and Zhang Wu, "On Corruption and Combating Strategies," *Jianghan
luntan* 11 (1993): 1–8; and He Xiaomin, "Factors Impeding Anticorruption Efforts and Strategies to
Deal with Them," *Fazhi Liaowang* 8 (1994): 16–17.
[67] Cited in Wang Huning, *Fanfubai,* 63–64.

Neoliberal economists fully endorse these views. Often admirers of F. A. Hayek, they are branded as "right-wing" (*you yi*) economists by their critics. As libertarian economists, they believe that corruption's destructiveness is positive in the Chinese context by helping to destroy the state economy. This view has been openly expounded in professional writings after 1992. As one such economist writes, "There are two ways to transfer or reallocate power: to seize it by compulsion (*qiang duo*) or by purchase (*gou mai*). . . . since officials do not easily give up their power and seizure is not possible, bribery—the exchange of money for power—becomes the only way to purchase power." "Reform," he continues, "should utilize corruption and bribery to reduce barriers to the transfer and reallocation of power."[68] Another neoliberal economist promotes such "spontaneous privatization" as a public policy. In a 1995 paper, he proposed a reform program under the banner "Use Capital to Exchange Power, Promote Privatization." In a 2000 speech, he remarked that "I have told the central government, it's best just to give these people a lot of capital to buy up the decision powers all at once, so they cannot abuse them anymore." One economist used mathematical modeling to prove that corruption was the necessary "toll payments" on the route to the market, or the necessary price for reform, preferable to monitoring costs and likely a second best strategy for development. For these neoliberals, corruption may give rise to a new system and as such, it is a driving force for reform.[69]

On the opposite side, their critics on the New Left have raised legitimate objections. As social democrats, they see an important role for government in reducing inequality, providing a social safety net, and intervening more in the market to correct its failures. At the core of their objection to the neoliberal proposition is the issue of who benefits and loses from a sale of government power. They ask, "Who would be capable of purchasing public power?" Would the process simply benefit a class of bureaucratic capitalists and entrench crony capitalism? Would not privatized power entail a new set of market barriers? Already, they argue, beneficiaries of corruption have become powerful interest groups with vested stakes in the current socioeconomic arrangements, uninterested in further reforms. Rather than being a lubricant of reform, corruption deprives reform of its motivating force.[70]

The impact of corruption in the Chinese case thus remains inconclusive and controversial. Given the visible paradox of high growth and high corruption, but equally notable variation in reform policies and outcomes across

---

[68] The cited economist is Zhang Shuguang. See a discussion of him and other so-called right-wing economists, in Lu Zhoulai, "An Economic Analysis," 34–36.

[69] Cited in ibid.

[70] Ibid.

time and locality, this impact is likely to be complex. The complexity certainly calls for a closer and more comprehensive examination.

RESEARCH THESES, SOURCES, AND DESIGNS

My objective is to explore post-Mao corruption in a systematic and comprehensive way, with the aim of clarifying some key questions raised in the literature but not adequately answered by it. These questions concern two clusters of issues. One is the causal linkage between economic reform and corruption, while the second is the consequential linkage between corruption and economic reform.

I make two arguments. The first concerns the interaction between reform and corruption: post-Mao corruption has largely been a by-product of economic reform. Path dependence in reform and development trajectories has been largely responsible for the structural opportunities and incentives for this corruption, and for its progressive aggravation in character, scope, and scale. The strong causal linkage is shown both synchronically across different periods of changing reform policies; and horizontally across different localities of diverse development trajectories. Correspondingly, structural disincentives against corruption have progressively weakened and this decline has been rooted in the same process.

My second argument concerns the interaction between corruption and reform: corruption may coexist with successful economic reforms and growth, but not necessarily for the standard efficiency reasons. In the short run, the uneven distributional implications of corruption may aid reform and growth through unintended and informal mechanisms. Over time, however, these mechanisms may take on a life of their own and undermine the central state's ability to implement its developmental policies, discipline its staff, enforce its regulatory infrastructure, and fundamentally transform the economy.[71]

I use collections of real corruption cases published by Chinese legal and disciplinary apparatuses (appendix 1). At the time of publication, between 1989 and 2003, the offenders had either been processed or were being processed by the penal system. Compiled by disciplinary offices, law enforcement agencies, and legal professionals, the casebooks are intended as legal and educational guidebooks during the uncertain transitional times. The ten casebooks complement one another: those by disciplinary agencies em-

---

[71] I thank Kellee Tsai for helping to sharpen these arguments.

phasize offenders from larger government agencies and affiliates, those by legal professionals emphasize offenders from smaller public agencies and firms (public organizations without monitoring agencies within or directly above them, nonparty officials not subject to party sanctions, collectives, and village administrations). The compilers selected the cases from around the country on the basis of their "currency," "representativeness," and "heuristic value," or cases reflecting features typical of the times that serve to show what behaviors constituted wrongdoing under reform conditions. The cases are factually presented, with details of the offenders, their offenses, the investigations, and punitive outcomes. Some casebooks also detail the legal proceedings, including defense arguments, appeals, and counterappeals. The majority of the volumes provide legal analyses and commentaries on definitional and legalistic matters. The casebooks are distinguished by their professional tone, systematic documentation, and relevant details, in contrast to more dramatized portrayals by commercial presses.

The most informative and valuable of these collections is the journal *Dangfeng Lianzheng* (DFLZ), a monthly digest of corruption reports, analyses, and policy discussions from periodicals around the country. Published by the Chongqing branch of the CCP's Discipline Inspection Committee (DIC), one of the journal's forums chronicles the latest roster of fallen officials at the *xian* rank and above.[72] Dated from 1990 to 2003, this digest is the most comprehensive and systematic source of primary data for this book. In addition, the author randomly interviewed workers, police officers, party disciplinary officials, factory managers, scholars, businessmen, and urban residents in Shanghai, Jiangsu, Sichuan, Chongqing, Shenzhen, and Beijing in the spring and summer of 1995, 2000, and 2003.

Important qualifications should be made of the data. First, the collected cases reflect those offenders caught by the system and may not be representative of the larger reality. More resourceful offenders may simply have escaped, and it is impossible to know the extent, ranks, and characteristics of this group. Second, the cases were not likely to have been selected evenly from across the provinces. Some provinces may be better represented not because they have more corruption, but because they have more effective control mechanisms or their legal professionals participated in the compilation of the casebooks. For example, there is not a single case from Tibet and the situation is only slightly better for the other ethnic regions of Xinjiang, Inner Mongolia, and Ningxia, or the frontier region of Gansu. Third, most of the cases include cadres at the rank of *xian* (the equivalent of the county mag-

---

[72] For a discussion of the CCP's cadre rank system, see ch. 1.

istrate) and above, thus underrepresenting cadres below the county level, that
is, those in the rural areas. Again the reach of the state's checking mechanisms
is simply weak beyond the county level so that the true extent of corruption
beyond this scope is little documented in the casebooks.

What these disclaimers entail is that the findings of this book may be more
true of the data used here than reliably of China as a whole and more re-
flective of the urban sector than of rural areas. These data also appear to rep-
resent larger and higher-level cases rather than routine and mundane ones,
because more of the former group are investigated and publicized. Corruption is certainly more widespread than available data can suggest because of
ineffective detection and uneven penal processes. But were the more visible
cases prosecuted for the political purpose of "killing the chicken to scare the
monkeys?" This is not the impression one gets from interviews with knowl-
edgeable sources. The general picture that emerges is that if the most scan-
dalous cases are not prosecuted, it would be hard to contain public outrage
and preserve the party's image. Further, like their counterparts in the United
States, overburdened Chinese prosecutors are forced to concentrate on the
most serious cases. Does the government neglect going after its high-ranking members to protect its image? The truth may be the opposite. Because
officials at the *sheng bu ji* (deputy provincial governor, deputy minister, and
above) are directly under the supervision of the central DIC, it is administratively easier to investigate and bring down officials at those high levels. By
contrast, local officials are not only shielded by local crony networks but are
often able to overpower local disciplinary agencies. Documentary and interview sources confirm that it is often the difficulty of pinpointing evidence
and carrying through investigations that hamper the exposure of corrupt
officials, not the deliberate efforts of the center to contain bad publicity. In
fact, the central government publishes collections of corruption cases found
within its ministries and departments.

Neither documentary nor interview sources give a clear indication of the
spread or level of corruption in the real world. According to a member of the
local prosecutor's office in Shenzhen, tolerable levels of corruption are no
longer serious obstacles to cadre survival or promotion, as long as job performance is satisfactory.[73] As a counterpoint, a mayoral aide for Shenzhen's
municipal government sees corruption as no longer a serious problem in the
local officialdom because of the increased parity of officials' income with the
private sector.[74] Mid-level officials interviewed in Suzhou and Shanghai

[73] Interview in Shenzhen, spring 2000.
[74] Interview in New York City, spring 1996.

confirm that they are reluctant to risk career prospects over graft, apart from their already handsome salaries and bonuses nowadays. Disgraced and disgruntled officials, however, tend to complain that every other official is worse but only the little fish gets caught. Despite all limitations, the casebooks give systematic and rich details, which are unavailable from interview sources given the secretive nature of the subject matter. The findings illuminate the kinds of cases that matter to the prosecutorial and legal establishment in the country.

Corruption is inherently hard to measure. The methodology to be employed will be primarily qualitative. A particular emphasis will be on how corruption works in the real world. To this end, the book combines macrolevel analyses with extensive documented cases of real-life offenders and actual processes of wrongdoing. Existing studies, by contrast, mostly deal with the corruption issue at the systemic level. The effect of a simultaneous macrolevel and microlevel approach is at once comprehensive while concrete, analytical while illustrative.

A few analytical points will help us navigate through the complex world of market and corruption. One is the distinction between those types of corruption that are based on two-way transactions and those that are not. Corruption, it is often assumed, involves two-way exchanges between officials and citizens (patrons and clients). While other types are noted, two-way exchanges receive the focal attention in the corruption literature. Typical is Joseph LaPalombara's claim, made quite recently, that corruption requires two or more parties to a transaction, at least one of whom holds a position of public trust and/or exercises a public role and another (others) of whom acts in a private capacity.[75] In reality, not all types need to involve a two-way exchange between officials and citizens. They may be just between officials and the public coffer. To focus on transaction alone would not give a whole picture of corruption. Nontransaction types may produce consequences as serious or worse than transaction corruption. As some students of Chinese corruption have noted, transaction types are common in market systems where two or more parties are usually involved and the rule of the game is "money" for power, whereas nontransaction types are common in systems where officials have direct access or control over the public coffer and the rule of the game is power for money. The latter are more typically found in the socialist period but remain important in the reform period.[76] The juxtaposition of transaction and nontransaction types captures the essential dif-

---

[75] Joseph LaPalombara, "Structural and Institutional Aspects of Corruption," *Social Research* 61:2 (1994): 328.
[76] Gong, "Jumping into the Sea," 26–33; and Lu, *Cadre and Corruption*, 237.

ference in the processes of two broad groups of corrupt behavior. The phenomenology of Chinese corruption is the subject of chapter 1. Transaction-type corruption is the subject of chapter 2 and nontransaction corruption of chapter 3.

A second point is the distinction of two stages of economic transition and corresponding patterns of corruption: 1978 (but especially 1984) to 1992 and 1992 to the present. The first period may be characterized as one in which state planners still tried to set commodity prices and production quantities, and decided who benefited from them. Though the erosion of such planning already began in various localities before reform, it was in 1984 that the state legally took many commodities off the system of central planning by formally allowing a "two-track system." This created a part-plan and part-market system in which firms could price and sell their products in the market after fulfilling state output quotas. The second period, initiated by Deng Xiaoping's famed southern tour of spring 1992 and continued since then, may be characterized as a period in which markets replaced state planners: the state in effect scrapped planned prices and production, except for military goods and a few key commodities.[77] In the ensuing empirical chapters, the evolution of market reforms and concomitant corruption will be organized, both chronologically and thematically, by the two major reform periods.

A third distinction is the differentiation of corruption across localities. Just as corruption has varied across reform periods, regional variation has existed in the scope, scale, and nature of corruption, thanks to degrees of market transition and state capacities. These structural factors are compounded by geographical ones that entail different opportunities for localities. I propose three regional models. The top-down model is usually found in less-developed and more geographically remote counties where the strength of the state and market opportunities are both meager. Here corruption starts from the top with ripple effects down the chain of the administrative command. The bottom-up model, by contrast, is usually found in more developed regions where societal and market forces are strong even while the central state may not be particularly weak or distant. Here, the vibrant activities of societal groups can engulf local officials, or alternatively, offer enticing inducements for the latter. The top-bottom model, finally, is usually found in metropolitan centers and provincial capitals where the reach of the central state may be close, but the strength of the local government and market forces can be just as strong. Here the local state and market forces are well matched, and the corrupt ac-

---

[77] I thank Professor Lynn White for helpful comments on characterizing the two periods.

tivities of officials and societal groups tend to interact with and reinforce one another. The dynamics of these three regional patterns is the subject of chapter 4.

A final analytical framework is the distinction of incentives/opportunities *for* versus disincentives/checking mechanisms *against* corruption. If the former motivate and encourage violators, the latter deter and constrain them. The deterrents thus may be as important as the stimulants. The disincentive mechanisms may be looked at from four dimensions. Structurally, the CCP's traditional instruments included the control of its agencies and agents through the hierarchy of administrative command, the power of appointment and promotion, and the disciplinary apparatus. Policywise, the traditional lack of local decision autonomy and policy flexibility minimized leeway for sectarian policy making, thus thwarting arbitrary local policies. Ideologically and morally, the party traditionally relied on ideological and moral exhortation, education, and ideological/moral criteria in personnel matters. Administratively, the grass-roots party branch, with its dominance over critical and routine decisions, was once the forceful and faithful enforcer of cadre discipline in the past. Periodic sessions of criticism and self-criticism meetings, political campaigns, and high political/personal costs also helped to ensure deterrence and compliance. How each of these dimensions has fared will be the subject of chapter 5.

Chapter 6 concludes by highlighting two major implications from the book: one regarding the relationship between corruption and the transition to the market, and the other regarding corruption and the state in the transition from a state-dominant to a market economy.

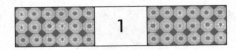

1

THE PHENOMENOLOGY OF REFORM-ERA CORRUPTION

Categories, Distribution, and Perpetrators

I will present in this chapter not abstract definitions but a comprehensive phenomenology of reform-era corruption. This systematic delineation, not yet made in the English language, can offer us a concrete and tangible understanding of corrupt acts in reality: What forms have been prevalent since economic reform and what has been their distribution over time? Who have been the major perpetrators, and what are the usual loci of their power? These basic questions are central to my theses about the linkage between evolving reforms, weakening state institutions, and attendant corruption. On the basis of Chinese casebooks, I first categorize corrupt acts in the reform era. Then I give an overview of their distribution—which have been more dominant in each reform period and over time. Then I explore the administrative background of frequent offenders. The phenomenology of post–Mao corruption, I suggest, has been essentially defined by features introduced by the market reforms.

CHANGING CATEGORIES OF CORRUPTION

Legal definitions and classifications of more than a dozen categories of corruption are delineated in the casebooks used for this book.[1] These delin-

---

[1] Casebooks #3 and 4 up to 1992. Updated versions in Zhu Lixin, *Chaban Tanwu Shouhui Anjian*

eations, rather than the criminal code, are used as reference here because not all forms of corruption are covered by the criminal code. There is also considerable flexibility in interpreting what constitutes corrupt behavior at the local level. The explications by professional analysts thus provide better practical guidance. The organizing principle for differentiating the categories is the type of deviation from official rules and duties, or the type of misuse of public resources. Of those under "common categories," negligence and moral decadence may not be considered as corruption outside the Chinese context. But they are important in China. Those falling under the "other categories" are insignificant to my theme and will not be treated in the book. The original Chinese terms are standard usages.

Common Categories of Cadre Corruption	*Other Categories of Misconduct*
embezzlement	violation of family planning policies
misappropriation	violation of diplomatic codes
bribery	disclosure of classified information
illegal profiteering	deserting overseas posts
negligence	
squandering	
privilege seeking	
illegal earnings	
smuggling	
moral degeneration	

Embezzlement (*tanwu*)

Embezzlement is a criminal offense referring to the theft of a minimum of Y2000 in the 1979 criminal law (but Y5000 after new laws in 1997) of public funds through accounting fraud (*Tanwu* means exactly embezzlement). Traditionally (referring to the socialist era) this involved small thefts through fraudulent bookkeeping. But a range of new methods have been made possible by the presence of independent contractors and private businesses since market reform, including:

1. Theft through contract fraud. An example of this is a manager of a state-owned enterprise (SOE) who contracts a construction project to an independent builder at 20 percent higher than the normal price. In return, the manager receives shares in the project, thereby indirectly embezzling a part of the project fund.

Zhifa Shouce (Manual for the Investigation of Embezzlement and Bribery) (Beijing: Zhongguo Jiancha Chubanshe, 2001).

2. Theft through payment fraud. In this case, an official could forward
   firm funds to a self-employed merchant for purchase payments. He
   recovers a bulk of the fund from the latter, thus embezzling it. Such
   illicit transaction is difficult to pull off between two state firms.

3. Theft through receipt fraud. For instance, an official or manager
   claims reimbursements by using receipts that itemize personal purchases as company ones. Again, private merchants are more than
   willing to provide such receipts.

4. Theft through managerial fraud. Here, a manager could put fictitious expenses in the books by overstating employee roster, bonus
   payment, and business expenses, or by understating pay deductions
   and other savings. Flexible remuneration and managerial autonomy
   under reform have facilitated such practices.

5. Theft through property transfer. In this case, a manager can transfer
   portions of the state assets under his control to a private business. He
   can also transfer portions of his state firm's revenues, bank loans, tax
   refunds, and such to private accounts. Almost impossible before reform and still difficult in much of the 1980s, such illicit transfers have
   become easy under managerial autonomy and shareholding reforms.

Bribe Taking (shouhui)

Bribe taking, a criminal offense if the amount of the bribe was at least Y2000
since 1979 but Y5000 after 1999, has evolved from petty gifts for personal
use before reform to a variety of creative and costly forms since then. Bribery
differs from most other categories here in that two-way exchanges are always
present and that the source of black money is the societal end of this exchange. Major new forms include:

1. Commission payments. Commissions are legal though their role remains controversial.[2] They are treated as bribe taking when (i) ex-
   torted or accepted against regulations and (ii) damages are incurred
   to firm or public interests. An example of this is when a manager orders substandard products from a township/village enterprise (TVE)
   because of commission payments from the latter.

2. Salaries and bonuses. Here, bribe givers put officials or their family
   members on their company's payroll as fictitious consultants or em-

[2] Chen Bo, "The Current State and Problems of 'Commissions' and How to Deal with Them,"
Jingji yu Fa 10 (1993): 13–14; Chen Xinliang and Huang Zhenzhong, "Commissions and Coping
Strategies," *Zhengzhi yu Falu* 2 (1993): 27–28.

ployees. Given high turnover rates in nonstate enterprises, it is difficult for state regulators to uncover such fraud. In the state sector, enterprises can give bonuses to their superiors in state agencies for their administrative "support." Such indirect forms of bribes are antidetection sensitive.

3. Loans, purchases, and reimbursements. These forms protect a bribe taker from possible evidence of wrongdoing. He can get "loans" from bribe givers with IOU slips, receive gifts with sale receipts attached, or reimburse personal shopping expenses.

4. Product trials. With the flourishing of new and luxury products, this form of bribe is regarded as appropriate and safe.

5. Special occasion gifts. Before reform a savvy briber looked for proper occasions like holidays, weddings, and funerals, now they also prize special occasions such as the departure of officials' children for prep schools, colleges, or overseas studies.

Misappropriation (nuoyong)

A criminal offense if the money involved amounted to at least Y5000, misappropriation is the unauthorized use of public funds by individuals. It differs from embezzlement in that the appropriated funds are intended to be returned later. Embezzlement charges ensue if they are not returned before the end of official investigations. This violation used to involve small amounts for personal or family needs, but has changed much in scale and purpose:

1. Loans for commercial use, either legal (business, stocks, and other uses) or illegal (smuggling, drug trafficking, substandard manufacturing, unlicensed business, among others). For instance, a self-employed person persuades a friend to lend him some public funds to start a business or repay an urgent debt.

2. Diversion of designated funds. Most notable are the "five relief funds" designated for the cases of natural disasters, emergencies, floods, social welfare, and families of disabled servicemen and martyrs. Heavy punishment is incurred if fund diversion results in human casualties or property losses.

Squandering (huihuo langfei)

Squandering, the wasting of public funds, traditionally conjured up images of lavish feasting and feudal rites (weddings and funerals). These practices are rooted in the ethos of Chinese communities. Adding to this ethos is the increased autonomy over finances and the greater pressures for cultivating connections under market competition. New forms are:

1. Feasting, gift giving and sight-seeing. The pretexts used to be special occasions, now they range from any business gathering to any occasion of celebration, such as the commencement of a new project, a new product, or a new contract. The grandeur of the occasion ranges from limousine pickups to fancy discos, aside from lavishing feasting.

2. Luxury amenities, for example, imported cars, fancy offices, latest models of cell phones, and residential construction for officials' consumption.

Privilege Seeking (yiquan mousi)
This is the seeking of favors for relatives, friends, and oneself. The favors may be economic or noneconomic in nature, but do not directly involve bribes. Once the most common form of abuse, it is still unrelated to reform in many ways—for instance, to secure a job for one's offspring, accept excessive gifts, or occupy larger residences than duly entitled. But reform has given rise to some new practices:

1. Allocating regulated goods to relatives and friends. The phenomenon is not new, but opportunities for profiteering from such goods have multiplied.

2. Paying private tuition. Under educational reform, those not qualified for regular admission can pay private tuition. Hence a variety of ways emerge to pay the private tuition of one's offspring, for example, asking subordinate agencies for a contribution, a legitimate request if trainees are to return to the sponsoring organization for employment.

Illegal Earnings (feifa shouru)
This is an offense where the accused cannot account for apparent discrepancies between his possessed assets and all possible incomes. A gap of a few thousand yuan suffices for disciplinary action, while "extraordinary" discrepancies warrant criminal prosecution. Actual cases before 1992 showed that a gap of Y60,000 or more resulted in convictions, while a gap of less than Y10,000 resulted in case dismissal. The bar was raised to Y300,000 in the late 1990s. This offense is often discovered accidentally, such as during the investigation

of another violation or through random tips. One burglar was so enraged by his discovery of startling wealth during one housebreaking that he brought the loot to the police. A little girl fetched some bank notes from under Grandpa's bed to buy ice pops, unaware of the high figures on them. One victim of burglary reported his huge losses, but could not explain why he was egregiously rich. Illegal income usually comes from profiteering, bribes, embezzlement, or smuggling.

Negligence (*duzhi*)

Negligence occurs when material or human damages result from neglect of official duties, for example, failure to perform one's duties, or to perform them correctly and competently, or acting recklessly outside one's duties. Traditionally negligence referred to bureaucratic laxity leading to disasters like building collapses or forest fire. Now it has become a serious economic offense capable of causing huge financial losses. Negligence is included in this book because the profit incentive is often behind deliberate or involuntary negligence, and public resources are always involved. Common forms are:

1. Negligence in business ventures and deals. An example of this occurs when an official's failure to conduct background checks or read fine prints results in defrauding or contractual breaches.

2. Negligence in supervision and regulation. Here production and marketing of harmful products can occur because of officials' failure to prevent and deter them.

Illegal Profiteering (*touji daoba*)

This becomes a criminal offense when it results in a minimum gain of Y10,000–200,000 in revenues for individuals, and Y300,000–600,000 in revenues for organizations, depending on the circumstances. Before reform, typical offenders were idle peddlers of small goods. But the scale and size of profiteering skyrocketed under the dual-track system in the 1980s. Public organizations and their employees became typical offenders. Funding for speculative activities expanded from private to organizational funds. Most common were the speculation of:

1. State-regulated goods, that is, goods allocated through state plans (key industrial and agricultural inputs), goods distributed through designated dealers (vehicles, imports and exports, mining and medical products), imports, and foreign currencies.

2. State-regulated permits, for instance, quotas and authorizing documents for controlled goods, services, contracts, delivery orders, and
   foreign trade licenses.

3. Illegal products and schemes, such as counterfeit products and contracts, provision of assistance to illegal profiteers, monopoly over
   supply and prices, and price hiking.

Violation of Accounting Procedures (*weifan caijing jilu*)

This applies only to public organizations, firms, and their executives, that is,
the work unit and its chief executive. Unlike the private sector, these public
actors must comply with state procedures governing the administration of
budgets, taxes, prices, wages, bonuses, revenues, and foreign currency. Yet decentralization, local autonomy, tax, and ownership reforms have greatly increased violations by local state agencies and firms. Most notably:

1. Retention of revenues due to the state. Common practices are concealed profits and other taxable income; unauthorized tax deductions and refunds; underreported or concealed foreign currency
   earnings; and falsely reported costs, profits, and losses.

2. Cheating the state out of financial allocation, subsidies, and other
   allowances: for example, overreporting of expenditures, losses, deficits, or staff size.

3. Illicit use and extraction of public funds. Examples of this include
   unauthorized diversion and use of designated funds and revenues;
   changing in-budget funds into outside-budget funds; unauthorized
   extraction of levies and fines, and their unauthorized disbursement.

4. Changing the nature of state assets: for example transferring state
   property to affiliated collectives or using unreported earnings to set
   up slush funds.

5. Price hiking, examples of which include the sale of plan-track inputs or products at market prices, or the sale of plan-track goods
   through affiliated trading companies.

6. Illegitimate increase of wages, bonuses and subsidies.

Smuggling (*zousi*)

This refers to the trafficking of controlled goods, or of legal goods by evading tariffs, import quotas, and entry inspection. It is criminal when the value

of such goods exceed Y20,000 for individuals and Y300,000 for organizations. If accompanied by special smuggling equipment, armed protection, and violent resistance to inspectors, any volume of smuggling is prosecutable.[3] The range of smuggling goods has evolved from small consumer goods in the early 1980s to inputs and household electronics in the mid-1980s and to big items such as automobiles and petroleum in the 1990s.

Moral Decadence (daode duoluo)

This offense covers a wide range of personal lapses: slandering and framing others, rape and other insults to women, disturbing public order, drug-related trespasses, soliciting prostitutes, gambling, spreading porno materials, wrecking marriages, domestic abuse, failing to provide for aging parents or young offspring, securing career promotions through fraud, fleeing scenes of imperiled humans or public properties, adultery, and sexual harassment. Many of these wrongs have no direct relation to reform, but those forms that involve bribery and misappropriation have become a significant part of corruption under reform. Notably:

1. Patronizing prostitutes. This becomes corrupt behavior when paid for by public funds or at bribe givers' expense. Since reform it has become not uncommon for officials to claim business reimbursements for visiting special saunas and discos. Savvy private businessmen have also found such treats to be among the most effective forms of bribe.

2. Sheltering mistresses. Common since the late 1980s, this has become a frequent motive for officials to assemble huge expense accounts through graft. The reason is to please the much younger, always insatiable, and often multiple mistresses. In fact, almost all of the offenders at the deputy provincial governor level and above fell for this trap: deputy governor Ni Xiance of Jiangxi (1989), deputy governor Tuohudi Shabi'er of Xinjiang (1992), mayor Chen Xitong and deputy mayor Wang Baosheng of Beijing (1995), deputy governor Meng Qingping of Hubei (1999), governor Cheng Kejie of Guangxi (2000), deputy governor Hu Changqing of Jiangxi (2000) and governor Li Jiating of Yunnan (2001).

Given the changing nature of what may be defined as "public" under economic reform, the definition of "public employees" culpable of corruption

---

[3] Casebook #4, 142–45.

has become complex. By occupation, any public employee has some access to or authority over public resources. This person may also be employed in organizations of varying degrees of "publicness," the identification of which has evolved over time. In the 1979 criminal law, two groups of public employees were defined culpable of embezzlement, bribery, and misappropriation: (1) employees in state agencies, the military, state firms, and nonbusiness public institutions (educational, cultural, and social) and (2) representatives of the state in "other public organizations," for example, neighborhood or village administrations.[4] With the rise of collective firms, employees of these companies came to be defined as "public employees" since 1985 and formally in 1988.[5] Illegal income and negligence may only apply to strictly defined state employees, not public employee of quasi-state and collective enterprises. The restricted standard is conceptually and empirically plausible. To determine illegal income requires meticulous documentation of all possible income resources in the court. So only state employees, with their fixed salaries, can have their incomes determined with some certainty. Like illegal income, negligence is hard to access in collective and joint-owned enterprise. Since ownership is mixed here, it is hard to prove that negligence has resulted in damages to overwhelming public interests.

The confines of "other public organizations" have expanded over time. The term now covers state and collective firms contracted to individual managers, joint-stock firms where the state or the collective has a major share, and Chinese-foreign joint ventures where the Chinese shares are owned by the state or collectives. Nonmanagerial employees in these firms cannot be accused of abusing public office as long as the nature of their occupation is labor (*laowu*), not decision making. They may only be charged with common crimes. Another difference is that Chinese managerial personnel are subject to both legal and administrative sanctions (and party sanctions if applicable), while ordinary employees are subject to legal sanctions only. In the revised criminal law of 1997, individuals appointed by state agencies to head joint ventures and contracted or leased state firms are formally defined as "state employees."[6] Of two other controversial groups, retired officials are treated

[4] Articles 126, 155, and 185 of the Criminal Law of the People's Republic of China, adopted at the second plenum of the fifth National People's Congress on July 1, 1979, and effective since January 1, 1980.

[5] The Supreme People's Court and the Supreme People's Procuratorate, "Explications of Some Legal Issues in Handling Economic Crime Cases at Present," announced on July 8, 1985; and "Amendment to the Laws on Embezzlement and Bribe-taking," adopted by the 24th Plenum of the 6th NPC in January 1988.

[6] Zhang Jun, "The Revision and Application of Laws on Embezzlement and Bribery," *Remin Ribao* (overseas edition), hereafter RMRB, August 30, 1997.

as state employees when utilizing their former positions for graft, while family members of officials are not when exploiting official advantages. The later may be treated as accomplices.[7] Other categories have expanded in meaning because they now apply to both individuals and organizational actors, in response to the rise of the latter since reform. Illegal profiteering, smuggling, and squandering are applicable to both individuals and organizations, while accounting violations apply to public organizations and their chief executives on the organizations' behalf. "Organizations" refer to work units (*danwei*). Their illegal activities are defined as corruption because they receive state budgets, plans, allocation, or tax privileges. Similar violations are considered as regular crimes for nonstate firms and employees. The revised law of 1997 introduced two new offenses for the work unit and its chief executive: unauthorized dispersion of state properties and unauthorized dispersion of confiscated properties and fines. The addition is due to the rise of privatization schemes among SOE managers and arbitrary fiscal extraction by state agencies. Other new categories added since the mid-1990s—tax fraud and failure to disclose overseas financial deposits—apply to both individuals and organizations.

Finally, moral misconduct is considered corruption only for public employees, subject to disciplinary sanction but seldom a criminal charge. The explosion of "decadent" temptations means that more and more public employees are likely to commit the offense. But the growth of the nonstate sector also means that proportionally fewer and fewer individuals will qualify for discipline. A summary of the foregoing categories, according to the type of actors, the relationship between officials and societal groups, and the source of black money, appears on table 1.1.

The peculiar circumstances of economic transition have led to variations in interpreting corruption at the ground level. Localities are given flexibility to apply central decrees according to local conditions. Standards are allowed to vary with different types of public organizations. This pluralism means that the same offense may be corrupt in one case but not another. Across regions, divergent implementation results from different levels of development and economic regionalism. For example, banquets and gifts at public expenses may be prohibited in one place but promoted as necessary measures in another. Using bribes to market products may be a corrupt practice in one setting but a creative one in another.[8] Many folk sayings testify to the looser standards in more developed regions. Most vivid is "a model worker in

---

[7] Case book #3, 39–40; and the Supreme People's Court, "Explications."

[8] Li Junchao, "Analyzing the Pluralization of Corruption Standards," *Beijing Shehui Kexue* 3 (March 1990): 136–41.

TABLE 1.1 Topology of Chinese corruption

Patron–client exchange/Source of black money

Type of actor	Essential/Nonpublic	Nonessential/Public	Mixed/Mixed
Organizational	Bribery	Accounting violations* Squandering Negligence Smuggling Illegal profiteering Tax fraud	Illegal Income

Individual	Bribery	Embezzlement
		Misappropriation
		Negligence
		Smuggling
		Illegal profiteering
		Tax fraud
			Illegal income**
			Moral
			  decadence
			Privilege
			  seeking

*This may be inclusive of the three new categories for public organizations: unauthorized dispersion of state properties; of confiscated properties, levies and fines; and unauthorized overseas financial deposits.
**This may be inclusive of the new category, undisclosed overseas financial deposits.

Guangdong may be a criminal in Shanghai, a chair of meetings in Hainan may be a bearer of handcuffs in Beijing" (*Guangdong dang mofan, Shanghai shi zuifan; Hainan nian jianggao, Beijing dai shoukao*). Another saying holds that "one can go to any kind of places in Guangdong, do any kind of business in Fujian, make any kind of money in Zhejiang, and hire any kind of people in Jiangsu." Across public organizations, standards are stricter on officials in the party and state apparatus than on those in SOEs. For instance, in regulations over gift giving and gift accepting, words like "small in amount, reasonable, and necessary" are used to modify the restrictions on SOE officials.[9] Across work units, divergent application can result from different forms of owner-ship. Standards are more stringent on publicly and collectively owned firms than on those of joint, village, or cooperative ownership. The public sector has to comply with state accounting procedures and has less nominal fiscal flexibility.[10]

There are even different standards for different individuals. While ordinary offenders are subject to regular sanctions, the so-called "able people" (*neng-ren*, or those who can generate profits) are measured by the "criterion of production forces" (i.e., economic contribution). After Deng's spring talk of

[9] Ibid., 136–137.
[10] Chen Bo, "The Current State and Problems of 'Commissions,' 13–14.

1992, the Prosecutors' Office in Shanghai pledged lenient consideration for such offenders, prompting a wave of appeal requests and a major public debate.[11] Supporters hailed such differentiated treatment as a "judicial progress." Critics objected on the ground that such pluralism would encourage more violations. Out of concern for moral consistency, the latter favored the centralization of standards through state legislation. For reasons of economic efficiency, supporters of legal pluralism favored continued regional and sectoral flexibility.

In December 1996, standards of honest conduct became a topic of heated debate on the floor of the National People's Congress (NPC) during discussions of a new anticorruption bill. Disagreements among delegates forced the bill to be withdrawn from voting. The major contention was over the scope of the law, or the scope of behavior and personnel to be defined as corrupt. Some lawmakers wanted a more restricted scope and supported naming the bill the Law on Administrative Supervision, thus limiting its application to state bureaucrats. Others argued on constitutional grounds that it should simply be called the Law on Supervision, without qualifying it to the administrative arena. The latter approach would extend the legal application to nonadministrative offenders and place everyone equal before the law. Another point of contention was over the treatment of SOE managers. If designated as state employees, they would qualify for the maximum penalty of death for corruption. Some held that they should be defined as public officials since they accounted for 75 percent of all violations. Others countered that this was unfair since managers of nonstate firms faced only a maximum of fifteen years in jail for corruption.[12] The bill was eventually passed in the May 1997 session of the NPC, under the name of the Law on Administrative Supervision. The narrower scope signified a victory for those who favored a more differentiated treatment of corruption.

In sum, the range of *individuals* culpable for corruption has broadened or shrunk in response to the changing nature of the organizations in which they are employed. So has the range of culpable *behavior* evolved under each category of corruption. Overall, the essence of each category remains, but the forms it takes and the degree of culpability have significantly evolved and diversified under economic reform.

[11] Ling Dun, "Can We Make Exception for Criminals Who Are Capable Individuals? A Major Legal Debate in 1992," *She Hui* 12 (December 1992): 9–10; and debates in *Fa Xue* 5, 7, and 10, 1992.

[12] "Disputes Prevent Passage of China Antigraft Law," Reuters, December 30, 1996; "Antigraft Law Delayed by Row on Name," *South China Morning Post* (Internet edition), December 31, 1996. "Dispute over Name Holds up Passage of Chinese Graft Bill," *Straits Times,* December 31, 1996.

DISTRIBUTION OF CORRUPTION CATEGORIES

Which corrupt acts have been more dominant in each reform period and over time? Why? As shown on table 1.2, embezzlement, bribery, and misappropriation top the list as the leading categories throughout the 1990s. They consistently account for around 80 percent of prosecuted economic crime cases each year. Because this table represents cases processed through prosecutors' offices, it does not include some important categories under the jurisdiction of disciplinary agencies, such as accounting violation, squandering, moral misconduct, and privilege seeking. The latter are better reflected in table 1.3, summarized from the ten casebooks used for this book. Rather than reflecting national trends, however, table 1.3 may be better seen as an indication of what type of cases got the attention of disciplinary agencies and casebook compilers. Consistently, bribery and embezzlement top both tables and make up more than half of all cases in both reform periods.

The contrasts between the two tables stem not only from the different data sets, but also from the changing reform landscape. One contrast is the larger presence of embezzlement than bribery in table 1.2, and the reverse in table 1.3. This may indicate two things. One, embezzlement involves larger or more verifiable amounts of loot, thus resulting in more prosecuted cases. Two, bribery may matter more to the case compilers of our casebooks. In reality, bribery may be far more widespread than reported data indicate. Embezzlement and misappropriation are often uncovered through routine reviews and random exposure of financial discrepancies. But bribery involves one-on-one exchanges that are impossible to detect unless the briber breaks the silence, or the bribee is implicated in separate investigations, or is suspected of unwarranted wealth. Not surprisingly, where citizen tips increase, bribery cases tend to rise more dramatically than other types. For example, in the first four months of 1989, a period of profiteering frenzy, citizen tips in the city of Suzhou increased by 120 percent. Correspondingly, bribery cases investigated by prosecutors jumped by 100 percent, embezzlement cases by 48.1 percent, and misappropriation cases by 71.4 percent over the previous comparable period. By contrast, the rate of increase for all three offenses in 1988, the year before, was only 2.2 percent.[13] Finally, the plethora of unconventional means by which bribes are given directly and indirectly, tangibly and intangibly, are being perfected daily—from paid prostitutes or sight-seeing trips to feigned losses at mahjong and gambling tables. Such schemes are hard to detect or difficult to prove in court.

[13] The Chinese Association of Prosecutorial Studies, ed., *Fan Tanwu Shouhui Lunji* (Collected Papers on Controlling Embezzlement and Bribery) (Beijing: Zhongguo Jiancha Chubanshe, 1990), 127.

TABLE 1.2 Top three categories among all prosecuted crime cases nationwide, 1990s

Year	All economic crime cases** prosecuted	Embezzlement: % of all economic crime cases	Bribery: % of all economic crime cases	Misappropriation: % of all economic crime cases	All three categories
1991	65,955	42.0	26.0	15.3	83.3
1992	61,476	40.8	20.6	17.1	78.5
1993	49,834	37.9	16.8	23.5	78.2
1994	62,875	36.1	24.3	22.8	83.2
1995	58,733	34.5	26.4	19.8	80.7
1996	66,501	32.3	24.8	18.9	76.0
1997	47,589	35.1	24.5	20.3	79.9
1998	34,081	34.9	24.4	23.0	82.3
1999	34,806	37.6	21.7	25.9	85.2

Source: Editorial Board of the Prosecutorial Yearbook of China, ed., *Zhongguo Jiancha Nianjian* (Beijing: Zhongguo Jiancha Cubuanshe, 1992–2000).
**Besides the above three, other categories include in "all economic cases" vary by year but usually encompass tax fraud, illegal income, counterfeiting, perversion of the legal and judiciary process, and negligence.

A second interesting pattern is the large presence of profiteering in the first period, as shown on table 1.3, and its almost absence in the second. This reflects the two-track system, which set off a speculative frenzy in the first period, and its demise after 1992. Illicit profiteering has existed in the second period, as in the speculation of stock shares and other capital goods. But such activities are more often associated with misappropriation and bribery,

TABLE 1.3 Distribution of corruption types over two reform periods based on ten casebooks**

Rank	Category (1980s–1992)	Sub-total	% of total	Category (1992–2002)	Sub-total	% of total
1	Bribery	234	35.6	Bribery	364	58.2
2	Embezzlement	111	16.9	Embezzlement	68	10.9
3	Profiteering	104	15.8	Negligence	47	7.5
4	Accounting violation	49	7.5	Squandering	34	5.4
5	Negligence	38	5.8	Misappropriation	28	4.5
6	Misappropriation	35	5.3	Smuggling	25	4.0
7	Privilege seeking	29	4.4	Sexually related offense	20	3.2
8	Sexual related offense	28	4.2	Privilege seeking	15	2.4
9	Squandering	19	2.9	Accounting violations	12	1.9
10	Illegal income	6	0.9	Illegal income	7	1.1
11	Smuggling	4	0.6	Profiteering	5	0.8
Total		657	99.9		625	99.9

Source: Casebooks 2–9 (1980s to 1994); Casebook 1 (1992 to 2002), Appendix 1.
**Each case can involve several individuals as culprits, and each individual is often convicted on multiple offenses. Only the first, or most important, offense cited in the casebook is counted in the above table.

and usually prosecuted under the latter offenses. This may explain the absence of profiteering cases on both tables after 1992. Third, there is a sizable presence of smuggling cases in the second period and very little of this in the first, as shown on table 1.3. The increase in smuggling cases after 1992 may not so much mean a dramatic jump in reality, but a visible growth in large-scale, organized activities. The reasons are again related to the changing reform course. The demise of the two-track system reduced speculative opportunities and induced changing needs of the domestic market. Consumer demands have increased for big items like automobiles, which, along with the growth of nonstate industries, have expanded the markets for petroleum, another major item in the smuggling trade. The smuggling of such big items, in turn, requires organized operations and insider protection. The result is the rise of large-scale, organized operations, whose executors are prosecuted more often than small individual ones.[14]

Two other categories, accounting violations and privilege seeking, are worthy of note. Both are transgressions typical of a planned economy. But accounting violations escalated in the first reform period thanks to increased firm autonomy, making up almost a third of all disciplinary cases in 1993.[15] Its decline in registered cases since then, in proportion to other categories, is understandable given the demise of the state economy after 1992. Two major changes have affected the level of accounting violation. One, as state financial allocation declined or disappeared, public organizations have found new ways to cheat the public out of funds. Examples of this include imposing fees for services an organization normally performs at no charge, exacting levies on unwarranted grounds, and evading taxes. Yet, such tactics, no less harmful than before and more pervasively felt by the public, are seldom disciplined as corruption. Second, in the rush to downsize state enterprises and diversify public ownership, firm executives have found more lucrative ways to enrich themselves, such as taking bribes, diverting bank loans, swiping state assets, or harboring profits. In other words, any decline of accounting violations by firms would mean a rise in individual abuse by firm executives.

Likewise, privilege seeking has been greatly outdone by bribe taking since reform. There are two essential differences between bribery and privilege seeking. (1) In bribery, an official seeks or receives a pecuniary bribe, in exchange for dispensing a usually profit-oriented favor. In privilege seeking, an

[14] See ch. 4 for more treatment of large-scale organized smuggling.
[15] "A Summary Look at the Efforts to Combat Corruption and Prosecute Major Cases in 1993," *Dangfeng Lianzheng Wenzhai* (hereafter, DFLZWZ) 6 (1994): 31.

official seeks a personal, usually nonprofit-oriented benefit for oneself or one's kin. (2) The exchange under bribery is more commercialized and impersonal, based at the very least on a mixture of *guanxi* and material incentives. In privilege seeking, one primarily explores *guanxi* to attain a goal. Even in the reform period, the leading favors pursued in privilege-seeking cases are excess housing and offspring's future—the sort of benefits pursued typically in the socialist period. Only now, "excess housing" no longer means an extra room or unit, but lavish renovation or new construction.

The data in tables 1.2 or 1.3, however, do not reflect the real rates of occurrence and detection. The latter are affected by reform policies and anti-corruption moves. This is clear from figure 1.1, which indicates clear cycles of corruption in the 1980s. As shown below, the first cycle started in 1978, or the first year of reform, and peaked in 1982. The year 1982 showed an abruptly high rate, because the previous two years of reform had unleashed a thrust of profiteering activities. This in turn led to the government's first *yan da* (tough crackdown) in April 1982, producing a high exposure rate for the year. The second wave of corruption peaked in 1986, two years after the launch of urban reforms in 1984 that ushered in a wider range of commercial and shady activities. In response, the second round of *yan da* came in late 1985, accounting for the abruptly high case rate in 1986. Then from late 1987, the resumption of reform after the Thirteenth Party Congress stimulated a new wave of commercial activity. The ensuing profiteering frenzy became destabilizing and culminated in the Tiananmen protests of spring 1989. This was in turn followed by the toughest round of crackdown since 1978. The bribery data for 1988–1989 vividly reflect this turn of events (see figure 1.1).

Table 1.4 shows that while all economic corruption cases doubled between 1988 and 1989, bribery rose almost fivefold in absolute numbers. The increase is logical given the key role of bribery in profiteering activities that were the hallmark of the late 1980s. Real occurrence could be even higher, if not for a universal amnesty on August 15, 1989, when the Supreme Court and the Supreme Procuratorate announced an amnesty for anyone who voluntarily surrendered to authorities by October 31. More than 52,800 cadres came forward and almost all were let go on the spot, their cases dismissed. This was more than two-thirds of the official figures for that year. In the 1990s, the fluctuations are reflected in table 1.2. The high case rate in 1991 and 1992 reflected official crackdowns in the wake of the Tiananmen protests of 1989. The rise again in 1994–1996 suggests both a return to profiteering activities after 1992 and a new round of *yan da* in the mid-1990s.

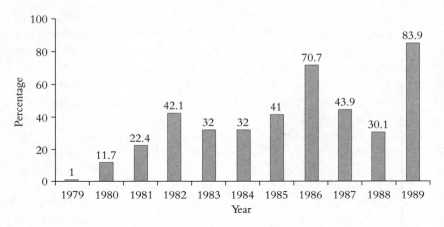

FIGURE 1.1 Percent of embezzlement and bribery cases versus all economic cases
Source: Wei Pingxiong and Wang Ranji, *Tanwu Huilu Zui de Rending yu Duice* (Beijing: Qunzhong
Chubanshe, 1992), 9.

BACKGROUND OF CORRUPT OFFICIALS

There is a clear contrast between the loci of offices where corrupt officials
came from before the early 1990s and where they concentrate since then.
These different loci indicate the changing areas of state power that engender
opportunities for corruption and are thus most affected by it.

In the first period, corrupt officials were typically found in the offices of
the traditional planned economy; these officials exploited reform policies designed to relax the command system. They served in branches of government
that controlled or regulated industries, agriculture, trade, and transportation.
These state functions were changing, but not disappearing. These officials still
administered state command over (1) economic plans and quotas, (2) production inputs and outputs, (3) supply and distribution, (4) finance and expenditure, (5) import and export quotas, and (6) trade and transportation.
Regulated goods and services here were now demanded by the market at a
higher rate than the state price. The main venue for graft was to allocate a
controlled good for a pecuniary benefit. Another was to set up an affiliate
company to sell the goods that should have been allocated through the state
track at controlled prices. The chief executives at each administrative level
faced similar opportunities by virtue of their capacity to place phone calls to
subordinate departments, though mainly the lower-level chiefs took advantage of the opportunity during this period. At higher levels, especially the

TABLE 1.4 Prosecuted bribery cases nationwide, 1988 and 1989

Year	All economic corruption cases nationwide	Bribery cases	Percent of bribery cases
1988	31,230	4,827	15.46
1989	71,587	24,597	34.36

Source: DFLZWZ 11 (1995):12.

county government and up, it was more likely that the spouses, offspring, and assistants of chief officials were directly engaged. Needless to say, it was the officeholder's clout and connections that played the key, helping role.

During the second reform period since 1992, the arena of abuse shifted to what the Chinese refer to as *san ji yi guan,* or three plus one agencies. The "three agencies" refer to party/state executive offices, law enforcement agencies, and judiciary organs. The remainder "one" refers to state economic agencies. Together they make up the state agencies that govern the new economy. The shift has accompanied the transformation of government roles and functions. Shedding off controls over industrial inputs and outputs, the state has turned to four new tasks: development, investment, marketization of factors of production, and transformation of state firms. Central ministries and local departments have been consolidated or reoriented. Personnel have been streamlined or voluntarily moved to the business world. Several new areas of public power have become significant and, likewise, lucrative. These include (1) determination and allocation of public investment, (2) assignment and pricing of land resources, (3) regulation and appraisal of levies and taxes, (4) reorganization and appraisal of state assets, (5) selection and financing of infrastructure projects, (6) regulation of business, labor, trade, and commercial disputes, and (7) provision of social welfare in an expanding market (even global) economy. Unlike in the first period, it is not only those located in specific areas of regulatory power who engage in illegal gain. Even more so do chief executives at local levels. As table 1.5 shows, officials from party and state agencies have become dominant violators, while violators from law enforcement and judiciary organs have also become alarmingly significant.

Beside the government organs (*guojia jiguan*), the other main source of corrupt officials came from what the Chinese refer to as the *guoying qiye* (state enterprises). Again, the marks of the two-track system were clear before 1992. Corruption occurred mainly in sectors that manufactured or retailed goods and services on the two-track system, as managers now had discretionary power over the above-plan portions of those goods and services. Like

TABLE 1.5 Distribution of offenders among "three plus one" agencies
nationwide, 1993–1997

"Three plus one" state agencies	Number of offenders, 1993–1997	Percent of period total
State/Party	16,177	29.5
Law enforcement	17,214	31.4
Judiciary organs	8,144	14.8
Economic governance	13,330	24.3
Period total	54,865	100.0

Source: Zhang Siqing, *Work Report of the Supreme People's Procuratorate,* at the Fifth-Plenum of the Eighth National People's Congress, March 11, 1997.

officials in state agencies, corporate officials exploited price differentials and supply shortages as the primary means to acquire illicit wealth.

This pattern changed after the early 1990s. With scarcity and planning disappearing, state manufacturers now faced a different ballgame. Instead of inputs and outputs, abuse shifted to things financial and far more profitable: loans, revenues, and assets. Instead of profiting from price differentials of goods, company possessions become the main source of illegal profiteering for SOE officials. A major new player, nonmanufacturing state firms, entered the corporate world after 1992. Hailing from capital-intensive sectors, these new SOEs encompass investment companies, property developers, banks, stock exchanges, and insurance companies. These new sectors are capable of generating far greater personal gains for officials than ever before. Not surprisingly, despite the declining importance of state manufacturers, SOE managers make up the largest group of corrupt officials. Table 1.6, based on information from individual provinces, shows that public firms contribute one-half to three-fifths of all economic crime cases, while the "three plus one" state agencies account for one-quarter to a third of such cases.

If the administrative rank of offenders gives any indication to the severity and spread of corruption, the two reform periods show a steady rise in the rank of corrupt officials. All employees of the public sector, whether in government, economic, or noneconomic organizations, attain a rank (*ji*) if they are in the *ganbu* (cadre) category. Here *ganbu* means professional or nonmanual staff, including administrative, managerial, technical, and educational personnel. A rank is determined both by seniority (years of service or the year when one joined the revolution) and by the professional nature of employment. A new entrant in a government bureaucracy usually starts with the *ke* rank. But only a sizable SOE is likely to have its managerial positions placed on the rank system. Officials are not assigned any rank order below the

TABLE 1.6 Distribution of offenders among "three plus one" agencies and public firms: fourteen provinces (Unless otherwise indicated, the figures are from 1996)

Province	"Three plus one" agencies: % of all state agencies and public firms	Party and government agencies: % of "three plus one" agencies	Law enforcement organs: % of "three plus one" agencies	Judiciary organs: % of "three plus one" agencies	Economic agencies: % of "three plus one" agencies	Public firms: % of all state agencies and public firms	SOEs: % of public firms*	TVEs: % of public firms
An'hui	25.8							
Fujian	25.6		18.2 (1998)	17.7 (1998)				
Guizhou	36.7							
Guangxi	32							
Hainan	20.6 (1997)							
Henan	27.6	27.9 (1997)	12.6 (1997)	35.1 (1997)	24.3 (1997)	58.4	44.9 (1999)	
Hubei							55	44.9
Jiangsu	15 18 (1997)	39.7	20.1	11.4	28.6	53.6 (1997)	58.6 (1997)	
Jiangxi	18.9	32.7	14.6	15.4	37.2			30.4 (1997)
Neimeng						33–50 (1999)		
Ningxia						62.5 (1998)		
Shaanxi		34.9 (1997)	14.4 (1997)	33.6 (1997)	17.2 (1997)			
Shandong	19.3 (1993)					66.04 (1993–97)	18.99 (1993–1997)	47.1 (all rural 1993–1997)
Zhejiang		37.8	17.6	30.4	18.9			

Source: Editorial Board of the Prosecutorial Yearbook of China, ed., *Zhongguo Jiancha Nianjian* (The Prosecutorial Yearbook of China) (Beijing: Zhongguo Jiancha Chubanshe), 1998–2000.
*Includes both SOES and TVES. Beside the traditional sectors (manufacturing, transportation, etc.), the SOE data often inclued the new financial, property, and insurance sectors as well. The latter usually make up 10% of all SOE corruption cases.

county level. A rank entails the concomitant benefits that one receives in terms of salaries and nonpecuniary privileges (vehicle usage, housing, phones, and other perks). With the highest rank being *zhongyang,* or central leadership, the hierarchy descends as follows:

1. Collectively known as *sheng-bu ji,* or *sheng-jun ji,* this is the administrative rank equivalent to the head of a central ministry (i.e., the minister), the governor of a province, and the mayor of the four top metropolises. *Jun ji* is the army commander level.

2. Collectively referred to as *di-ting ji, ting-si ji,* or *ting-ju ji. Ting ji* is the rank equivalent to the head of a department in a central ministry or in a provincial government. *Di ji* is the rank equivalent to the head of a *di-qu,* a special government entity between the province and the county. *Si ji* is the regiment commander below the army commander. *Ju ji* is the rank equivalent to the head of a bureau parallel to a department in a central ministry or in a provincial government.

3. Collectively referred to as *xian-tuan ji* or *xian-chu ji. Chu ji* is the rank equivalent to the head of the office (*chu*) under the *ting* level, or under the bureau (*ju*) level in a municipal government. *Xian ji* is the rank of the county magistrate. *Tuan ji* is the regiment commander below the *si* level.

4. *Ke ji* is the rank equivalent to the head of the section under the *chu* level.

A mayor usually has attained a *ting* rank, unless he or she heads a small city or is still early in his or her career. A government bureaucrat in his or her forties usually has attained a *chu* rank. The CEO (*zhong jingli*) or the senior engineer of a large SOE can have a *ting* rank, whereas the manager or senior engineer of a mid-size firm usually has a *chu* rank. (An assistant professor has a *ke* rank, an associate professor a deputy-*chu* rank, and a full professor a *chu* rank.) What these ranks entail is the level of power available to an official, the level of comfort and constraint one feels about the bounds of behavior.

As noted before, the number of violators in a given period fluctuates with the larger context of reform policies and anticorruption campaigns. Nonetheless, tables 1.7 and 1.8 show a steady rise of cadre disciplined at the *xian-chu* level and above. Offenders without a reported rank were usually found in the rural, industrial, and commercial sectors, at the staff level in govern-

TABLE 1.7 Five-year trends in the discipline of Party members

Period	Total number of members investigated	Given penalty	Expelled from the Party	Criminally convicted	Offenders at *xian-chu* rank	Offenders at *di-ting-ju* rank	Offenders at *sheng-bu* rank
1982–1986	N/A	650,000	152,000	N/A	635 (1985 and 1986)	74 (1985 and 1986)	N/A
		100%	23.4%				
1987/10 –1992/9	874,690*	733,543	154,289	42,416	16,108	1430	110
		100%	21%	5.8%	2.2%	0.2%	0.0015%
1993/1– 1997/6	731,000	669,000	121,500	37,500	21,000	1673	78
		100%	18.2%	5.6%	3.13%	0.25%	0.0012%

Source: "Minutes of Anti-corruption Efforts, 1979–1997," *DFLZWZ* 5 (1998):23.
*Figures in this row include disciplinary actions associated with the post-Tiananmen crackdown in 1989. They should thus be higher than normal levels.

ment agencies, or among ordinary ranks of law enforcement agencies. This was especially true in the first reform period when corruption concentrated at lower levels. Here are also where the bulk of the offenders are in the national figures, shown in the two tables below. In fact, interviewees usually attribute the bulk of offenders to the county level and below, where only

TABLE 1.8 Nationwide trends in the discipline of corrupt officials, 1989–2001

Year	Total number of cases investigated by monitoring agencies	Individuals disciplined at *xian-ch-tuan* rank or over	Individuals disciplined at *di-ting-ju* rank	Individuals disciplined at *sheng-bu* rank
1989	38,908 (Jan.–Oct.)	1,212*		3
1990		1,188*		
1991	52,039	1,530*		
1992	150,000+	2,700+		
1993	120,000+	2,462		
1994	116,582 (Jan.–Nov.)	1,833	252	
1995	122,476	3,084	279	24
1996	135,000	3,695	321	13
1997	N/A			
1998	158,000+	5,357	410	12
1999	130,414	4,092	327	17
2000	134,693 (Jan.–Nov.)	4,146	331	21
2001	174,633	6,076	497	16

Source: Liao Wang, 1 (1990), 4 (1992); CCPDIC plenums, Jan. 1993–Jan. 2002.
*These figures include only cases from the Ministry of Supervision. Data from DIC agencies and prosecutors' offices are not included. The three branches began to work together after 1992. The figures after 1992 include data from all three agencies.

county governors are ranked in the cadre hierarchy. Among officials from state agencies, the bulk of offenders fall between the *ke* and *chu* ranks in both periods, or in other words, the lower and middle levels. After the early 1990s, there has been a marked rise of offenders with the *ting-ju* rank, such as chief and deputy executives of cities, government bureaus, law enforcement, judicial agencies, state banks, and large SOEs. Overall, officials ranked at *xian-chu* levels and above account for about 1 percent of prosecuted economic criminals, lower than their share among cases disciplined by DICs.[16]

Tables 1.9 and 1.10 summarize the highest level of officials disciplined for corruption since reform, at the rank of the minister and provincial governor (including deputy levels) and above. All were at the deputy ministerial level and above. The contrasts between our two periods are clear and illuminating. One is the level of bribes. In the first period, the lowest bribe was the equivalent of Y5000. Most bribes were not cold cash but gifts in the form of home electronics. In the second period, the lowest amount was Y62,000 in cash, almost double the highest bribe for the first period, Y38,000. The highest loot in the second period exceeded Y40 million (excluding Wang Baosheng, who committed suicide), an astronomical figure in the Chinese context. Another contrast is the nature of transgression. Among those disciplined in the first period, almost half did not directly engage in corruption. Rather, they merely tolerated, or failed to restrain, the corrupt behavior of others. Even if they did take bribes, these were few and small. By contrast, in the second period, all but Chen Xitong were found directly engaging in bribe taking, with numerous bribe givers and huge material rewards. Even for Chen Xitong, whose downfall is often interpreted as political, the size of his booty more than warranted his fate. The gifts he accepted (gold jewelry, video cameras, and other items) were far more numerous and valuable than the home electronics and boxes of liquor received by the two highest ranking offenders in the first period. Just the two private villas, where Chen and Wang Baosheng spent leisure time and kept their mistresses between January 1993 and February 1995, cost the public nearly Y40 million. These include Y35.21 million in construction costs, Y2.42 million in maintenance fees, and Y1.05 million in catering expenses. The villas were filled with luxuries ranging from gold doors and agate floors to extensive maintenance and security.[17]

[16] Editorial Board of the Prosecutorial Yearbook of China, *Zhongguo Jiancha Nianjian* (The Prosecutorial Yearbook of China) (Beijing: Zhongguo Jiancha Chubanshe), 1991–99.
[17] "Beijing's Highest Court Sentenced Chen Xitong to Prison," DFLZWZ 9 (1998): 21; Chinese Academy of Social Sciences et al., eds., *Zhongguo Gaoguan Fubai de Tedian he Bianhua Qushi* (Characteristics and Evolving Trends of High-ranking Officials' Corruption in China), abridged in *Qiao Bao,* June 5, 2003.

TABLE 1.9 Highest ranking corrupt officials since reform, pre-1992 (deputy *sheng-bu* ranks and up)

Year/ loot	Name	Highest position	Transgression	Penal outcome
1986	Hong Qingyuan	Secretary General of Provincial Council, member of Standing Committee of Provincial Government of An'hui	bribe taking	10-year jail term
1987	Ni Xianche	Deputy Party Secretary and Governor of Jiangxi	helped protect mistress's brother from prosecution for smuggling electronics	2-year jail term
1989	Yang Huiquan	Deputy Governor of Hunan, 1983–1989	failed in his job to clean up '*guan dao*' (official profiteeing) companies, including the company of his son-in-law	Recalled by PPC*, first in the country
1989 Y16,000	Tuo'erti Shabi'er (Uighur)	Deputy Chairman of Xinjiang Autonomous Region	took bribes to allocate state-tracked goods and rail quotas for two (both Han ethnic) mistresses	Dismissed from office
1989	Liang Xiang	Governor of Hainan Province 1987–1989	permitted spouse in speculating two apartment units / supported son in speculating import quotas	Dismissed from office
1989 Y5000	Luo Yunguang	Deputy Minister of Rail Transportation, Early 1980s–1989	overlooked corruption of local officials and accepted bribes from them	Dismissed from office
1990 Y22,000	Zhang Xintai	Deputy Minister of Rail Transportation, 1982–1990	while on assignment to investigate Luo's case, accepted gifts for allocating rail quotas	3-year prison term with a reprieve of 5 years
1990 Y38,000	Han Fucai	Deputy governor and Deputy chairman of Provincial People's Congress, Qinghai Province, 1987–1989	took bribes from building contractors	8-year prison term

Source: Yu Min, *Gongheguo Fanfu Fengbao* (Beijing: Tuanjie chubanshe, 1993), 263–65; Casebook #5, 173–75; Casebook #2, 49–51.
*Indicates the Provincial People's Congress.

CONCLUSION

In this chapter I have enumerated the major categories, distributions, and perpetrators of post-Mao corruption, and in the process, have established that these have changed not only from the prereform period but also across China's two reform periods.

TABLE 1.10 Highest ranking corrupt officials, post-1992 (deputy *sheng-bu* ranks and up)

Exposed/loot	Name	Highest position	Transgression	Penal outcome
1994 Y64,000	Li Xiaoshi	Deputy Director of the State Commission on Science, late 1980s–1993	Y52,000 in bribes for support of a pyramid financial scheme Y12,000 embezzled	20-year jail term
1995 Y113.3m $25m	Wang Baosheng	Deputy Mayor of Beijing (deputy ministerial level), late 1980s–1995	Y300,000 embezzled Y100m and U.S. $25m appropriated for other business activities Y13m for private villas	Suicide, April, 1995
1995 Y555,000	Chen Xitong	Mayor of Beijing 1980s to 1995	Y550,000 in gifts protected Wang Baosheng	16-year jail term
1998 Y550,000	Xu Bingsong	Deputy Governor of Guangxi, 1993–1998	Y550,000 in bribes from businessess	Life in prison
1998 Y240,000	Meng Qingping	Deputy Governor of Hainan 1989–1992; of Hubei, 1993–1998	Y240,000 in bribes from contractors, real estate developers, etc.	10-year jail term
1999 Y7.1m	Hu Changqing	Deputy Governor of Jiangxi, 1997–1999	Y5.5m in bribes for contracts, loans, licences Y1.6m unaccounted for	Death
1999 Y40m	Cheng Kejie (Zhuang minority)	Governor of Guangxi 1992–1998; Deputy Chairman of NPC Standing Committee 1998–1999	$40 million in bribes for loans, land, contracts, and promotions helped mistress's business win allocations and loans	Death, first national leader since 1949
2001 Y5m	Li Jizhou	Deputy Minster, Ministry of Public Security, 1994–1998	Y5m from Yuanhua Co. intervened in smuggling investigations	Death, with reprieve
2001 Y18.1m	Li Jiating (Yi minority)	Deputy Governor and Governor of Yunnan, 1994–2001	Y18.1 million in bribes and gift money secured Y3 million in loans for mistress	Death, with reprieve
2001 17m	Cong Fukui	Deputy Governor of Hebei, 1996–2000	Y17 million in bribes for contracts, projects, etc.	Death, with reprieve
2001 Y697,700	Shi Zhaobin	Deputy Party Secretary of Fujian	intervened in smuggling investigations for bribes	13-year jail term
2001 Y866,322	Liu Zhibing	Deputy Governor of Guangxi Autonomous Region	Y866,322 in 53 bribes for loan guarantees and intervening in smuggling investigations	15-year jail term
2003 Y9.97 m	Wang Huangzhong	Deputy Governor of Anhui, 1994–2001	Y5.17 m in bribes and Y4.8 m in illegal income	Death

Source: DFLZWZ and DFLZ, various issues, 1994–2004 and http://english.peopledaily.com.cn.

In her book about Chinese corruption during the socialist period, Julia Kwong observes several peculiar forms. One was the fabrication of reports or output to please upper echelons and gain honors. Another was the hoarding and bartering of goods to avoid the consequences of inelasticity and scarcity of supplies. A third was organizational corruption, that is, illicit activities for the collective interest of the work unit on which the individual depended for his many needs. Finally, state property was the major target of illegal activities.[18] In his paper about Chinese corruption in the socialist period, Alan Liu classifies three categories of corrupt acts, including those universal among nations (embezzlement and bribery); those typical of the plan economy (misappropriation, illegal trade, and housing irregularities); and those peculiarly Chinese Communist (illegitimate feasting, feudal rites, false models, or illegal imprisonment).[19] Both scholars place the blame on central planning, the concentration of resources in the state sector, shortages of supplies and goods, and multifunctionality of public organizations.

This chapter has shown that the characteristics of corruption have changed in major ways in the reform period. While still marked by degrees of universal and Chinese features, they have been significantly reshaped and expanded. The ten categories of corruption delineated in the chapter can be further divided into three groups, along Alan Liu's framework. The first group, such as embezzlement, bribery, and misappropriation, is universal in all political systems. Not surprisingly, they remain prevalent in the reform context. But their features have changed in fundamental ways. While state property is still a major target of this category of crime, it is no longer the sole target or venue. Rather, it is the greater inducement from and dependence on the market that now defines the forms and methods of a transgression. The second group of corrupt acts, such as profiteering, accounting violation, squandering, negligence, and privilege seeking, is germane to a centralized economy. These acts have continued to thrive after reform. But they are no longer fueled by the old dynamics of economic scarcity or the desire to please or cheat upper echelons. Rather, it is decentralization, autonomy, increased resources, and new sources of exploitation that have driven newer and more severe forms of corruption of this type. The third group of corrupt acts, broadly characterized as moral decadence, may be peculiarly Chinese. Even here the marketplace has stimulated distinctive forms of moral deviation in recent years.

[18] Julia Kwong, *The Political Economy of Corruption in China* (Armonk, N.Y.: M. E. Sharpe, 1997).
[19] Alan Liu, "The Politics of Corruption in the People's Republic of China," *American Political Science Review* 77:2 (1983): 602–21.

The distribution of corrupt forms has evolved in response to changing reform policies. Those forms associated with the two-track system of the early
reform period receded in the second period, while dominant forms in the
latter period have stemmed from the transfer of the allocative and distributive mechanisms of the plan to the market. Further, the violators of public
duties are no longer mainly officials located at public enterprises, as was the
case before reform. Though this group has remained sizable, offenders are just
as likely to come from state agencies and nonbusiness public organizations,
and at all ranks of the official strata. Further, officials no longer need to have
physical control over public resources to seek private gains. They are more
likely to have regulatory and allocative powers, and, increasingly, decision
powers over such matters as credits, trade, contracts, land, and privatization.

Clear departure from prereform patterns is only part of the evidence for
the strong linkage between economic liberalization and new forms of corruption. Another part is the changing patterns of corruption across post-Mao
reform periods. The type of public office and resources available to corrupt
officials, as well as the loci of state agencies and agents vulnerable to abuse,
has evolved along with progressively deepening marketization and state retreat from the economy. At state agencies, the range of offices open to abuse
has shifted from economic and regulatory agencies to executive branches, developmental agencies, and legal/judiciary organs. At state enterprises, the
type of sectors vulnerable to abuse has expanded from the allocation, production, and retail processes to the financial, property, and extractive arenas.
In all, the linkages between reform and post-Mao corruption emerge as the
basic characteristic in the phenomenology of contemporary Chinese corruption.

2

BETWEEN OFFICIALS AND CITIZENS

Transaction Types of Corruption

In transaction-type corruption, "transaction" refers to the presence of two-way exchanges between officials and citizens. The former supplies an official service in return for a material reward from the latter. The receipt of this reward is a main motive to supply the service, although this can be mixed with affective motives. Transaction, as used here, does not include such actions as the splitting of funds among members of a work unit, transfer of public assets to private accounts, levying of arbitrary fees and fines, or negligence that results in shady business dealings. Though some form of transaction in a general sense does take place in the above instances, in none of them is bribery the deciding factor. These nontransaction types will be treated in chapter 3. Transaction-type corruption, for this chapter, involves mainly bribery, perhaps the most prevalent type of violation in the post-Mao period. Thanks in large part to its dominance, bribery is often synonymous with corruption in the revisionist, rent-seeking, and other major theories of corruption. But bribery is at most synonymous with transaction-type corruption.

I shall show that reform policies have created new contexts for bribery, resulting in incentives, mechanisms, and consequences that differ from those in the prereform era on one hand, and from those across reform periods on the other. In the reform period from 1978 (but especially from 1984) to 1992, corruption largely exploited the loopholes of a mixed plan and market system, playing more mixed roles, thanks to its corrosive effects on the irrationalities of a mixed economic system. In the period since then, corruption has largely exploited the disintegration of the socialist economy and the process of its handover to the market, playing far more damaging roles, thanks to its obstructive effects on the functioning of a fledging market system. Revisionist arguments about economic efficiency and social integration, thus, are more relevant to the first reform period than to the second.

REFORM AND CORRUPTION: WHAT INCENTIVES AND OPPORTUNITIES?

This section addresses the first question of the chapter: what are the causal linkages between economic liberalization and transaction-type corruption over China's two reform periods?

Bribes are paid for two reasons: to obtain government benefits and to avoid costs. When the government distributes or buys goods and services, it creates such benefits as contracts, below-market prices, credits and interest rates, exchange rates, and subsidies. When the government imposes regulations, levies taxes, and enforces laws, it creates such costs as regulatory barriers, tax burdens, and delayed services. Economic liberalization creates many new government benefits, such as multiple prices and credit rates, the contracting of public projects, the organization of privatization, and foreign trade. The costs that the government imposes are critical for fledging businesses in emerging markets: license approval, regulatory restriction, property disposal, and tax/ tariff rates. Simply put, new government benefits stimulate incentives for obtaining exclusive access, while newly imposed costs generate incentives for favorable interpretation and enforcement of rules.[1]

The exchange of material rewards for official favors is by no means exclusive to the reform period. But the role of commercial advantage as an incentive makes the key difference. Two contrasts are particularly relevant. First, a reform official usually takes a pecuniary reward in exchange for dispensing a profit-oriented advantage. By contrast, his predecessor usually took a nonmonetary gift for a personal, nonprofit-oriented advantage. Second, reform-era exchanges are more commercialized and impersonal, based at the very least on a mixture of *guanxi* (affective ties) and material incentives. Preform exchanges primarily involved *guanxi,* along with noncash gifts. In fact, during the prereform period, the exchange of private gains and official favors was categorized as "privilege seeking," a lesser violation than bribery. "Priv-

[1] Susan Rose-Ackerman, "The Political Economy of Corruption," in Kimberly Elliot, ed., *Corruption and the Global Economy* (Washington, D.C.: Institute for International Economics, 1997): 34–36.

ilege seeking" has survived as a category, referring to such actions as using official access to pursue "excess housing" or "offspring's future"—the sort of benefits typically sought in the socialist period. Market reform, in short, is directly behind the commercialized forms of favor seeking.

The Within-Plan Reform Phase: Mid-1980s to 1992

During this period, both the *incentives* and *opportunities* for bribery were largely rooted in the within-plan reforms. Among the structural opportunities were a dual-track for goods and financial allocation, a continuation of basic plan quotas and inputs, and a parallel economy of a state and a nonstate sector. In short, at least two sets of prices, distribution channels, and players existed for the same goods and loans.[2] One may call these "distortionary policies," as government manipulation of demand, supply, and price produced an artificial state price and channel, spurring "rent-seeking" activities. The new incentives for bribery, on the other hand, concentrated in the following areas: competition for goods and prices on the state track, for market access, for building and management contracts, for favorable enforcement of market-regulating rules, and for trade rights.

By far the most pervasive incentive was competition for access to favorable prices and regulated items on the state track. Examples of this include durable and scarce goods, plan quotas, agricultural and industrial inputs and many outputs, rail transportation, and bank loans. All bribers wanted to gain these items at the cheaper, regulated prices. Microlevel examples best illustrate how the two-track system actually spurred the incentives and mechanisms for corrupt exchanges. The first example shows the opportunities in the allocation of regulated output and funding. Mr. Li Mingfu was a deputy director of the "112 Special Project" Office (*chu*) in the Economy and Trade Bureau (*si*) of the State Commission on Planning, an equivalent ministry in the central government. As the headquarters of the planned economy, the agency retained some allocative powers in the first reform period. In mid-1988, Li was asked by an acquaintance to help procure color television sets for her trading company. Li telephoned a state television factory in Chengdu, claiming that he had made efforts to give the factory an opportunity to bid

---

[2] See Chen Jun of the State Bureau of Taxation, "An Analysis of Price Developments in 1992–93," in Liu Guoguang, ed., *Zhongguo zai Yijiujiusannian: Jingji Fazhan de Fenxi yu Yuce* (China in 1993: Analysis and Predictions of Economic Development) (Beijing: Zhongguo Sheke Chubanshe, 1992): 182–92. And Gao Shangquang, "The Paths and Lessons of China's Economic Restructuring," in Ye Sheng and Wang Haijun eds., *Jingji Tizhi Zhuanbian de Guoji Bijiao* (An International Comparison of Economic Restructuring) (Beijing: Gaige Chubanshe, 1993): 146–56.

for foreign currency quotas and even disclosing the criteria for a successful bid. Thereby he secured a thousand color TV sets at the factory price. Back in Beijing, his friend sold the sets and passed Y13,300 of the earnings to him in "appreciation fees." The friend's profits, calculated at a minimum markup of Y100 per set, would have amounted to Y100,000.[3]

The second example shows the opportunities in the allocation of regulated services and supplies. From April 1985 to February 1989, three individuals used bribery to win rail cargo quotas at the Zhengzhou Rail Station so they could transport coal to other provinces for profiteering. Situated in the capital of Henan Province, the station is a major junction point in the nation's rail system. The trio—a manager of the station's retail service corporation, an official from the provincial utility company, and a private businessman—managed to secure cargo allocation above central plans from the deputy head of the Zhengzhou Railway Bureau, along with approval from the head of the Transportation Bureau at the Ministry of Rail Transportation in Beijing. The three individuals also bribed layers of other officials so they would ignore their activities. Between April 1985 and February 1989, their profits reached several millions of *yuan*. The case eventually implicated more than fifty rail officials, including thirteen at the *ke* level, nineteen at *chu* level, fifteen at *ju* level, and a deputy minister of transportation at the central level, Luo Yunguang (1982–1989). Extraordinary in its scale and level of cadre involvement, the case became the biggest bribery scandal in the rail history of the PRC and brought down the highest-ranking official in the central government before the 1989 Tiananmen protests. Another deputy minister, Zhang Xintai, assigned to investigate the case, fell two years later in 1991 for the same misconduct of allocating rail quotas for bribes.[4]

A second area of incentives for bribery stemmed from market competition. Because reform policies had fostered a nonstate sector alongside the state sector, competition resulted between and within the two sectors for purchase orders. Before reform, purchase agents were responsible for the leading forms of corruption in the planned economy. Since reform, abuse in this area no longer resulted from government distribution or regulation per se, but from interaction among state and nonstate sectors. Typically, a private or village firm bribed a SOE agent, who then placed orders with the briber at above-market prices. The two parties then shared income from the price hikes. Alternatively, a SOE agent would retail company products at below-

[3] Casebook #2, 68–69.
[4] Dong Fang, "A Rare Case in the History of China's Railroad," in *The Research Department of the DIC Office of Chongqing,* ed., *Fanfu Changlian Lu* (Chongqing: the DIC office of Chongqing, 1991): 263–267. Also Casebook #2, 49–51.

market prices, in exchange for bribes from a buyer, usually a nonstate firm. Both practices benefited the nonstate firm at the expense of the state firm and led purchase agents to neglect quality issues. Two examples illustrate typical purchase and sale transactions in the mid- and late 1980s. Mr. Teng, a planner at a state plant, originally signed a contract with a county factory to buy eighteen decelerators for Y35,000. The salesman asked to raise that price and promised Mr. Teng a share of the higher payment. Thereby Mr. Teng bought the same products for Y87,000, at extra costs of Y52,000 to his plant, which resulted in Y1,500 in personal gain. In the second case, Mr. Wan, contract manager of a welding product plant, sold ninety tons of scarce input materials (and some output) at below-market prices to a township/village enterprise (TVE). In return he received Y7,120 in twelve separate bribes. It is noteworthy that the contractor found it more profitable to undersell his inputs for bribes than to sell outputs at market prices.[5]

A third incentive for bribery was access to contracts, especially building and management contracts. Again, reform policies provided the context. Construction contracts flourished once autonomy and decentralization allowed public organizations to hire their own contractors to complete construction projects, such as plant expansion, office renovation, and residential buildings. At the same time, the mushrooming of small, nonstate building teams boosted the growth of a new, private construction sector in the market. Because they were often from rural areas, new to the business, inexperienced, and rarely state certified, those new teams often resorted to bribes to win building contracts. Management contracts emerged in the mid-1980s with the introduction of contract production, whereby SOEs could be contracted to individuals to manage. Medium and large firms were usually contracted to existing managers experienced with the SOE, but small firms and retail stores were more open to outside bidders. The latter again often resorted to bribes. For contract managers, successful bidding was not the only motive. New contract practices had glaring policy defects and faced almost no monitoring and accounting mechanisms. Contractors of small firms and stores could easily embark on short-term self-enrichment at the expense of the firm. Some loaned out firm funds at high interests, others made reckless business decisions or simply nibbled away at firm assets. Abuse was still moderate in the 1980s among building contractors. Most winning builders did not grossly overcharge, skimp on quality, or delay completion, as was common later. And only a small minority of officials overlooked quality problems because of bribes. In fact, some bribers went out of their way to ensure

[5] Casebook #3, 52–54, 55–57.

quality, for deficiencies could easily arouse public suspicion about possible corrupt exchanges, worrying bribe takers and affecting long-term reciprocal relationships. Fear of inquiries restrained both parties and was a strong disincentive against outright abuse at this time.[6]

The case of Mr. Xi is illustrative. Mr. Xi headed the Construction Department of a state-owned food processing plant. When the plant planned to build a freezer storage-house in 1987, it wanted a top-grade builder certified by the state. One TVE, lacking such credentials, begged Mr. Xi to contract the project to a qualified firm from the city but let the TVE subcontract it. As incentive the TVE offered 2 percent of the Y5 million budget in back payments to the primary contractor and to the food plant. Mr. Xi mediated the deal after accepting a bribe of Y100,000 from the TVE, but he strictly monitored the quality of the construction work. In 1988, when a pig farm was planned by his plant, Mr. Xi again picked a TVE out of five bidders to do the Y1 million job, this time without prior bribes. The winning TVE agreed to do the project for 10 percent less than the proposed budget and did complete it with speed and quality. Afterward the TVE gave Mr. Xi Y10,000 to thank him for the job. During the annual quality appraisal at the plant in May 1989, both projects won "all-around excellent" rankings from experts. But three months later, amid the anticorruption campaign after Tiananmen, Mr. Xi was arrested for bribe taking. Legal analysts recommended a light sentence.[7]

The second case offers an opposite example, but is not common among pre-1992 violations. Mr. Xin was an engineer and deputy head of the Construction Division (*chu*) at a state shipping factory. In 1990 the plant sought open bids for the construction of a computing center. Days before the bidding, one building team sent its manager to visit Mr. Xin at home and after leaving Y1000, asked Xin to "take care" (*zhaogu*) of his firm. Thereafter the plant halted open bidding and chose the said builder. Inspectors later stopped the construction for quality problems, but the builder was allowed to continue after offering Xin's daughter an imported, Y670 motorcycle. Minor repairs were made but inspectors still uncovered quality problems after completion. Mr. Xin not only ignored the problems but agreed to the builder's request that extra payments be made in light of the repairs undertaken. This resulted in Y140,000 in additional costs above the Y1.08 million in the original budget. Xin's family of three, meanwhile, received an all expense-paid tour of the scenic Yellow Mountains.[8]

[6] See especially cases in Casebook #7.
[7] Casebook #7, 98–103.
[8] Casebook #3, 68–71.

Another opportunity for bribery stemmed from government agencies that enforced new market-regulating rules. With new economic activities, many state agencies began to play regulatory (as opposed to command) roles. The Industry and Commerce Management Bureau (hereafter ICMB) oversaw business licensing and commercial violations, monitored and disciplined price irregularities, and handled tax collection and evasion. Police departments administered vehicle licensing, an important area of power because illegally smuggled or acquired vehicles required illegal registration. Finally, courts arbitrated commercial disputes and enforced contracts. Each of these regulatory functions provided occasions for bribes because officials had discretionary power over license approval, legal registration, taxable amounts, reduction or withdrawal of fines, and the outcome of business disputes. While many bribes acted as speed money, others did lead to more harmful acts of unwarranted approval, neglect of violations, and arbitrary regulation. It was not uncommon, for example, for tax agents to accept bribes from village industries in exchange for overlooking tax evasions.[9] Yet it was difficult to uncover such irregularities because of individual encounters between tax collectors and small businesses, and because of scanty accurate information about nonstate businesses.

Foreign trade rights were another government good that fueled bribery. Import and export rights used to be granted to intermediary state agencies. Under reforms, the Ministry of Economy and Trade set up regional branches to grant rights directly to qualified local firms. Along with the central ministry, these regional agencies controlled import and export quotas, foreign currency allowances, and currency exchange rates for state firms. All this opened the gates to a flood of favor seekers who wanted to win trade quotas, hard currency, and favorable exchange rates, with the goal of importing scarce goods and speculating in them in the domestic market. Popular items included cigarettes, electronic gadgets, television sets, industrial inputs, and gold jewelry. Compared with the smuggling frenzy of the 1990s, these early activities were still benign. In most cases a work unit was the culprit, and bribery was designed to gain official quotas rather than to bypass official procedures. The scale of illicit importing was moderate and rarely well organized.

The Beyond-Plan Phase: After 1992

After Deng Xiaoping's spring tour of 1992, the new leadership under Jiang Zemin endorsed the idea of a "socialist market economy." The policy impact

[9] Casebook #5, 6–7.

was to take the "plan" part out of the earlier framework, "integration of the plan and the market." The two-track system was phased out and replaced by market allocation of goods and finances. State firms lost plan allocation and were thrust into the market. In a further retreat from command mechanisms, the government turned to macrodevelopmental and indirect regulatory roles in the economy. These new policy contexts created new opportunities for rent seeking in the new reform period. The resulting incentives for favor seekers, in turn, shifted to the following areas: competition for public investment projects, for bank credits, for land and properties, for building contracts, for market access and exclusion, for partial enforcement of rules and laws, and for public offices.

First and foremost, the source of government benefits shifted away from plan allocation of goods and finances, and toward public investment projects with developmental objectives. For this purpose, the central government administers four "special project funds" (*zhuan xiang jijing*): poverty relief funds, state bonds for infrastructure construction, hydraulic construction funds, and higher education funds.[10] Along with provincial governments, central ministries support large public projects such as mass transit systems, energy and utility facilities, urban and frontier development programs, industrial zones, and rural relocation and poverty reduction. Recipients may be local governments, state firms, and other public organizations. At a time when traditional sectors are stagnating and state firms waning, public investments provide a crucial way to develop the local economy and revitalize state firms. Lofty as these goals may seem, the subjective determination of investment entails ample room for arbitrary decisions.

Thus since 1992 winning these state projects has motivated attempts at bribery, with organizational bribers as the main players. Whereas earlier bribes had served to distort policies already made, now bribes are used to influence the policy-making process by local agencies, firms, and other organizational recipients of public investments. Many popular sayings attest to this shift. According to one gibe, "*Dapao da xiangmu, xiaopao xiao xiangmu, bu pao mei xiangmu*" (major lobbying [*da pao*] wins major projects, minor lobbying [*xiao pao*] wins minor projects, and no lobbying [*bu pao*] wins no projects). Here *pao*, literally "running," refers to lobbying around the bureaucratic departments. Another saying derides "pao bu qian jin" (getting ahead by running). *Bu* (step) is a homonym of ministry (*bu*), while *qian* (ahead) is a homonym of money (*qian*), so the phrase means "run around ministries and get ahead

[10] "Work Report of the State Accounting Agency Shows Violations by 36 of 55 Central Ministries and Commissions," DFLZ 12 (December 2000): 18–19.

with money." Still another saying describes the practice as "*jin jing song bao*" (come to Beijing to present treasures). One experienced local official advised that "you should not spread out your (lobbying) expenses. Do not just treat the (project) official with a fine meal. Nothing will come out of that. You need to focus your targets. Give (him) so much that his hands burn and his heart aches."[11] Since ministries no longer need to make allocation according to plans, lobbying becomes crucial in determining the destinations of government funds. Not surprisingly, liaison offices of local governments have mushroomed in the capital city.[12] By late 2002, there were 54 liaison offices representing provincial and city governments in Beijing, and 597 such offices representing lesser agencies and larger SOEs.[13]

Like the earlier efforts of TVEs, these bribes are paid with collective funds for collective interests. To win a project, some localities and firms are willing to spend 5–10 percent or more of the potential project budget on lobbying, calling it *huodong jingfei* (activity fees). Many localities have an unwritten rule that any local agency or administrator that wins financing from higher agencies will receive a proportional share, or else a monetary bonus. In one county, the Department of Civilian Affairs gave Y60,000 in bribes to the Bureau of Civilian Affairs in the provincial government, before winning Y500,000 in antipoverty funds. The bribe payment was 12 percent of the return, an especially high ratio for a county that should deserve antipoverty funds. Since the primary motive is to advance local collective interests, such bribes are usually justified with a nice-sounding rationale, economic development.

Another key incentive for bribery is to acquire bank credits, a leading source of funding for SOEs since 1992. While the shift from state allocation to commercial loans marks a major progression to the market, state and commercial/cooperative banks coexist on a dual-track credit system. Loans from state banks, which rely on government supply of credits and control of interest rates, can mean negative rates for clients (after adjusted for inflation). For nonstate banks, interests can go as high as 20 percent. This dual credit system, observes the economist Wu Jinglian, is to the 1990s what the dual-track price system was to the 1980s in fueling corruption.[14] Another problem is discretionary loan supply. Bank officials can decide what and whom

---

[11] Wei Hongqian, "Bribing with Public Funds," DFLZWZ 11 (1998): 12.

[12] Ibid. and Liu Ya, "The Abuse of Approval Powers and Its Remedies," DFLZ 11 (1999): 13–14; "Institutional Reforms Should Incorporate Anticorruption Mechanisms," *Zhongguo Jingji Shibao* 3 (1999): 20.

[13] "An Expose of Liaison Offices in Beijing," *Wenzhai Zhoubao*, December 2, 2002.

[14] Wu Jinglian, "Combating Corruption Must Start from the Roots," *Xinhua Wenzhai* 11 (November 1994): 24–25.

to fund. Money supply can become tightened whenever the government decides to cool down the economy. The massive entry of SOEs has increased loan shortages. In addition, individual speculators can secure cheap loans with bribes and relend them in the market for higher interests. Finally, credit application fuels bribery because bankers will be reluctant to go after bribe givers who delay or evade repaying loans. A case in point is Zhu Bingquan, CEO of a leather shoe factory in a small city in Jiangsu Province. Zhu's plant had been in steady decline since 1991. Rather than improving production and management, he used bank loans to keep his workers paid. By the late 1990s, Zhu had spent Y300,000 on nine bank officials, including the head of the local bank, the head of the city's Bureau of Resource Allocation, and the head of the city's Foreign Trade Commission. In all, he raised over Y150 million to have his factory maintain a façade of boom, popped up by loans and bonds alone.[15] With loans in hand, borrowers like him often try to dodge payments. Lenders are either unwilling or afraid to pursue such debtors, for fear of disclosing the bribes involved.

Another incentive for bribery has been provided by new policies that allow the sale, lease, and development of land and properties. Much of the country's land, long held publicly, is now under the jurisdiction of local governments. Local officials thus have discretion over the granting of ownership and user rights. For an individual to win such rights, extraordinary official patronage and bribes are necessary at every step. First, he needs to pay a large bribe to a well-positioned official, or a patron, who is able to find local officials willing to give up some local land. Second, the patron often needs to intervene to help find financing to pay for the land. Next, the patron steps in to help clear the complex hurdles of zoning approvals, ownership transfer, and building permits. Finally, the patron brokers a below-market price for the property and may even arrange an exemption of taxes due from the land transaction. Such complexities require exorbitant bribes, which creates tremendous pressure for land speculation (*chao di*) once the bribee secures a piece of land. Steep profits from speculation, in turn, fuels more competitive bribery to win land concessions from local officials. Not surprisingly, land seizure has become one of the hottest activities of the 1990s, making it the fastest track to overnight wealth. The noted social critic, He Qingliang, has likened it to the enclosure movement of the landed gentry in modern English history.[16]

A dramatic case in point is Cheng Kejie, deputy chairman of the Stand-

[15] Xiao Li, "Tracing Bribe Giving," DFLZWZ 8 (1998): 28–29.
[16] He Qinglian, *Xiandaihua de Xianjing* (Traps of Modernization) (Beijing: Xiandai Zhongguo Chubanshe, 1998): ch. 2.

ing Committee of the National People's Congress in the late 1990s and the highest official ever prosecuted for corruption in the PRC. In 1994, a Guangxi developer asked Cheng, then chairman of the Guangxi Autonomous Region, to approve a piece of land for developing a shopping mall. He promised generous "consulting fees" for Cheng's mistress. When Cheng was told that the eighty-five *mu* of land had already been assigned to the region's Department of Civilian Affairs for an ethnic theme hall, he testily insisted that the location be reassigned to the mall developer. Eventually Cheng was able to grant the land at a below-market price to the developer. In return Cheng received a briefcase loaded with so much cash that thoughts of the death penalty raced through his mind. Nonetheless he accepted it. The developer then probed Cheng to help secure bank loans for the construction of the mall. These came through and eventually reached Y188 million. For these two favors, Cheng and his mistress received Y17.30 million and HK Y8.04 million, or more than U.S. $3 million.[17] In 2000, Cheng received the death penalty for these and other bribes that totaled Y40 million.

The case against Zhu Rong offers a convoluted example of bribe for land rights. In 1992 Zhu quit his state job to become an agent for a foreign property developer in Shanghai. At the time, foreign businesses were not allowed to buy land or sell real estate in China. Using connections, Zhu gained user rights to land owned by a domestic real estate company. He then leased it to his foreign company for development (while the land rights remained with the domestic company). With huge profits earned from the "lease" deals, Zhu paid generous bribes to officials at the domestic real estate company to keep the deals afloat. By the time the scheme was exposed in 1998, Zhu had paid Y1.7 million to those officials. The amount was more than three-quarters of the Y2 million in total bribes accepted by the company's officials from all sources. For a crime that is seldom prosecuted, Zhu received twelve years for bribe giving.[18]

The case of Chen Xiaotong, once head of Beijing's Travel Bureau and son of then Beijing mayor Chen Xitong, offered an example of bribes for building permits. In 1994, a year before Deputy Mayor Wang Baosheng's suicide brought down Beijing's political establishment, the junior Chen was offered a chance to invest in a construction project. Estimated at Y1.5 billion in costs, the project was to be a compound of high-end apartments not far from the heart of Beijing, in the choice neighborhood of the State Guest House and the Shangri-la Hotel. Because a dozen domestic and foreign companies vied

[17] Cheng Jia, "The Fall from Power, Facts from Cheng Kejie's Crimes," DFLZ 10 (2000): 10–12.
[18] Xiao, "Tracing Bribe Giving," 28–29.

for the location, it was difficult to win an exclusive building permit. So Mr. Wang, CEO of the company that wanted to build the compound, courted Chen Xiaotong. With Chen on his side, he hoped to sail through city agencies that oversaw regulatory hurdles, from urban planning, land management, to environmental protection. He offered Chen a 5 percent share in the project, at a worth of Y7.5 million, and promised a 100 percent profit yield within a year of the project's completion.[19] These shares were in effect bribes.

Associated with the developmental frenzy of post-1992 and the marketization of financing and real estate is the building boom across the country. The boom has given a new boost to bribery in the construction industry. In 1994, about one-fifth of all economic corruption cases involved this sector.[20] By 1999, a third of such cases stemmed from it.[21] And of these cases, a majority involved bribery.[22] While the overriding incentive for bribers is still to compete for a contract, the market has become tougher thanks to several new developments. The bigger sizes of construction projects, the highly lucrative nature of the sector, and the proliferation of nonstate builders have intensified the fight for a slice of the construction pie. It is reportedly routine to spend 3–5 percent of the potential budget of a project on bribing, and the amount can go as high as 10 percent.[23] According to one private contractor, when his city planned to build a new residential area, almost all local builders privately went to the mayor and the city's party secretary to win "support." The race was determined by the strength of personal relations and the size of bribes. In the end, the contractor mentioned above won the contract, even though he had only an uncertified, makeshift company. The project was supposed to require a certified builder of at least a third grade by government certification. This requirement was already lowered from the second grade certification originally proposed. City officials had lowered the standard for the sole purpose of accommodating many unqualified bidders.[24]

Bidders are also brazen about reselling a contract repeatedly, unlike earlier times when many uncertified bidders bribed to overcome their lesser status and lack of access and tried to do a reasonably good job afterward. According to the contractor mentioned above, when his building team first started

---

[19] Zhong Shi, *Nie Hai Chen Zhou* (Buried by the Evil Sea) (Beijing: Sifang Chubanshe, 1998).

[20] According to figures from the DIC of Baoji city, Shaanxi, in Ji Wen, "Serious Violations in the Construction Industry Requires Immediate Actions," DFLZWZ 7 (1995): 13.

[21] Yao Zhenghua, "Severely Punish 'Construction Corruption,'" DFLZ 5 (1999): 16–18.

[22] E.g., in Hubei Province from 1990–1992, 54 percent of violations in the construction sector were bribery cases; see Ji Wen, "Serious Violations," 13.

[23] Xiao Li, "Hunting Down Bribe Giving," DFLZWZ 8 (1998): 28–29.

[24] Liu Huai'eng, "My Dealings with Monsters," DFLZ 9 (1999): 29–30.

out, he would get a project only after the contract was resold four or five times. Each round of subcontracting would take away another 15 percent of the expected budget of the project, leaving him practically no profits to make.[25] In fact, some major building companies, with top certification from the state, make a living simply by contracting projects with their good name and then subcontracting them to lesser builders. One city, for example, had only one top-grade building company, but the city government helped to affiliate four hundred more builders to that certified company. With the affiliation, the lesser companies were able to win contracts outside the city in the name of the top firm. Together they earned more than Y2 billion in revenues annually. The top company, meanwhile, collected Y50 million annually simply by supplying tens of thousands of photocopies of its certificates to subcontractors. Its director, credited for "actively carrying out city decisions and generating remarkable economic results" went on to become the secretary general of the city government.[26]

After winning a contract, a builder goes on to face a new round of officials whom he has to pay off. Depending on the ownership of a project, these officials can be from the local government or the contracting work unit, including accreditation officials who check builders' credentials, budget officials who decide the size of funding, resource allocators who make progress payments, accountants who track revenues and expenditure, and inspectors who frequent the sites and control quality. At each juncture the contractor is motivated to smooth relations, ranging from cash gifts to meals and paid prostitutes. If these arrangements are not made, the contractor may face delays or rejection of a request.[27] Not surprisingly, a construction scandal usually unravels a ring of violators at a time, from a few dozens to more than a hundred individuals. In one city, a road construction project brought down one corrupt official for every twelve kilometers of finished road, more than the number of workers injured on the job. Nationwide, a daily average of 6 individuals ended up at the Prosecutors' Office from the construction industry. Fujian Province alone caught 727 violators between January and October of 1998, or more than 2.5 persons daily; 420 of the 727 were officials.[28]

In commercial competition, bribery is no longer mainly an instrument of nonstate firms, as state firms now flood the market, and there is no longer a shortage economy in the country. The issue of "commissions" is no longer a

[25] Ibid.
[26] Qun Yi, "When Would the Speculation of Construction Projects End?" DFLZWZ 7 (1996): 11–12.
[27] Wei, "Bribing with Public Funds," 12–13; and Liu, "My Dealings with Monsters."
[28] Yao, "Severely Punish 'Construction Corruption,'" 17.

controversial one, though the Bureau of Industrial and Commercial Regulation bans any promotional incentive to retailers, in the form of cash, goods, advertising expenses, research funds, consulting fees, or paid travels. But manufacturers have made their promotional incentives more subtle in the effort to win retailers. A case in point is the retail company of the Telecommunications Bureau of Chengdu, capital city of Sichuan Province. The retailer, with its monopoly rights over the commercial sale of mobile phones, negotiated a base price with a supplier. Then it asked the supplier to raise the price of each phone *on paper* by Y1000–Y1500 apiece. The supplier tacitly did so and provided receipts for the inflated price. The retail company then paid the higher prices, but covertly received most of the extra payments back from the supplier.[29] These refunds were in effect kickbacks from the supplier, since the retailer went on to "legitimately" sell the cell phones at inflated prices. If added prices are the main harm here, other practices are less benign. The most notorious involves pharmaceutical products, where inflated prices have made medicine unaffordable to many who have lost socialist health care and now depend on the market. The lure of commissions has also made some hospitals and doctors lose professional ethics, dispensing more "profitable" medicines rather more suitable ones.[30]

Among the areas of government power that imposes costs on society, tax bureaus, judiciary organs, and law enforcement agencies have spurred the most lucrative avenues for bribery. Tax rates used to be more vital to the fortune of small-scale, nonstate firms than large SOEs. But with the expansion of *li gai shui* policies since the early 1990s (i.e., changing the policy of turning profits to the government to one of turning in taxes), tax burdens have also become vital to the profit margins of the vast number of state enterprises. Yet the tax system is rampant with flaws and idiosyncrasies because of its short history, lack of routinization, and technical deficiencies. Smaller businesses especially have many incentives to pay off tax agents. Bribes can gain exemptions or reductions from obligatory amounts; cause agents to ignore violations and evasions; help bribe payers avoid fines and penalties; gain the cooperation of tax agents in tax scams; result in inside information and tips; and lead agents to look the other way when they encounter fraudulent payment receipts, false claims of closedowns and dissolution, and most absurdly, loans from tax agencies for business or personal use.[31] Among the sectors

[29] Ma Liqun, "The Phenomenon of 'Collective Bribery'," DFLZWZ 3 (1998): 12–13.

[30] Liu Jianhua, "Attack Both the Symptoms and the Roots; Curb Illegal Commissions in the Pharmaceutical Market," DFLZWZ 5 (1998): 9–10; Chen Jing, "The Inside Stories of Pharmaceutical Salesmen's Bribery to Hospitals," DFLZWZ 10 (1998): 28.

[31] Fu Lanyu, "The Causes of Corruption in Tax Agencies and the Remedies," DFLZ 8 (2000): 15–16.

most susceptible to tax-related bribery are the construction, manufacturing, and retail industries.

Judiciary and law enforcement organs have become important institutions in the postplanned economy. In place of government bureaus and departments, courts now serve as arbitrating mechanisms in the marketplace. But as economic interests and actors compound in the new market economy, even courts engender incentives for favor seeking. Above all, bribes are used to induce preferential judgment in business disputes, such as those involving contracts, payments, or debts; or to avoid delays in judiciary processes and decisions, which have important economic consequences for businesses. In fact, some court officials have become so accustomed to bribes that they expressly prefer to process economic cases, where they would be more likely to share a cut from the settlement. Cases without apparent economic interests for court officials may be delayed or shuffled aside. In some localities, it has even become a common practice to levy a share of the economic settlements reached in the court.[32] For law enforcement agencies, the types of favors sought from them have expanded and with much higher stakes. Although bribes for vehicle registration, Hong Kong entry visas, and urban resident permits remain common, protection for organized crimes has become a key goal for criminal groups who enlist the collusion of police officers and coastal guards. Organized criminal activities, from smuggling and underground entertainment industries to drug trafficking and money laundering, have become prevalent and even menacing along some coastal cities.[33]

Finally, to retain or obtain public offices has become a notable goal for bribe givers since the 1990s. While the phenomenon is not new, two developments have measurably intensified it. One is the weakening of influence of higher agencies in cadre recruitment and promotion, part of the broad devolution and retreat of the state. The other is the increasingly lucrative nature of public offices in the new economy. Popular sayings attest to the new upward path. One goes that "no seeking and giving, stay where you are; merely seeking and no giving, move sideways only; seeking and giving, climb up and about" (*bupao busong, yuandi budong; zhipao busong, pingji diaodong; youpao yousong, tiba zhongyong*). Another saying mocks this phenomenon by asserting that "from the deputy *ke* rank to the full *ke* rank, it costs you Y10,000; from the *ke* rank to the deputy *chu* rank, it costs you Y100,000."[34] Though it is not clear how pervasive the problem is nationwide, it seems to affect poorer

---

[32] Zhou Qingwen, "Punishing Corruption in the Judiciary Front," DFLZWZ 8 (1998): 9–10 and "Deliberate Delay Is Also Corruption," DFLZ 8 (1999): 22.

[33] Zhou, "Punishing Corruption," 9–10.

[34] Wei, "Bribe Giving with Public Funds."

regions more than others. This phenomenon will be discussed among the regional dynamics of corruption in chapter 4.

CORRUPTION AND REFORM: WHAT BENEFICIARIES AND COSTS?

This section addresses the second question of the chapter: what role has the transaction-type corruption played in China's reform process over the past two decades? I will demonstrate two claims. One, on the supply side of the exchange (officials), the rent-seeking behavior of officials entailed some trade-offs between policy distortions and bureaucratic support and policy implementation in the early reform period. But cadre abuse has done more harm in the second reform period. Second, on the demand side (bribees) of the transaction, the favor-seeking activities of societal actors entailed trade-offs between unfair competition and the participation of underprivileged and enterprising groups who circumvented structural barriers and contributed to reform's success, again in the early reform period. But the expansion of favor-seeking behavior across sectors, the explosion of the sizes of favors, and the change in the type of favors sought have served to undermine the major reform goal of a more open and free market.

Impact of Official Behavior

In a comparative analysis of local elite support for economic reform in China and India, Chibber and Eldersveld find that China's local elite have been more supportive of reform than India's because institutional changes introduced by reform has transformed incentives faced by local elite.[35] Local elite are important to the day-to-day process of economic reform in China because, first, the party and bureaucratic structure provide them with influence over local areas, and second, the weakness of organized interests enhances their power as cadres who serve as the key link between the state and society. Incentives that have generated local elite support for reform in China include the decentralization of fiscal authority, the ability of the local elite to retain revenues through local enterprises, and the political decentralization that accompanied economic reform. Thus, not only are local elites more powerful politically but they retain control over resources at the local level.[36]

[35] Pradeep Chibber and Samuel Eldersveld, "Local Elites and Popular Support for Economic Reform in China and India," *Comparative Political Studies* 33:3 (April 2000): 350–73.

[36] For a discussion of these incentive changes, see Susan Whiting, *Power and Wealth in Rural China: The Political Economy of Institutional Change* (Cambridge: Cambridge University Press, 2001); Gariella

The last point is reinforced in the discussion of changing opportunities for bribery in this chapter. Moreover, not only have officials' legitimate authority over the new economy been enhanced, their avenues for illicit material gains have multiplied. In another words, both formal and informal incentives have changed for the Chinese cadre, especially the local elite who have been the primary beneficiaries of the two-decade long decentralization and devolution. The informal, unintended advantages may be seen as one important impact that corruption has had on economic reform.

Did rent-seeking activities help solidify reform in any way by mitigating potential cadre resistance to reform? An affirmative answer is shared among Chinese analysts, especially for the early reform period. They often compare the private incentives for Chinese officials to the financial compensations enjoyed by Japan's feudal elite during the Meiji Restoration. Indeed, like the old Japanese elite who utilized feudal privileges and financial incentives to become a new economic elite, Chinese officials have combined official power and private-interest seeking to become nouveau riches. Some turn from the bureaucratic to the business elite.[37] Others become "bureau-preneurs."[38] Still others profit from local governments' role as shareholders, quasi-owners, and/or tax authorities. More have become rent collectors. The data for this study do not directly provide evidence for a link between corruption and cadre support for reform, but they do show that decision powers have remained easily available to officials. In other words, they have lost little politically under economic reform, but have gained much in economic authority and benefits. Indeed, the relative ease of doing a favor from one's formal position appears to be a strong impetus to succumb to temptations. The prerogative may be seen both as an incentive for supporting reform measures and a disincentive for honest behavior. In the early reform period, reform did not take away *yi yuan hua ling dao* (centralized leadership under the chief executive), making it easy for key individuals to dole out favors using old and new authorities. By the 1990s, a much wider range of officials could make economic decisions, yet still without added supervision from above or

---

Montinola, Q. Yinqyi, and B. Weingast, "Federalism Chinese Style: The Political Basis for Economic Success in China," *World Politics* 48:1 (1995): 50–81; Jean Oi, "Fiscal Reform and the Economic Foundations of Local State Corporatism in China," *World Politics* 45:10 (1992): 99–126; Oi, "The Role of Local State in China's Transitional Economy," *China Quarterly* 144 (1995): 1132–49; Jonathan Unger, *The Transformation of Rural China* (Armonk, N.Y.: M. E. Sharpe 2002); and Louis Putterman, "On the Past and Future of China's Township and Village-owned Enterprises," *World Development* 25:10 (1997): 1639–55.

[37] Ting Gong, "Jumping into the Sea: Cadre Entrepreneurs in China," *Problems of Post-Communism* (July–August 1996): 26–33.

[38] Xiaobo Lu, "Booty Socialism, Bureau-preneurs, and the State in Transition: Organizational Corruption in China," *Comparative Politics* 32:3 (2000): 273–94.

below. When an individual can approve hundreds of thousands of *yuan* in loans or contracts at the stroke of a pen, laments one disgraced banker, "This kind of power cannot stop anyone from being tempted."[39] Based on the data for this study from both periods, about half of the times officials did favors as part of their routine duties, such as assigning a project or loan. The ulterior incentives made a key difference as to which recipients were selected. About a quarter of the times, officials illegitimately performed special favors, such as allocating below-market-price quotas or cheap land. Only when unwarranted approvals were given or frauds were purposely overlooked was a violation of duty formally committed. This outright violation occurred in about a quarter of the cases. In other words, generally officials did not have to go out of their way to profit personally. Deliberate violation occurs usually under two circumstances. One is when direct peril seems small, such as a license for an unqualified businessman. Another is when the payoff is enormous, as in the case below.

Chen Junqiu, a model employee with provincial and city honors, was the chief executive of the Local Produce Imports and Exports Corporation in Shantou, a coastal city of Guangdong Province. In 1986, when a private business partner could not repay a Y1 million debt owed to Chen's company, he offered ten *mu* of land in the city's special economic zone as equivalent payment. The land was not worth the value of the debt, but he expected Chen to overrate its value. After all, Chen's public firm, not himself, would take the loss. Chen initially declined, but was visited many times between 1986 and 1988 by the debtor. Each time the latter escalated offers of kickbacks. Chen remained hesitant until the offer rose to Y200,000. Thereafter the land transferred hands for Y2.25 millions, from its original price of Y14,000 four years earlier. At the expense of Chen's state firm, the briber was overnight debt free and Y2 millions richer! The outrageous deal made Chen apprehensive enough, so when he was detained for investigation, he committed suicide. His four codefendants, members of his executive team who accepted between Y10,000–Y40,000 each for the scheme, gave themselves up to the authorities before the amnesty deadline of October 1989. All were pardoned and received no punishment.[40] In this case, the key official had no difficulty within his authority to wipe off a debt willfully.

The exchange of power for pecuniary gains has further consequences than securing cadre acquiescence for reform. If indeed officials are motivated by the maximization of bribes in illicit exchanges, as critics of corruption argue,

---

[39] Xiao Li, "Tracing Bribe Giving."
[40] Casebook #4, 42–45,

then they are more likely to manipulate policies, erect bureaucratic barriers, and create delays. The resultant market-hindering corruption would be more harmful by aggravating entry barriers and destabilizing the business environment. If, however, officials are motivated by mixed affective and materialist incentives, they are more likely to maintain more predictable services and rates. In this context corruption's worst effects could be mitigated and in some cases entry barriers be eased, as some revisionists would contend. The extent of affective versus material incentives in the Chinese setting is influenced by the strength of affective ties, the nature of the exchange, and the size of the favor and its liabilities.

Officials granted favors in more affective ways prior to the 1990s, which in turn entailed more limited costs on favor seekers. When the bribe giver and the taker shared community ties, as in a village, officials were usually constrained by local customs and neighborhood opinions. The patron-client networks were well established, as were the terms of the deals and tacit understandings. Payoffs could come after a service, especially after the bribe givers had earned profits, and were settled amicably. Here both the services and rates were normally calculable and the work environment stable for both parties. In such a context it is in fact counterproductive for officials to violate conventions. When a favor seeker was a relative, gifts, rather than cold cash, usually arrived afterward or on special occasions. (Because family members need not pay bribes, doing favors for them constitutes the lesser violation of privilege seeking.) When favor seekers were hometown natives, former classmates, neighbors, or old buddies from the army, the impulse to help was also stronger. Payoffs were still accepted, but usually after the service and not at excessive levels. When favor seekers were introduced by family members or others with strong ties, services also tended to be performed first, and on amicable terms. At the very least, a promise of "consideration" (haochu) was often sufficient for gaining a service when some sort of affective ties or guanxi were present.

In the example of a Zhejiang village, village businessmen were generally willing bribers. Initially it was they who cultivated the cadre's habit of taking gifts. Over time, trust was built. During one negotiation over a contract, village cadres reasonably raised the share of profits that the contractors had to turn in to the village. After the work was finished, the village head queried the contractors if they had "made money." On hearing the affirmative, he preceded to scribble 3 × 3 and 3 × 1 on a slip of paper, meaning three cadres should each receive Y3000, while an additional three cadres would get Y1000 each. When the village head was asked to reduce the Y1000 to Y800, he casually waved "you decide." It is notable in this example that potential dividends did not act as an incentive for officials to lower tax rates earlier. But cadres could change their expectations over time, thus destabilizing the exchange relationship. In the same village, when six village entrepreneurs completed a log business deal, they were told by the village head (who had helped them win the log permit from county authorities earlier): "The Y2000 you gave me (before applying for the permit) has been spent. Why don't you give me another six doses (Y6000) today!" The villagers had only intended to offer another Y2000 and cursed at the "merciless man." They had to give in. But the village head did not fare better: in the next anticorruption drive launched from above, the entire village leadership was cleansed, though not because of complaints from villagers. The villagers did cooperate with authorities during investigations.[41]

Officials have benefited from corrupt exchanges in more direct and material ways since the 1990s, when a decline of affective exchanges increasingly has removed incentives to temper graft. One cause for the decline is the growing commercialization of social relations as the market deepens. Another is the proliferation of bribers, which means that increasingly fewer of them have direct affective ties to officeholders. In this context, the intervening factors in determining the level of bribes are whether the exchange is a haphazard, one-time deal, and what its size and liabilities are. Thus the gains are weighed against the likelihood of exposure and punishment. When visited by an eager stranger seeking a short-term deal, an official expect sizeable payoffs. When the favor requested is large and risky, the bribe demanded is usually proportional, as if to compensate for the potential costs faced by the taker. Typically a mixture of lure and coercion characterizes the process of non-*guanxi* exchanges. The official needs to establish that he is able and willing to deliver the favors, while appearing hesitant enough to induce maximum kickbacks. Before the early 1990s, outright extortion was infrequent and hints about "family needs" were usually made. Since then, explicit payoffs have become part of the matter-of-fact bargaining process.

Do bribes act as incentives to delay services so officials can maximize chances of graft? This is a key argument about the harmful consequences of corruption, or against the alleged merits of "speed money." The reality seems to be affected by many circumstantial and human factors, such as the type of favors, fear of exposure, and the relationship between the parties involved. When both deterrence and affective ties were stronger in the 1980s, officials appeared eager to return favors after accepting bribes. They were not excessively greedy in demanding bribes, if not out of reciprocity but at least out

[41] Casebook #5, 27–30.

of fear of retaliation and exposure. One deputy county governor, on seeing the gold necklaces his wife and daughter were wearing, asked where they came from. On learning that they were from an overseas returnee, he flew into a rage: "Why didn't you tell me earlier? Her request for housing has been delayed for long!" The request was soon settled.[42] In another case, an official at a coal mine would only write out invoices after bribes were paid. But the practice backfired. One purchase agent grew tired of paying bribes before each order and became a willing witness against him.[43] As bribery becomes pervasive and routine since the early 1990s, favor seekers and bribe takers have also become brazen in mutual dealings. The terms of exchange have become well understood, such as a 3–5 percent rate (of the total budget) for construction contracts, or a 5–10 percent rate (of the total funding) for loans and development/investment projects. Two ironic consequences result. One is that with less fear of retaliation or exposure now, officials expect high rates for favors. The other is that with such high rates, favors are usually performed. The higher rates, nonetheless, exert tremendous costs and entry barriers for doing business.

In routine interactions with officials, interviewees view small gifts as positive mechanisms to get things done. Many reform policies, interviewees report, are vague on specifics. Officials do not feel obligated to lend an extra hand to small businesses, or to get something approved promptly for them. Holiday gifts, mainly on the two most important holidays of the Lunar New Year and the Autumn Moon Festival, warm up the relationships between petty officials and small businesses. One Shanghai woman interviewed reveals that she gave more than two hundred gifts on a Lunar New Year to officials of a township where she has been building luxury villas on a scenic hill along a scenic lake. The value of each gift ranged from a few hundred *yuan* (e.g., a cashmere sweater) to a few thousand *yuan* (e.g., a digital camera). The gifts were not coerced, but "it's just easier when you go to them later for some approval and see a smile on their face." The gifts, plus occasional meals and entertainment for officials, amount to 5 percent of her revenues. Her experience, if not the number of her gifts, seems typical. After Shenyang's mayor and other key officials were arrested for bribery in 2000, other city officials no longer dare to take gifts. They are more cordial toward private entrepreneurs, but also much less efficient and helpful. For fear of arousing suspicion of bribe taking, they would not address the needs of the entrepreneurs promptly, let alone go out of way to help them.[44]

[42] Casebook #7, 30.
[43] Ibid., 104–5.
[44] Shuang Mu, "Six Symptoms of Corruption," DFLZ 8 (2002): 14–15.

Are services usually performed after bribes are paid, as implied above? This is again an important consideration in evaluating the impact of bribery, including social tolerance for corruption. If services are defaulted, corruption's effects are more aggravated. It has been argued that the lack of clarity in the chains of command, such in the independent monopoly model under decentralized systems, can lead to uncertain outcomes for bribers. In the cases examined by this study, favor seekers usually know whom to approach, thanks to the role of *guanxi* that ensures information flows. And due to the culture of reciprocity and the motive of self-protection, rarely is a service *not* performed *after* bribes are paid. In the only case among my casebooks where service was defaulted, the breach turned out to be self-defeating. The details are an eye opener. Wang Zhengfu was the head of a borough branch of the People's Bank in Kunming, capital of Yunnan. In 1989, he was asked by two eager self-employed merchants for a huge loan to pay off business debts. Over an invited feast, he asked them casually, "What is the best VCR brand lately?" Upon hearing "G-33," Wang asked to trade one with an older model, paying the difference. Overnight a G-33 arrived at his house. Neglecting to inquire about its cost, Wang expressed another "family need": the construction of his new house required an additional Y5000. The two agreed to "lend" the money but were then told that Wang's son wanted a drive's license. They agreed to pay for driving lessons, at Y4000. But Wang was insatiable: "Can you find a couple of girls?" A prostitute was sent over, but Wang continued to balk by claiming that the Y5000 promised earlier had not been paid in full. The merchants pledged another Y1600. But this proved to be the last straw. At their tip-off, Wang was arrested ten days later.[45] In this case, the extortion was driven by the vulnerability of the two self-employed entrepreneurs.

The more typical process of nonaffective exchanges is reflected in the following complaints from a village building team, made at one Prosecutor' Office:"During bidding, if we don't give the project's officials some advantages, we won't get it. During construction, if we don't please the contracting organization, they will give us obstacles. During inspection, if we don't loosen some joints, they will pick on us. At every point you have to pay tributes to these Gods."[46] While there is ample evidence of "no pay, no service" here, there is also little indication that no service is performed *after* pay. In other words, bribery has not become the most damaging form of pure extortion. And it has not decapitated economic reform or continued growth. This may partly explain Chibber and Eldersveld's surprising finding that the percep-

[45] Casebook #5, 35–36.
[46] Casebook #7, 51.

tions of the extent of corruption in China did not affect popular support for the reform process in that national context.[47]

In the post-1992 period, the problem is no longer largely at the microlevel of individual exchange, but more important, at the macroeconomic level of policy making and implementation. Influence-peddled competition, thus, leads to many public "bads" in project allocation. It skews the project selection process, leads to reckless or redundant investment, drives up the costs of winning or losing for everyone, and reduces real funds for investment. Worse still, those localities actually in need of antipoverty funds may have difficulty getting them. Unprofitable ventures, in turn, have contributed to serious problems of wasteful undertakings, nonperforming loans, and insolvent banks. These are the legendary conditions that have been blamed for the Asian currency crisis, and they are also largely responsible for the stagnation of China's financial sector and her SOE reforms. Influence peddling has further resulted in disregard for merits, efficacy, and equity in contractual, regulatory, extractive, and judiciary decisions. Lax and arbitrary enforcement of standards, regulations, laws, and taxation, in turn, have contributed to serious problems of public hazards, social injustice, and fiscal aggravation. Most of all, bribe taking by judiciary and law enforcement agencies serves to undermine government legitimacy and the basic fabric of law and order. Nothing can do more damage to public confidence than the image of gun-totting soldiers safeguarding smugglers on the high seas.

Impact of Societal Behavior

The revisionist literature has cited two major positive functions of corruption for social groups. One is the efficiency of individual decision over cumbersome bureaucratic policies and the flow of corrupt money into investment. The other is the integration of social groups into the economic process, especially the less privileged and otherwise socially alienated. Has corruption indeed been conducive in these two aspects, in other words, economically efficient and socially integrative? The answer appears to be different for each phase of China's economic reform.

In the first period, nonstate actors emerged as the main beneficiaries of corruption at the buyers' end. Foremost among these were the TVEs, an assessment widely shared by Chinese academic and legal analysts.[48] First de-

[47] Chibber and Eldersveld, "Local Elites and Popular Support," 368–69.
[48] The Chinese Prosecutorial Association, ed., *Chengzhi Tanwu Shouhui Lunwenji* (Collected Papers on Combating Embezzlement and Bribery) (Beijing: Zhongguo Jiancha Chubanshe, 1990): 117, 136–37, 332–33; Wei Pingxiong and Wang Ranji, *Tanwu yu Shouhui de Rending he Chuli* (Identify-

veloped under Mao outside the planned sector, TVEs were sanctioned as part of local initiatives, protected and supervised by local governments. As non-state actors, they were not included in the state plans and had no access to resources from the state. Under reforms, they were allowed to develop on a much larger scale and to compete directly with the state sector. Yet during the 1980s and early 1990s, under the dual-track system, TVEs still had no formal access to cheaper and more secure supplies of inputs, financing, trans-portation, and marketing outlets. Less established, they also faced misgivings from bankers, retailers, and consumers. Thus they resorted to bribery to level the playing field and compensate for their lack of access. In one hotbed of TVEs, Suzhou city of Jiangsu, 20 percent of prosecuted bribery cases involved TVEs in 1987 and 1988. The figure jumped to 39.2 percent in the first quarter of 1989.[49] To say that TVEs played a major role in the bribery activities in this period, however, is not to say that bribery played a major role in the spectacular growth of rural industries. It played a greater role for some TVEs than for others, and the ones resorting to corruption may not have been the more successful in the first place, as the following two cases illustrate.

In 1987 Feng Xiangsheng was a new manager of a township liquor dis-tiller, located in an ethnic region of Guizhou. Faced with capital shortage and stagnate sales, Feng secured a Y40,000 loan and held a press conference in Beijing to publicize his products. There he was introduced to an official from the Ministry of Agriculture in charge of certifying high-quality products. Af-ter careful cultivation and a gift of a carbon box of bottled *maotai*, China's most famed liquor, to the official, Feng won a seat at an award competition for liquors. Though the event was for liquors with a different alcohol level, Feng managed to receive a "fine-quality" award for his products. He thanked his benefactor with additional gifts and cash totaling Y10,000. The award made it easier for Feng's plant to promote its products. It also earned the Bei-jing official three years in prison.[50] In the second example, a metal process-ing TVE had been laying idle for lack of raw materials since its founding in 1987. In late 1988, its director met the head of a state resource supply com-pany, Mr. Zhu. The contact was so valued that the TVE convened an executive meeting to discuss proper "gifts" for Mr. Zhu. The participants—including

---

ing and Handling Embezzlement and Bribery Cases) (Beijing: Qunzhong Chubanshe, 1992); Mu Ye, "A Summary of Discussions on Combating Corruption," *Lilun Xuexi Yuekan* 2 (February 1992): 72; and Li Junchao, "Multiple Standards of Corruption," *Beijing Shehui Kexue* 3 (March 1990): 137.

[49] Economic Crime Section of the Research Division at the Suzhou Prosecutors' Office, "Gen-eral Trends of Embezzlement and Bribery at Present and their Causes," in the Chinese Prosecutor-ial Association, ed., *Chengzhi Tanwu*, 137.

[50] Casebook #3, 33–35.

the TVE's party secretary, chief executive, accountant, and teller—agreed to offer Mr. Zhu an imported color TV and a cash advance of Y10,000 at company expense. The scheme worked: Mr. Zhu allocated steel to the TVE at state prices and helped to market its products.[51] But rents have their own logic, as the theorists of rent seeking would assert. The TVE, as it turned out, did not put all the input into production: it resold two-thirds of it at higher prices.

Were the efforts by TVEs to overcome structural hurdles, overall, a "positive" impact on economic reform? The behavior of the TVEs in this period has received mixed reviews. Chinese analysts are generally critical of the corrosive effects of TVEs' corrupt activities. Products of SOEs, they argue, were superior in quality (at least in the 1980s when SOEs still dominated). Yet unlike TVEs, SOEs had to follow state accounting procedures, pay higher taxes, and did not have the fiscal flexibility to give out bribes. Thus they had difficulty competing with marketers from TVEs. Slow sales, among other problems, led to lower production and closedowns. With their advantageous size, equipment, and technology, the downfall of SOEs entailed a great loss for the country. Chinese analysts are careful to place the primary blame on the contradictory policies of a dual economy, with discrepancies in institutional and financial support.[52] Both Chinese and Western analysts, nonetheless, are highly approving of TVEs' upsurge and credit them for playing a central role the success of China's economic reform.

Another prominent group of favor seekers in the first period were contractor managers of SOEs, especially of retail stores and small plants. Though more advantaged than TVEs, such contracted firms faced similar pressures of having to hunt for supplies, loans, and markets for the portion of their business that sold goods at market, not state-set, prices. Like TVEs, they had to survive in the market on their own, rather than relying on the mechanisms of central planning. Bribery became a convenient instrument of commercial competition and survival, as reflected in the types of bribers in the case below. Mr. Xue Shangli headed the Shanghai's No. 2 Refrigerator Factory in the 1980s and was prosecuted for bribe taking in 1988. As shown on table 2.1, all his bribe givers came from the surrounding localities of the Jiang-Zhe (provinces of Jiangsu and Zhejiang) regions best known for thriving TVEs

---

[51] Casebook #9, 193.

[52] The Tianjin Prosecutors' Office, "Sources of Embezzlement and Bribery and Coping Strategies," in the Chinese Prosecutorial Association, ed., *Chengzhi Tanwu*, 117; Chen Bo, "The Current Status and Problems of 'Commissions' and How to deal with Them," *Jingji yu Fa*, 10 (October 1993): 13–14; Chen Xinliang and Huang Zhenzhong, "Commissions and Coping Strategies," *Zhengzhi yu Falu* 2 (February 1993): 27–28; Ou'yang Tao and Qin Xiyan, "The Harms and Characteristics of Bribery and How to Deal with It," *Faxue Yanqiu* 2 (February 1990): 30–31.

TABLE 2.1 List of bribe givers to Xue Shangli, CEO of Shanghai No. 2 Refrigerator Plant

Bribe giver	Position/occupation	Bribe amount	Favor secured
TVE manager	Manager of a refrigerator parts plant from Jiangyin county, Jiangsu province	Y6000	Subcontracting jobs
TVE manager	Refrigerator packaging plant from Jinsan county, Zhejiang province	Y503	Subcontracting jobs
Contract store manager	Contract manager of a Shanghai retail store	Y12,000	Wholesale of 200 refrigerators
Contract store manager	Manager of a retail store from Wenzhou, Zhejiang province	Y11,000	Wholesale of 3,200 refrigerators
Out of town store manager	Deputy manager of a retail store from Zhangjiagang, Jiangsu province	Y3000	Wholesale of 100 refrigerators
Total	5 sources of bribes	~Y31,000	Sentence: 8 years in prison

Source: Wang Jian and Zheng Jie, eds., *Fan Fubai Anli Xuanbian* (Beijing: Zhongguo Caijing Chubanshe, 1989), 23–24.

and other nonstate businesses. Motivated by competition and commercial interests, the bribe payers were from underprivileged groups at the time and faced tough market barriers vis-à-vis established SOEs. Typical of most violations before 1992, both bribers and bribees were relatively restrained and the size of each bribe was moderate. As such, they did not appear to have done severe social harm.

The self-employed were another major group of favor seekers in this period. As unaffiliated and often despised individuals, this group was in an even weaker position than TVEs and individual contractors. Indeed, there was a wide public perception, especially in the early days, that the self-employed tended to be the scum of society, unemployable or unemployed elsewhere, at least those in the urban settings. Their greater vulnerability and flexibility combined to make them both adept payers and easy targets of extortion. The data from one bank is not untypical. Out of fifty-five bribery cases uncovered from the branches of the Commercial Bank of Liaoning between 1985 and 1990, 51 percent of the bribe payers were self-employed, as opposed to 25 percent that were cooperatives (usually TVEs) and 23 percent that were small state firms.[53] The case of the Zhejiang village, cited earlier, shows how bribery helped the self-employed in their business dealings. The self-employed in the village, who were lumber dealers and building contractors,

[53] Zhao Fengxiang and Qiao Biyang, eds., *Jinrong Jiancha Lilun yu Shijian* (The Theory and Practice of Monitoring Financial Institutions) (Beijing: Zhongguo Jinrong Chubanshe, 1991): 199–200.

relied on village officials for permits, quotas, inspection, pricing, and profit-sharing arrangements. The officials accommodated every request of theirs, since these rural entrepreneurs made it very easy for them: "approval notes out from one hand, cash in the other." The folksy men frequently "insisted" on filling officials' pockets with "cigarette money," their kids' pockets with "candy money" or "New Year's money," and their aged parents' pockets with "medicine money." In this way, a few self-employed villagers managed to corrupt an entire body of the village leadership of eight officials.[54]

The self-employed are vulnerable in many ways, which made them highly dependent—even if reluctantly—on paying dues to officials. A typical example is shown in the case against Ms. Gu Chaoying, ICMB director in a county outside Shanghai. Although a veteran model worker, Gu turned to the self-employed in her district when she was making arrangements for her son's wedding in late 1988 and early 1989. She asked for contribution from merchants, visited a retailer for deep discounts, and sternly imposed her banquet order on a caterer whose restaurant was already booked full. In each instance, the merchants involved had previously gone to her or was expecting to go to her for licenses or other regulatory matters. In the end, the wedding banquet lasted two days and served thirty-nine tables, with grandeur unprecedented in the area. Most guests were local business managers and the self-employed, who felt obligated to show up with handsome gifts.[55] Despite the victimization of the self-employed such as is shown in this case, bribery may still be seen as helping to "integrate" a vulnerable group into the new economy.

Well-connected but unproductive speculators were yet another group of bribe payers during the dual-track period. With a regular job, these individuals moonlighted independently as go-betweens between suppliers and buyers, exploiting all sorts of social and business ties to gain information and access to profitable goods. Their activities contrasted with those of the other groups in that their original intention was solely to profiteer, rather than to meet business needs or to overcome entry barriers. This group created "public bads" by adding superfluous and costly links between the supplier and consumer. A case in point was Mr. Gui Guangqing, director of the Metallurgy Research Institute of Wuhan, capital of Hubei Province. In 1988, when a severe shortage of electrolyte nickel swept the country, Gui went out of his way to cultivate ties with a ministerial official in Beijing, in the name of securing plan allocation for his institute. With bribes ranging from paid travels for the official, jewelry for his offspring, and a monthly salary for his wife,

---

[54] Casebook #5, 27–30.
[55] Ibid., 34–35.

Gui managed to receive thirty tons of the material at state prices. He resold five tons for a hefty profit of Y403,110, pocketing it himself. On another occasion, Mr. Gui allocated nickel plates from his institute to two acquaintances at moderate prices. The buyers resold the items and passed on Y13,000 of the profits back to him.[56] The presence of speculators like Mr. Gui attested to the underdevelopment of the market at the time, which allowed speculators to play the role of information and access facilitators. In this sense, their role was not totally negative.

Overall for the first period, bribery and the attendant speculative activities, while distorting the goals of reform, did not result in overwhelming harms that strangled reform. While they entailed unfair access, hiked prices, and led to income inequality, they also contributed to the flow of goods and information, an overall constructive role in a system just breaking away from its irrationality.

After 1992

Since 1992, however, leading actors have changed. Nonstate bribe givers persist, but they have been eclipsed by the massive entry of SOEs into the market. While still privileged in size, established status, and administrative ties to the state, SOEs now face similar pressures in having to compete for loans, supplies, markets, and consumers. Not surprisingly, Chinese analysts compare the causes of bribe-giving by SOEs in the 1990s to those of the TVEs in the 1980s.[57] SOEs, moreover, face additional incentives. Since public-funded projects—at national, provincial, or local levels—are no longer plan-allocated, they are now open to lobbying and bidding. SOEs are also subject to more systematic fiscal and tax inspections by state authorities. All these factors motivate SOEs to turn to collective bribe-giving as a way to reduce entry and regulatory barriers. In addition, the greater need of SOEs for large projects and their greater financial capacities and stakes also aggrandize the game and the size of the bribe. *Gong kuan hui lu,* or bribe-giving with organizational financing, became a category of corruption all by itself in the 1990s. According to prosecutorial agencies, as many as 80 percent of all bribery cases involved this type of "collective bribery," accounting for a hefty 90 percent of the total bribe money by the end of the decade.[58] Although these figures include "nonbusiness" public entities, such as the local "three plus one" state

---

[56] Ibid., 121, 122.
[57] See especially Wei, "Bribe-Giving with Public Funds"; and Ma, "The Phenomenon of Collective Bribery."
[58] "80 Percent of Bribe-Giving Is Collectively Funded," DFLZ 2 (1999): 12.

agencies, SOEs are at the forefront of bribery activities since the 1990s (see table 1.6).

Like TVEs, SOEs have justified collective bribery by the interests and survival of their firms, even though they are not overcoming the kind of unfair, market-obstructing barriers faced by the nonstate sector earlier. SOEs cover up the culpability of their activities by holding collective meetings and reaching collective decisions. They record their bribes in accounting books as part of business expenses. In this way the work unit as a whole shares the risks.[59] Moreover, once discovered, "collective bribers" are rarely punished and if so only lightly. By the mid-1990s, Chinese law came to define dozens of work unit transgressions as crimes, including bribe giving, tax evasion, and counterfeiting. The work unit may be named the chief defendant and its executives as secondary defendants. But it has proven to be a weak deterrent. In the case of Zhu Bingrong, the shoe factory manager who used loans to prop up his failing factory, prosecutors were hard pressed to find any illegitimate interests gained by Zhu himself. As Zhu stated in his own defense, "My family has no savings over the past ten years. We still use the fourteen-inch black-and-white TV set from fourteen years ago. We live in the same house. . . . If I did not give gifts, I would not have gotten those loans, but then the firm would have halted its production. What would the thousands of workers do? I have been after only collective interests, not private ones. What crime have I committed?" Zhu's plight is indeed typical of many struggling SOEs and captures the complexity of incentives facing various actors. Nonetheless, his bribes brought indictments to a dozen officials, who had lent his factory hundred of thousands and even millions of *yuan* at a time. Zhu received five years in prison, uncommon for such offenders, but his firm was fined a mere Y20,000.[60]

The proliferation of organizational bribery has been facilitated by the multiple forms of bribes that SOEs, as large organizations, are capable of offering. Besides direct monetary and material rewards, the more subtle forms include stocks and IPO shares, overseas travels, educational sponsorships, insurance payments, "work convenience" amenities (cell phones, vehicles, etc.), residential renovation, urban residential cards, and job placements.[61] These indirect forms are "antidetection sensitive" (*you fang zhencha yisi*), as they are easier to explain away and harder to prove as evidence of bribery. The rise of

[59] "Collective Plotting—Corruption at the End of the Century," DFLZ 12 (1999): 12–13; Wang Bing et al., "Corruption is Hard to Eradicate without Prosecuting Bribe Taking," DFLZWZ 1 (1998): 12–13.

[60] Xiao, "Hunting Down Bribe-Giving," 28–29.

[61] "Beware: Do not Allow Bribe-Takers to Safely Reap Rewards," DFLZ 6 (1999): 26; Wei Hongqian, "Bribe-Giving with Public Funds"; and Ma Liqun, "The Phenomenon of Collective Bribery."

SOEs and their chief administrators as bribe givers is well reflected in the roster of bribers in the case against Li Chenglong, mayor of Yuling, a city in Guangxi Autonomous Region, summarized in table 2.2. Until Cheng Kejie, Li had the honor of being the official with the largest bribe take in Guangxi.

Organization bribery affects reform outcomes in far more harmful ways than bribery by nonstate actors. In contrast to reform's goal of eliminating administrative command, the activities of institutional bribers contribute to new kinds of administrative intervention. In contrast to the first period, when bribe givers interacted mainly with the allocating and distributing offices at local levels, organizational bribers interact with more complex webs of offices, ranging from those of chief executive offices to those of more specialized developmental, fiscal, technical, and financial branches of the government at local, intermediate, and provincial levels. Collective bribery also tends to involve larger amounts of payments, as public entities are generally after larger prizes and capable of affording big bribes. Finally, the "legitimacy" of collective bribery can also make it more unproductive, as some executives devote their energy not to the management of their businesses, but how best to explore the loopholes in new financial policies and to induce more bank loans. In short, while the bribery of TVEs and the self-employed contributed in part to clearing certain market barriers, SOE bribery contributes to new market barriers. Moreover, the behavior of public organizations exerts more legitimizing and exemplary effects on society than that of nonstate actors.

Land- and loan-related bribery has helped to distort the functioning of the property market and financial institutions. Repeated speculation of ill-gotten land grossly inflates land prices. Sometimes speculation becomes an end in itself and the land eventually is left undeveloped when the speculative bubble bursts and nobody is seriously interested in developing it. This can leave a chain of bad loans, as speculators fail to reap returns from commercial usage of the land. Even when the land is eventually developed, the commercial or residential complexes can be so expensive as to be unmarketable. Even in more benign scenarios when the land is not speculated time and again, the land buyer may feel that the land was obtained with such high payoffs that he must get high returns from expensive projects. The result is often the lack of affordable housing for the average consumer and the over-construction of high-end buildings. Finally, the combination of land- and loan-related bribery may have contributed to the very top tier of China's nouveau riches. Among the hundred richest people of China ranked in 2002, half are real estate tycoons. Of the three nouveau riches investigated by Shanghai's prosecutors in 2003, including the city's richest man Zhou Zhengyi, all come from the property sector. All three started from ordinary

TABLE 2.2 List of bribe givers to Li Chenghong, mayor of Yuling City, Guangxi Autonomous Region

Background of briber	Position/occupation of briber	Amount of bribe	Favors secured by bribers
Local state agencies	Deputy head, city electricity and water bureau, and city electricity corporation	Y45,000	Promotion and patronage
	Head, city foreign trade bureau, and city foreign trade corporation	Y10,000	Positions safeguarded
	Head, city commercial regulation bureau	Y10,000	Position protected
	Head of a township, also businessman	Y200,000	Approval for setting up a Chinese medicine marketplace
Public firms	Head of a city cement factory	Y2,100,000	Spouse's job upgrading, bank loan, joint venture fraud, contracts
	Chief executive of a provincial cement company	Y700,000	Promotion to deputy head of city's enterprise bureau, mayoral aide, and PCC member; securing of land, bank loan, capital
	Chief executive of a corporation	Y220,000	Promotion, bank loans and capital raising
	Middle school principal	Y150,000	Contracting rights to a plant expansion project
	Manager of a crop cultivation company	Y80,000	Promotion to deputy head of city TVE bureau, member of PCC and assistant to mayor; bank loans
	Head of a cigarette factory	Y70,000	147 *mu* of land; Y2m in budget allocation; Y12m in other funds
	Manager of a trade and industry corporation	Y70,000	Brother's promotion to deputy head of city senior cadre bureau
	Manager of a regional investment corporation	Y60,000	Y5m in bank loans
	2 staff members of an electronics corporation	Y10,000	Promotion of cadre rank, building projects, loans; land
	Official in the city electricity corporation	Y5,000	Promotion to company's deputy head
Private firm	Manager of a tea house	Y200,000	Bank loans totaling Y4 million
	Manager of a printing material company	Y39,800	34.8 *mu* in land allocation; Y3 million in bank loans
	Manager of a holiday resort	Y20,000	Business license in the city
	Farmer	Y10,000	8 *mu* in land allocation
	Grower of special fish	Y10,000	Y1 million in bank loans
	Agent for a Hong Kong corporation	Y10,000	Highway construction contract
Total	22 sources of known bribes	Y4,000,000	Sentence: death for Y16 million in bribes and unaccounted income

Source: "A mayor who takes in Y10,000 daily," DFLZ 7 (July 1999), 27.

backgrounds and acquired wealth overnight. In one instance alone, Zhou—ranked by Forbes as China's eleventh richest man in 2003—obtained an illegal loan of U.S. $227 million from the Hong Kong branch head of Bank of China, a state-owned bank. Instead of development, such loans are often used for speculation in the property markets or the stock market—sometimes buying the shares of one's own company so as to send its prices higher, and for acquiring smaller companies.[62]

Still more socially destructive has been the bribery in the construction sector. Shoddy builders have been responsible for poorly and even dangerously constructed projects, with short-term and long-term consequences. For all the emphasis that the state places on infrastructure construction, whole buildings, bridges, and dams have collapsed, roads sunken, railways cracked and airports wasted, impairing the major economic functions that they were supposed to serve, not to mention the tremendous losses in human lives and construction costs. Added costs for builders, thanks to the layers of bribes, have led to corner cutting in using construction materials, from low-grade concrete to subsized frames, and from counterfeit parts to scrap metals. According to figures from the State Construction Bureau, during the eighth five-year plan period from 1991–1996, eighty-six severe building collapses occurred nationwide, or an average of seventeen per year. Appendix 3 shows some of the worst construction incidents in the country. In an inspection of housing construction in provincial capitals by the Ministry of Construction in 1995, 56.25 percent of the residential projects in Nancang, Jiangxi Province, failed to meet standards. In 1996, state construction authorities checked 190,000 residential projects nationwide and found 1,245 with serious problems, of which 210 required partial or total rebuilding. In 1995–1997, the Department of Construction for the municipal city of Beijing carried out an inspection of the city's housing construction projects in recent years, and found a stunning 98 percent with defects.[63] These problems seriously undermine the credibility of the state's new market approach to construction matters.

CONCLUSION

The many characteristics and outcomes of bribery over two reform periods confirm the claims I laid out at the beginning of this chapter. One, the dom-

[62] "Why Are There So Many 'Problem Nouveau Riches' in China?" and "How Can China's Nouveau Riches Shake Off their 'Original Sin?'" *Qiao Bao*, June 27, 2003. See also "Banking, Chinese Style," *The Wall Street Journal*, June 11, 2003.
[63] Ji Wen, "Serious Violations," 13.

inant forms, incentives, and opportunities for bribery have been spurred by changing reform policies and the larger systemic environment, shifting its arena from the bottlenecks of the planned economy to the loopholes of the two-track system in the early reform period, then to the voids left by the disintegration of the socialist economy. Second, the effects of bribery have progressively worsened, shifting from partially helping to corrode the planned system to being a major hindrance to reform and developmental efforts.

Of the incentives and opportunities for transaction-type corruption, one set of mechanisms may be grouped under competition for favorable access to the goods and services under government allocation, distribution, or administration. Though long present in the Chinese system, the opportunities for access competition differ markedly from the prereform context. It is no longer the rigidities of central planning that induced the use of back doors, but the contradictions and imperfections in the fledging market. During the dual-track phase of the 1980s, the type of goods and services subject to corrupt exchanges concentrated in the industrial planning, manufacturing, and distribution processes. During the market phase since the 1990s, the type of goods and services subject to corrupt exchanges have shifted to the decision processes of the capital-intensive sectors of investment, finance, land, property, and construction. A second set of mechanisms for both periods can be grouped under competition for favorable enforcement of regulatory, extractive, and judiciary rules. In this set, the aim of corrupt practices is to reduce regulatory burdens, extractive obligations, and legal responsibilities. For officials, opportunities for rent seeking have grown with reform measures aimed at implementing new regulatory functions and overseeing new economic activities. For favor seekers, activities to purchase official advantages have expanded from low-level, moderate, and individual-based instances to higher-level, serious, and often organizational violations.

What has been the balance of bribery's effects over the two reform periods? The relative position of privilege in the plan versus the market has determined the type of winners from corrupt exchanges. On the buyers' side, the social groups least advantaged in the plan part of the dual-track economy before 1992 were most active in competing for access, namely, TVEs, small collectives, contractors, the self-employed, and small overseas investors. Since then, the groups that lost their privileged position in the planned economy have become dominant players in bribery, that is, SOEs and even local state agencies. Changing reform policies are a key explanation of this evolution over time. If incentives for buying access stem fundamentally from the state's administration of economic assets and activities, then the changing objectives of favor buyers have resulted from changes in the form of state administration and the types of goods and services administered by the state. On the suppliers' side of corrupt exchanges, officials have not lost their power and stature under reform. The components and methods of their authority may have progressively changed, but not their prerogatives over economic and regulatory decisions. If anything, the expansion of economic activities and corresponding government functions has only increased individual officials' power over time, especially at local levels.

Do the incentives and the actors who exploited them, then, produce not just costs, but also certain "positive" outcomes in the sense that they constitute "rational" responses to policy inconsistencies and systemic deficiencies? This may be cautiously and partially argued for the within-plan phase before 1992. Influence peddled notwithstanding, extraplan allocation and distribution helped further loosen up central monopoly, while nonstate actors found ways to survive and thrive through the "cracks" of the public economy. In this sense, corrupt exchanges helped to circumvent formal barriers to equal access and entry into the new economy to some degree. Cadre involvement, on the other hand, also meant de facto acquiescence to and participation in market-related activities, helping to neutralize potential bureaucratic resistance. Moreover, the more affective nature of two-way transactions, prevalent in the first period, also helped to temper their worst effects, leading to a more stable environment and moderate rates of payment for favor seekers. At the same time, the process of favor-seeking did create different kinds of market barriers that may be just as inequitable and obstructive to competition. On balance, it may be safe to argue, the negative impact is not absolute and total during the early reform phase.

The same, though, cannot be said of the post-1992 period. Bribery, now involving economic actors from all sectors and all ownership forms, can no longer be seen as individual efforts that chip away at a dominant planned economy and circumvent formal barriers to equal access. Rather, it undermines a dominant market and thus the reform program itself, making unequal—rather than equal—competition the rule of the game. Moreover, cadre support is no longer critical to reform's survival and implementation at this stage. But cadre's rent-seeking behavior, meanwhile, has become entrenched and a formidable obstacle to the goals of reform. With affective motives waning, finally, the material impetus has become dominant for officials in corrupt exchanges, bringing about a more unpredictable environment and highly variant rates of payment for favor seekers.

BETWEEN OFFICIALS AND THE PUBLIC COFFER

Nontransaction Types of Corruption

Several major forms of Chinese corruption fall into the nontransaction group of corruption: embezzlement, misappropriation, accounting violation, squandering, and negligence. Common to these types is always the loss or diversion of public funds and often the absence of two-way exchanges between officials and citizens. Needless to say, the distinctions may not be always clear, especially in cases where the principal culprit may have negotiated with allies and confederates. But it is the preying on public resources, rather than private ones, that is the defining characteristic of the categories here. Moreover, it is not essential for two-way exchanges to be present in these corrupt acts. Smuggling and illegal profiteering also belong in the nontransaction group, as they derive black money from sources that should accrue to the state coffer. I discuss smuggling in chapter 4 along with the regional dynamics of corruption. Illegal profiteering has largely ceased with the end of the two-track system and will thus not be examined. Of the five nontransaction forms to be discussed in this chapter, embezzlement and misappropriation are exclusively committed by individuals. When committed by organizations, they fall under accounting violations. Accounting violations and squandering are mostly carried out by organizations or by individuals in the name of organizations. Negligence may be by both individuals and organizations.

In this chapter I address the question of interactions between reform and corruption with reference to nontransaction corruption. I intend to demonstrate that first, like bribery, nontransaction corruption has evolved markedly, thanks to the changing, if largely unintended, opportunities and incentives created by the reform process. Second, nontransaction types can generate more serious consequences than transaction types, at least in the Chinese context. Most important are its greater financial and fiscal impact and its function as a disincentive against more productive activities. Revisionist arguments about economic efficiency and social integration are not relevant to nontransaction corruption.

CORRUPTION AND REFORM: WHAT INCENTIVES AND OPPORTUNITIES

Embezzlement and Misappropriation: From Petty Thefts to Grand Larceny

Embezzlement and misappropriation share the common violation of taking funds from the public coffer by individual officials. They differ in the intentions of the act: the former entails intention to steal public funds, while the latter only the use of such funds temporarily. The divergent intentions are determined by evidence of attempts to eliminate physical traces of arrogated funds, which is logical in embezzlement cases, or the lack of such attempts, which is common in misappropriation cases. Misappropriation may also be determined by evidence of attempts to return partially the original funds. Though these two violations are less discernable to the public, they can account for much larger losses than bribery in financial terms. Nationwide data below show that the number of exorbitant bribes remained small in the mid-1990s, in comparison with embezzlement and misappropriation, which saw larger increases in the size of funds involved. By the 1990s, the scale at the higher end reached hundreds of thousands of *yuan* and over the million range more frequently than bribery cases. As table 3.1 shows, most of the Y1-million–plus cases fall under misappropriation and embezzlement, and only misappropriation cases broke the Y10 million and the Y100 million mark. The unusually large amounts are often due to the perpetrators' access to bank and investment funds.

The dramatic increase in the size of appropriated and embezzled funds is in part due to changes in the type of corrupt actors over time. Before the urban reform of the mid-1980s, most offenders were petty staff members at SOEs such as accountants, treasurers, cashiers, and guards who were directly involved in handling money. They were often motivated by the personal difficulties of their families, friends, or boyfriends. Since the mid-1980s and especially in the late 1980s, SOE directors and contractors became dominant violators. Endowed with new authority to make most decisions, sign all pa-

Table 3.1 Largest prosecuted cases of top-three categories, nationwide

Amount per case	Misappropriation			Bribery		Embezzlement and bribery			
	1994	1996	1993–1997	1996	1995–1997/8	1989–1992	1994	1996	1993–1997
Y10,000–50,000									86,616
Y50,000–100,000			27,698*		29,923*		2,239		11,656
Y100,000–500,000				109	187	1,728	1,654	2,227**	8,539
Y500,000–1 million		383		17	72	122	154		797
Y1 million and up	366	417		9		81	103	156	617
Y10 million and up	29	57							
Y100 million and up		5							

Source: Editorial Board of the Prosecutorial Yearbook of China, ed., *The Prosecutorial Yearbook of China* (Beijing: Zhong-guo Jiancha Chubanshe, 1995– 1998).
　*From Y50,000 to Y1 million
　**From Y100,000 to Y1 million

per work, and appoint most personnel at the firm level, factory managers could virtually appropriate and embezzle at will. Their motives were no longer personal ones but the business activities of relatives, friends, and occasionally their own. Appropriated funds were often used for buying low and selling high in and out of the dual-track price system, for starting up new businesses, or for paying troubled business loans. Overall, the scale of appropriation and embezzlement remained modest before 1992, the methods tempered, and the culprits not too reckless. But the motives and methods were to change dramatically in the 1990s.

Misappropriation after 1992

Since the 1990s embezzlement and misappropriation have shifted to commercial activities and increasingly have been directed by officials themselves. Moreover, such activities no longer mean a small, one-time profiteering deal but major operations such as stock trading, subcontract manufacturing, real estate investment, and even organized smuggling. A survey of misappropriation cases processed in the first six months of 2000 by the Prosecutors' Office in Chengdu, capital of Sichuan, showed that 73 percent of the appropriated funds were used for private business activities. The same survey also showed the SOEs as the primary arena for this offense, accounting for 57 percent of surveyed cases. Moreover, 67 percent of the offenders held the top managerial position at SOEs, such as head of the board of directors, chief executive, general manager, or party secretary. The rest were SOE cadre at middle and lower levels in charge of individual departments such as purchasing, marketing, finance, and accounting.[1] The outside businesses, where appropriated money is often diverted to, may be run by officials themselves, their family members, friends, or others with whom officials share partnerships. The seeming temporality of the arrangement abates psychological tensions over punitive prospects, while the potential reward aggrandizes the risk-taking mentality. Sometimes the pressure to return the money creates further pressure to appropriate. This desperate gambler mentality results in a panic cycle of "borrowing," losing, "borrowing" more, and losing more. Often, the scheme falls apart and comes to light when money fails to be returned partially or totally.

There are several opportunities for appropriating SOE funds for private commercial activities, all made possible by increased managerial autonomy and reduced administrative supervision from above. One is to transfer, through false pretense, a SOE's bank account to that of a private firm, a joint venture, or an individual. The Chengdu survey cited above revealed that as many as 82 percent of the misappropriation cases employed this scheme, and at millions of *yuan* per case. At Southwest Airline, a major airline in the country, the head of its Accounting and Finance Department, along with the head of a lower Finance Office, transferred Y7 million from the company account to a private construction business in one month. Another avenue is to divert funds through subsidiaries of SOEs. Two chief executives at the Chengdu Xinda Corporation, from the same survey, transferred Y2.08 million from the parent company to its subsidiary, in the name of property purchase by the latter. The funds were then used to purchase private villas. Still another way is to forward bank loans acquired in the name of SOEs to alternative destinations. In one case, three top executive/financial officers at the Hebei Pioneering Machinery Plant secured three bank loans totaling Y4 million in the name of the plant. Instead of entering the plant's account, the money was mailed to a friend's company in faraway Guangxi, where the fund was used to speculate in real estate and petroleum.[2] Yet another mechanism is to make private copies of SOEs' official seals and deposit company funds in separate accounts using the counterfeit seals. One can also forge loan agreements, so that appropriated funds appear to be legitimate loans to another party. One can even invest SOE funds in other firms in the name of the SOE, but pocket the earnings personally. Increasingly, CEOs employ family members or relatives as accountants and treasurers in their firms to facilitate appropriations.[3]

[1] Rong Lin and Gu Ping, "How Are State Resources Appropriated," DFLZ 10 (2000): 17–18.
[2] Zhang Yan, "Reflections on Establishing and Perfecting Supervisory Mechanisms for SOE Managers," DFLZ 3 (2000): 6–7.
[3] Rong and Gu, "How Are State Resources Appropriated," 17; and Chen Xiling, "The Major Junc-

Chen Xiaotong, son of former Beijing mayor Chen Xitong, provided a good example of business-related misappropriation. As first introduced in chapter 2, a building contractor offered Chen high returns on a 5 percent share in an exclusive project, so as to enlist his support in the licensing process. Chen tried to come up with his part of the investment funds by "borrowing" Y5 million from the New Century Hotel, a joint venture where he was the Chinese manager. The money was originally set aside by the hotel to pay back a long-standing loan. Chen "borrowed" the funds in the name of another company he headed, with the intent to return it later. The deal failed after corruption scandals brought down the city government. The loan was returned, but Chen was still convicted on a misappropriation charge and given seven years in jail, on top of six years for bribe taking.[4] Compared with deputy mayor Wang Baosheng, Chen was actually a cautious violator. Wang had appropriated more than Y100 million, plus U.S. $25 million, for the business activities of his mistress and his brother. Losses from his appropriations totaled U.S. $13 million. In addition, Wang had embezzled Y250,000 and U.S. $20,000 for himself and built two luxury residential complexes with public funds.[5]

An increasing new form of misappropriation involves employees of banks, investment firms, and stock exchanges. Individually or through small group collusion, they temporarily appropriate firm funds to speculate in the market. A few may even use the ploy to run smuggling operations. The profits are then pocketed personally. Though big cases still remain limited, small ones appear to be not infrequent.[6] The schemes usually come to light when an offender fails to make enough to cover the original funds. In Shanghai's largest case of this kind, Jiang Jiehua, deputy director of trading at the Shanghai branch of a provincial investment firm under the Agricultural Bank of China, made as many as 230 separate illicit appropriations, for a total of Y36.08 million. He lost Y1.39 million in the stock market before giving himself up to authorities.[7] Like Chen Xiaotong, Jiang received a relatively mild sentence of fourteen years, compared with what one might expect of bribery or embezzlement cases, where similar amounts of graft could warrant life sentences. Differences in intent, process, and outcome of the offences account for the punishment.

---

tures Where the Exchange of Power and Money Takes Place in SOEs and Coping Strategies," DFLZWZ 2 (1997): 10–11.

[4] Zhong Shi, *Nie Hai Chen Zhou* (Buried by a Sea of Evil) (Beijing: Sifang Chubanshe, 1998).

[5] "Emergency Chase of Wang Baosheng's Mistress," DFLZWZ 6 (1998): 28–30.

[6] "An Analysis of Crimes in the Financial Sector," DFLZWZ 10 (1994): 18–19.

[7] "Major Events in the Anticorruption Work of 1996," DFLZWZ 2 (1997): 25.

Embezzlement after 1992

The new round of SOE ownership reforms, initiated since the Fifteenth Party Congress in October 1997, has spurred extraordinary opportunities for plundering state assets. The push to "marketize" SOE ownership rights openly sanctions the transfer of state assets into nonstate hands. SOE officials have responded in various and creative ways.

One common scheme is for SOE managers to maintain a separate and secret account for profits earned from covert sources. These range from hiked prices, extra orders, and overseas earnings to underground contracting and undocumented sales. In one case, a large plant made agreements to contract production orders to its branch shops. The latter were supposed to fulfill orders for the parent plant before accepting orders from other clients. But at one branch, executives busily fulfilled orders from outsiders, ignoring those of the parent plant. In two years the branch netted over Y1 million into its own account. Some of the money was spent on gifts for officials from state agencies, presumably to buy their oversight, while most was split among the branch executives. Their employees received only Y100 per person in annual bonus besides regular salaries.[8] At a branch of the Shanghai Lights and Lamps Plant, three top executives and two accountants made a full-time job of profiteering from the plant's assets. They speculated them in the market, set up small treasuries, and held frequent meetings about how to split more company assets for themselves.[9] Unlike the case of Chu Shijian, discussed below, these officials did not appear to deserve higher compensations than their regular salaries.

Chu Shijian was the head of the Yuqi Tobacco Company of Yunnan Province since 1979 and later CEO of the expanded corporation, Red Pagoda Group, Inc. Known as the "king of tobacco," Chu stewarded his company from an unknown plant in 1979 to the largest tobacco manufacturer in Asia and the fifth in the world by the mid-1990s. Its asset value increased from a few tens of million of *yuan* in 1979 to Y7 billion in 1996, with profits and tax payments approaching Y20 billion annually. Over the years the plant maintained its leading status in equipment, exports, profit earnings, and tax payments among over 180 tobacco companies in China. Chu in turn received many honors, including Model Worker of Yunnan Province, All China Model Worker, All China Excellent Manager, All China May-Day Medal Recipient, All China Excellent Entrepreneur, and one of the ten All China Top

[8] Guo Ji, "Pay Attention to Economic Violations during Enterprise Reforms," DFLZ 4 (1999): 15.
[9] Liu Zhiwu, "Rampant Corruption at Unprofitable SOEs: Who Will Punish Their Destroyers," *Beifang Shichang bao,* December 29, 1997.

Reformers. With his supreme authority at the plant and a perennial seller's market for tobacco, Chu increasingly treated firm assets like personal property. Using unreported revenues, he set up a slush fund with his chief accountant and deputy manager. His downfall came in 1995 when he ordered the fund be split among the three of them. Chu received U.S. $1.7 million of the $3 million total. During his trial, additional "illegal income" of Y5 million was traced to him, as was nearly Y40 million in bribes to his daughter and Y3 million in bribes to his wife and other relatives. These bribes were paybacks for the phone calls and handwritten notes Chu helped to place in the bribees' favor. In 1999, twenty years after he first headed the Yuqi Company, Chu was sentenced to life in prison for embezzlement.[10]

Another opportunity for embezzlement comes by way of assisting outside businesses at SOEs' expense. Managers have done this in a variety of ways. Some pass on the more profitable production lines, equipment, capital, and input to their cronies' plants. Some buy products from other plants at above-market prices, including substandard products, but sell to them at below-market prices. Others contract or lease a SOE in whole or part to cronies at discount prices, under terms highly unfavorable to the SOE, such as the absence of open bids, guarantees for the retention and growth of SOE assets, or penalties for losses. Still others set up "joint ventures" with private firms, but pass profits mainly to the latter. In all of these arrangements, managers receive a variety of overt or covert kickbacks.[11] At a major petrochemical plant, for example, two executives made a covert alliance with a private partner to speculate in petroleum. As a large SOE, the plant received petroleum from state allocation even in the late 1990s. The inexpensive supply was then passed to the local partner, who sold it at market prices. The scheme earned them Y14 million in profits, most of which they shared privately.[12]

Yet another avenue is to "privatize" state assets partially to firm executives themselves. Ownership reforms require the appraisal of SOE assets, whether it is for auctioning, "stockfication" (*gufen hua*), mergers, buyouts, or joint operation (*lianying*). But the well-intended reforms have also spurred opportunities for "insider privatization" by managers, who have the best knowledge of their firm assets. Common schemes include siphoning off assets to private savings and profiteering; concealing the real size of a firm's resources, revenues, and credits; inflating firm expenditures and debt burdens to depress

[10] Liu Siyang and Zheng Hongfan, "The Downfall of the King of Tobacco," DFLZWZ 4 (1998): 22–25; and "The King of Tobacco Chu Shijian Is Sentenced to Life in Prison," DFLZ 4 (1999): 20; and "Red Pagoda CEO Chu Shijian Expelled from Party," DFLZWZ 4 (1998): 16.
[11] Bo Chuanbao, "The Loss of State Assets and the Coping Strategies," DFLZWZ 4 (1998): 8–9; and Zhang Xinjiang, "How State Assets Are Lost and the Remedies," DFLZ 7 (2000): 16–17.
[12] Zhang, "How State Assets Are Lost," 16–17.

the price of a buyout; and excluding land and other elusive assets from appraisal. To ensure that cronies become new owners at below-market prices, some executives set price ceilings for buyouts, discount asset values, limit open bids, collude with appraisers, or falsify data.[13]

A growing opportunity is to embezzle through the distribution of SOE shares. Some executives turn firm assets into shares in ways contrary to government regulations or market mechanisms. After splitting majority shares among themselves, they offer gift shares to officials in state agencies, so the latter would overlook the irregularities. CEOs also pressure employees to buy shares, threatening them with layoffs for failure to do so. Yet employee participation is not present in shareholder meetings or management boards, so that management styles remain unchanged after a firm has issued these shares. Some executives squander employee contributions by spending them on entertainment and amenities, or worse, privately pocket the money.[14] For still others, their earnings from shares are fixed at high rates, regardless of firm performance. Even if operating at losses, they still collect handsome dividends financed by slush funds or bank loans.[15]

Two examples illustrate embezzlement via stock shares. Dongguo (East Boiler) Shareholding Group, Inc., a large SOE in Zigong, Sichuan Province, was chosen as one of the first experimental sites for the shareholding system in 1992. Its stocks were allowed to go public in 1996, the same year when China's stock market reached the height of frenzy. Dongguo's stocks shot up quickly after going public. Tempted by the good prospect, four top executives—the head of the board of directors, the CEO, and two deputy CEOs—colluded to divide up 1.32 million shares of IPOs among themselves. They paid for the shares only after selling them in the market. The scheme earned the four executives a total of Y9 million, or over Y2 million each. Though all four officials were highly regarded by employees as competent and generally honest, two were given a suspended death sentence and the other two a life sentence.[16]

The second case involved Daqing Joint Shareholding, Inc., of Daqing, a city in Heilongjiang Province. The company first started out as a TVE with no relation to the famous Daqing Petroleum Plant. Benefiting in part from its namesake and its formidable founder, the firm grew from its meager base in 1985 to a complex corporation by the mid-1990s, specializing in the production, refinement, processing, and transportation of petroleum and petro-

---

[13] Bo, "The Loss of State Assets," 8–9; and Zhang, "How State Assets Are Lost," 16–17.

[14] Wang Ruogu, "Corruption and the Shareholding Reforms," DFLZWZ 5 (1998): 23.

[15] Sheng Xiaoping, "A Look at the Schemes to Transfer Public Money into Private Pockets," DFLZ 9 (2000): 23–24.

[16] Guo Xiping, "The Investigation of Dongguo's Big Embezzlers," DFLZ 10 (1999): 22–23.

chemical products. Its stocks went public in May 1997. On the first day of its appearance on the Shanghai Stock Exchange, it was the best-performing company among the more than five hundred firms listed. But its prices fell steadily thereafter. Before long its founder and CEO was mysteriously murdered. In 1998 the plant joined with ten other firms to form a shareholding conglomerate, with a deputy chair of the city's People's Congress, Xue Yongling, chosen as board director. Xue's major move in the new company was to deliver gift shares to city officials. Totaling Y10.94 million in cash value, these gifts included Y200,000 in share value for the chair of the city's People's Congress (about to become the mayor), Y66,000 for the city's deputy party secretary, and Y284,000 for the deputy director of the local office of the National Tax Bureau. The tax official brokered nearly Y1 million in additional gift shares for the tax office's director and six other colleagues. The Tax Office, in turn, ignored back taxes owed by the company. Other firm executives came up with their own lists of people to receive gift shares, including fictitious names. In all, sixty-one company officials and city agencies acquired or purchased shares illicitly, among them seventeen ranked at *ting* and forty-four ranked at *chu* and higher. Thirty-nine of them received disciplinary actions, of whom ten were also prosecuted.[17]

Still another convenient way to loot company assets is to place relatives in charge of bookkeeping and financial disbursement. As managerial autonomy has extended to most personnel appointments, the practice has become more common since the 1990s, especially in less-developed regions and in smaller SOEs. In a survey of SOEs in one Shandong city in the mid-1990s, the largest number of workers (43.7 percent) cited "kinship appointment" as the leading problem of state firms.[18] At the Shanxi Knitwear Factory, 80 percent of top-level officials had their children placed in managerial or accounting positions; 60 percent of these had little professional knowledge. Founded in 1968, this plant was once a flourishing business with four thousand employees and Y40 million in fixed assets. Yet the unceasing expansion of managerial autonomy had sent the plant on a downward slope since 1990. Twenty-eight of the plant's officials had gone on overseas sight-seeing trips in the name of "study tours," at a cost of more than Y400,000. Another Y100,000 or more disappeared without records. Accountants kept books not according to receipts but by managerial instructions. Eleven executives took more than Y100,000 in bribes from subordinates within the company. By 1996, pro-

[17] "Daqing Co. Corrupted 39 Officials," DFLZ 3 (2000): 26–27; Wen Xuedong, "A Burrow of Moths in the National Tax Bureau," DFLZ 7 (2000): 25–26; "39 Officials Disciplined in the Case Involving the Stock Shares of Daqing Co." DFLZ 2 (2000): 23.

[18] Jin Bo, "Anticorruption Work at SOEs Should Be Strengthened," DFLZWZ 1 (1995): 5–6.

duction all but ceased. Its employees, owed eighteen months in back pay totaling Y20 million, had to be laid off."[19] In another case, the manager and
three other officials at the Shenzhen Coastal City Trading Company placed
130 relatives in the firm, or 17 percent of the employee roster; 18 of them
served in middle-level management positions, or 32 percent of company officials at that level. The arrangements made it possible for the four top officials to loot the company at will and flee overseas after their crimes became
known.[20]

Violation of Accounting Procedures: From Diversion to Extraction of Public Funds

Public organizations and their chief executives may be guilty of accounting
violations. It would not be much of an exaggeration to assert that all state
firms and local state agencies are guilty of some violation of state accounting regulations. These rules govern the administration of budgets, taxes, profits, prices, credits, wages, bonuses, and foreign currencies. Nonstate firms are
obligated by laws regulating taxes and prices, but not state budgets or expenditures. The essence of accounting violations is to divert state funds to alternative use or to retain funds that are otherwise due to the state.

In the partially plan-governed days of pre-1992, violations centered
around state allocation and distribution. The misused funds came mainly from
the state, such as financing and subsidies from the plan, profits from regular
or above-plan production that were partially due to the state, above-budget
allocation for special causes, and excess allocation from inflated budgets and
expenditure claims. The two-track system and increased firm autonomy,
above all, broadened both the space and channels for misusing public funds.
Common violations included diverting designated production funds for
nonproductive usages, concealing real business incomes, selling plan-track
items at market prices, and setting up trading companies to market controlled
goods. Contract and leased production, additionally, gave managers the autonomy to make false claims about costs, profits, rosters, losses, and deficits.
The usage of diverted funds was also typical of the days of the planned economy: wage increases and bonuses, and benefits-related projects such as residential expansion, office renovation, entertainment facilities, and company
vehicles. Only occasionally did the siphoned funds go into business expan-

---

[19] Xiao Li, "The Power of Public Organizations and Firms Must Be Checked," DFLZWZ 7
(1998): 25–26; and "11 Factory Officials Ruined in 11 Years What a Factory Had Built in 60—'Collective Corruption' Must Be Severely Punished," DFLZWZ 3 (1998): 26.
[20] Jin, "Anticorruption Work at SOEs," 4.

sion or other productive activities. By and large the violations in the first reform period may be characterized as diversion or redistribution of public
funds.

With the replacement of the plan by profit sharing and then taxation, accounting violations have shifted to two new areas since the 1990s: diversion
of revenues that should be due to the state and extraction of funds from the
public. The first is often practiced by SOEs by way of concealing profit earnings from unlicensed business activities, making unauthorized tax reductions or evasions, underreporting foreign currency earnings, transferring firm
properties to outside businesses, and not least, setting up small treasuries.[21]
The second, the extraction of funds from the public, is commonly practiced
by local state agencies. Under a loose policy of *zichuang zishou* (keep the revenues you levy), these agencies arbitrarily levy fees—often determined by
the agencies themselves—from the routine services they administer on behalf of the state. These services have not only multiplied with the expanding
market economy, but are crucial to economic activities: land transaction,
property rental, permit application, vehicle and residence registration, job
placement, law enforcement, and other services. Although the need to make
up for the fiscal cutbacks from the center is an important cause of increased
local levies, the autonomy to set and levy fees has presented opportunities to
hike fees and broaden levies at will. These are often imposed against central
regulations and without the knowledge of higher authorities, and no local
mechanisms exist to control them. Corrections come about usually after the
eruption of a major scandal or a change of local administration. The arbitrariness of local sectarian policy making, such as levying, will be discussed
in greater detail in conjunction with the decline of disincentives against abuse
in chapter 5.

The destinations of the illegitimate gains from accounting violations are
no longer centered on welfare functions of the work unit. The extra incomes,
universal for managers and work units nowadays, often pay for entertaining
and amenities. Increasingly, they are also deposited in private accounts, so individuals can earn the interests and have access to the capital, but handily give
up the funds when suspicions arise. Or the booty is privately divided up
among a small group of individuals, such as in Chu Shijian's case.[22] Officials
from higher administrative agencies are also notorious for digging into the
slush funds of subordinate units, be they a factory or a village, to cover ex-

[21] See a treatment of the problem in Andrew Wedeman, "Budgets, Extra-budgets and Small Treasuries," *Journal of Contemporary China* 9:25 (November 2000): 489–512.
[22] "Pay Attention to the Negative Effects of Private Banking of Public Funds," DFLZWZ 3 (1997):
13.

trabudget expenses for feasting, travel, and bonuses. Based on a survey of the cases used in this study, the average amount of an accounting violation exceeded Y2 million per case in the 1990s, much higher than the average for embezzlement, misappropriation, or bribery cases. Even this data may be misleadingly moderate, as the number of prosecuted cases is unrealistically low and does not reflect the real extent of violations.

Tax fraud is another common accounting violation. In place of central plans and command, tax measures were introduced under economic reform to coordinate fiscal relationships among SOEs, local governments, and the central government. While taxes may be more efficient incentives than plan quotas, enterprises quickly learned to take advantage of the new system. Various schemes may be carried out by a firm collectively or its officials in collaboration with members of tax bureaus, customs offices, and banks. The most pervasive one is tax evasion. According to data from the National Tax Bureau in 1994, 50 percent of all state firms and 60 percent of collective firms evaded or cheated on their taxes. The figures for the nonstate sector are still higher, estimated at 60 percent for Chinese-foreign joint ventures, 80 percent for private enterprises, and 100 percent for self-employed vendors.[23] By one estimate, if calculated at a low evasion rate of 6 percent of the GDP, out of China's total GDP of Y3,138.03 billion in 1993, tax evasions would amount to Y188.28 billion, or 42.6 percent of the country's fiscal revenues for the year. Though state firms are not alone in this violation, the fact that half of state-owned firms cannot be controlled is significant enough.[24]

A related scheme is the false claim of tax rebates. Introduced since 1985, the rebates were incentives for export-bound producers, traders, contractors, and shippers. Firms that paid the product tax and value added tax (VAT) were entitled to rebates after exporting occurred. Many firms took advantage of the policy to file false claims. In 1994, 115 cases of violations by state firms were investigated and disciplined nationwide, involving eight hundred firms from twenty-three provinces, with illicit rebates totaling Y800 million.[25] Counterfeiting documentation was common in fraudulent rebate claims: concocting customs documents to fabricate exporting, altering sale receipts to upgrade exports, or even fabricating production and VAT payments. The last fraud is especially prevalent in some poor regions, a problem to be examined in more detail in the next chapter.

[23] "A Look into the Violations and Transgressions of Firm Heads and Managers," DFLZWZ 4 (1994): 18.
[24] "Public Funded Consumption and Tax Cheating Are Serious Problems," DFLZWZ 10 (1995): 13.
[25] Jin, "Anticorruption Work at SOEs," 5–6.

It may be added as a final note on accounting violations that even anti-SARS funds spurred similar patterns of transgression. The allocation of Y2 billion for the campaign, in the spring of 2003, turned out to be another windfall for some officials and work units. An auditing review of SARS-designated funds among the most-affected boroughs of Beijing, by the Ministry of Treasury on June 10, 2003, showed familiar forms of abuse. In place of prevention supplies and special vehicles, many organizations went on a shopping spree for office supplies, computers, and ordinary vehicles. Or they doled out employee bonuses. Administrators who worked on SARS prevention and inspection were quick to claim extra allowances designated by the central government for SARS-related medical workers (Y100–Y300 for "frontline" medical personnel per day; Y50–Y100 per day for nonfrontline health workers). Inspections in Inner Mongolia, Hebei, Hunan, Jiangsu, and Heilongjiang showed similar problems.[26] A national tragedy and the wide display of patriotic heroism occasioned by it, it turned out, were insufficient to overcome the weakness of checking mechanisms against abuse.

Squandering of Public Resources: From Modest Amenities to Ostentatious Indulgence

The essence of squandering is wasteful consumption of public funds for private enjoyment. Like accounting violations, squandering in the reform era is often committed by work units or in the name of such collectives. The two categories are also linked in that accounting violation is a main funding source for squandering. In the early and mid-1980s, squandering was small in scale and rarely received discipline. Larger cases increased in the late 1980s, but compared with the 1990s, the frequency of occurrence and level of waste were still moderate.

Two trends were dominant from the urban reform of 1984 to the early 1990s. One was officials' growing willingness to accept free offers from subordinate agencies, professional counterparts, and business clients. With professional relationships no longer based on administrative command, entertaining and gifts became important to cultivating business contacts. But the scale of squandering was yet modest, as shown in the two worst cases reported in this period. In the first, a "quality and management" inspection team, staffed by the State Technical Supervision Bureau and the State Quality Control Bureau, accepted free offers during their inspection tour of state firms across five cities. These offers included free hotel stays, banquets, meals, sight-seeing

[26] http://www7.chinesenewsnet.com, June 18, 2003.

tours, and gifts totaling Y42,900 for the entire team in a one-month period. Though a modest amount for the size and duration of the tour, it was treated as a serious matter because the offers came from the very businesses being inspected.[27] In the second case, a former district magistrate in the poor province of Shaanxi, Wei Shizhong, made a farewell trip to sixty subordinate agencies before leaving for a promotion in the province's capital. During the eight-week trip, Wei and his wife were treated to nineteen banquets, thirty-two farewell parties, along with nineteen gifts.[28] The total cost of Y5,337 was hardly exorbitant, but the effort to solicit entertainment and gifts created much bad publicity and potential conflicts of interests. After all Wei was to assume the deputy directorship at the province's Economic Commission. The errant officials in both cases received disciplinary sanctions.

The second trend was the increased use of public funds for entertainment and unauthorized construction. The surge was due in part to the expansion of firm resources and control over these resources since urban reforms in 1984 and then in 1987. One common practice was to feast and entertain at the slightest pretext of an occasion, as in the launching of a new project, product, or contract. In 1988, the Northeast Pharmaceutical Plant, in Hebei's capital city of Shi Jiazhuang, spent Y365,000 on celebrating its thirtieth anniversary. This extravaganza by a model plant headed by a model director took state authorities by surprise. The manager defended his spending as in the best interest of his firm: half went to guests from state agencies important to the plant's administrative and financial support, while the rest to gifts for members of the pharmaceutical regulation agency in his province and a distribution company in Beijing.[29] Financial and administrative autonomy also encouraged the unauthorized construction of new office buildings and cadre residences, sometimes at exorbitant expenses. The Ministry of Light Industry exceeded its original budgets by fourfold to construct a luxury office complex. With the latest construction materials and interior decorations imported from Europe, including gold and marble fronts, the complex took four years to complete, and even in the inexpensive era of 1984–1988, cost a total of Y1.16 billion.[30]

Squandering has become routine and rampant since the early 1990s. Many factors led to its upsurge in scale, frequency, and grandeur. Aside from a competitive psychology to display and impress, eased access to diverse public funds and weakened accounting controls removed the carefulness the Chi-

---

[27] Casebook #3, 222–24.
[28] Ibid., 220–22 and Casebook #4, 216–17.
[29] Casebook #4, 208–10.
[30] Ibid., 218–19.

nese traditionally had with spending money, while aggrandizing the typical regard the Chinese have for equating pomp with status and sincerity. Hence showy entertaining has become the biggest part of squandering. Figures from the State Statistics Bureau are staggering. In 1980, public-funded entertaining was estimated at Y18.6 billion for that year. The amount reached Y74.12 billion in 1990, or a fourfold increase in a decade. The figure shot up to Y128.35 billion in 1993, or nearly doubled in three years.[31] Operational expenses for nonenterprise public institutions grew at a 21 percent annual rate, or over Y4 billion a year, according to the Treasury Ministry's 1996 data. The bulk of these "operational expenses" went into entertaining. Township and village governments spent Y8 billion a year on entertaining, according to a 1996 report.[32] By mid-1990s estimates, industries across the country (state and nonstate) spent more than Y150 billion a year on feasting and gift giving, an amount equivalent to 40 percent of the annual output value of all state firms' fixed assets and 20 percent of all self-governing village industries' annual revenues.[33] To put the figures in perspective, Y150 billion was a little more than half of the country's annual budget for education in 1998 (Y294.906) and would likely grow at a faster rate than the educational budget's 16.48 percent rise from the previous year.[34] At local levels, educational and developmental funds may be further depleted by entertaining costs. One Hebei university had meager research funds but managed to spend Y360,000 a year on entertaining. A Hubei village council dined and wined away Y20,000 a year, despite the village's annual income of Y600 per capita.[35]

Feasting is the most visible part of public-funded entertaining and the part with the most "Chinese characteristics." Besides economic and cultural factors, feasting fever is driven by a calculation to escape anticorruption regulations: dining and wining do not violate any laws and nobody is pocketing any money personally. Operating on this logic, institutions and cadres of all sorts have little qualms about spending their funds and time on feasting or being fed. In 1993, such feasting totaled Y87.5 billion nationwide, or more than 65 percent of public-funded consumption that year.[36] According to estimates by the State Statistics Bureau in 1997, 70 percent of all large- and medium-size restaurants' income depended on public-funded consumption,

[31] "Public-funded Consumption and Tax Evasion Are Very Serious," DFLZWZ 10 (1995): 13.
[32] "An Analysis of the Phenomenon of 'Guest Accompanying' in Township and Village Governments," DFLZWZ 2 (1996): 8.
[33] "The Annoying Convention of Entertaining and Gift Giving," DFLZWZ 1 (1997): 31.
[34] "The Chinese Government Increases Investment in Education," RMRB, November 26, 1999.
[35] Li Haiyun, "Beware! Dining Expenses—The Sources of Overspending," DFLZWZ 5 (1997): 17.
[36] "Public-funded Consumption and Tax Evasion," 13.

30 percent of which was spent by public organizations.[37] A local survey, conducted in Jinzhou in Liaoning Province in the same period, showed the proportion of public funds to be still higher, at 80 percent or 90 percent of caterers' revenues.[38] Surveys from Guangzhou, Haikou, Fuzhou, Nanjing, and Xi'an suggested that 60 percent of all business in luxury places of entertainment was paid by SOE funds.[39] By 2002, about 20 percent of restaurant earnings came from public organization consumption, thanks to the rise of private consumption, but the total volume remained daunting, at Y100 billion for that year.[40] Apart from dining and wining, feasting often includes karaoke sing-alongs, ballroom dancing (and the hiring of female dance partners), and hors d'oeuvre. The time consumed is equally costly. One source puts the average time that business and government executives spend on feasting and gift giving at a hundred hours a month. This means two and half weeks in one month for an eight-hour day schedule. Even calculated at the wage rate of the lowest paying regions, Y3.5 an hour, the salary costs to firms and the government would be billions of *yuan*, while the efficiency loss to production and public administration may well be in hundreds of billions of *yuan*, if measurable at all.[41]

Second to feasting in waste and ubiquity is the public funding of automobile use. Cars have become a must acquisition for top officials at all kinds of public institutions and firms. Were vehicles necessary for their work, this may be justifiable, especially in the countryside. Yet the primary incentive is often competitive consumption and the acquisition of a status symbol, enabled by fiscal and administrative autonomy. So luxury cars, not just any cars, become prized. Unwritten rules at the gate of one city government say much about the social climate: jeeps must park outside the gate, domestic cars must be registered to enter, imported cars drive through freely.[42] If cars are treated so differently, one can imagine the different treatment their riders receive at business and social functions. Relatedly, car maintenance costs escalated to 70 percent of public administration expenditure at some work units. Nationwide, such expenditure reached Y11.4 billion in 1992 and doubled to Y20 billion in 1993. Gas and maintenance alone cost between Y20,000–30,000 a year for one vehicle, more than the annual income of most citizens.[43]

[37] "Members of the National Political Consultation Committee on Combating Corruption," DFLZWZ 9 (1997): 10.

[38] Li, "Beware! Dining Expenses," 17.

[39] "An Analysis of the Phenomenon of 'Poor Church with Rich Monks,'" DFLZWZ 8 (1997): 15.

[40] Cited in *Zhongguo Fazhi Bao*, February 17, 2003.

[41] "The Annoying Convention," 31.

[42] "Worrying Thoughts on Public-funded Car Consumption," DFLZWZ 4 (1996): 21.

[43] Ibid., 21.

The gap between car possession and financial realities often betrays misplaced priorities. One county was perennially in deficit, yet all eighty-four agencies in the county government had at least two cars (not including vans and trucks) and nearly all bureau heads (*ju zhang*) and above were equipped with a car. In fact, at the funeral procession of the Tax Bureau chief in this county, the streets were lined up with singularly imported cars, prompting a local newspaper to headline its report "A Long Trail of Deficits, A Long Track of Imported Cars." One impoverished county owed its hundreds of teachers six months in back pay, thanks to "financial hardship." Yet the county government managed to purchase eight luxury cars earlier in the year. One northeastern county owned more than seven hundred cars by 1989, with gas and maintenance costing a staggering Y10 million annually. Yet the same county received Y13.76 million in poverty relief annually from the central government.[44] A deeper problem is how public-funded vehicles are actually used. One survey finds that they are used for private purposes 20 percent of the time, with a mixture of public and private purposes for another 15 percent. During random stings at nightclubs, police even found customers with "Antipoverty Office" plates on their cars. And it is no longer usual to see officials transport their ladies of the night in official vehicles. When public vehicles are used for such questionable purposes, social inequities are magnified in the public eye.

Cell phones contribute to another form of squandering. Anyone who has been to Chinese cities or even counties will be impressed by a presence of cell phones greater than in many developed countries. Cell phones may not be luxuries per se, since telephone systems are going directly to cellular in China as in many late-developing nations. The problem is the public funding of privately consumed phones. Surveys in the mid- and late 1990s showed that about 60 percent of all cell phones were not privately owned, and of these, another 65 percent or so were purchased at public expense without proper authorization. Examples abound of situations where levies are exacted, taxes evaded, business losses ignored, loans misused, or subordinates coerced, all in an effort to finance what the public refers to as "ear-side corruption." The costs are significant. According to calculations by the provincial government of Hunan in the mid-1990s, the total number of public-funded cell phones in the province, at Y4000 a piece, cost Y576 million to purchase and another Y432 million annually in phone bills.[45] That is more

[44] "The Hot Waves of Automobiles," DFLZWZ 7 (1994): 9–10.
[45] "Cell Phones in Violation of Regulations—A Black Drain to which Public Money Flows," DFLZWZ 1 (1998): 12; and "Reflection on the Heat Wave of Public-funded Cell Phones," DFLZWZ 1 (1996): 12–13.

than Y1 billion combined for a province that is not even considered a developed region. Calculated at this rate, the total costs of public-paid cell phones easily exceed Y30 billion for China's thirty-some provinces in a given year, or about one-tenth of the country's educational budget in 1998. (With declining prices for cell phone services, however, there has been strong growth of private cell phones more recently.)

The explosion of business trips, conferences, inspections, and other perks, while signaling greater mobility and open exchange, has become both a cause and result of widespread abuse. Business trips often turn into extended sightseeing travels, especially the so-called overseas study and observation tours. With few substantive goals, such trips have become official prerogatives. Those from urban and well-off rural areas feel entitled to at least one trip to one or more Western countries during their tenure. Those from rural or poorer regions feel entitled to one Southeast Asian tour of Hong Kong, Macao, Thailand, and Singapore. In one extreme case, the Bureau of Meteorology in a poor city of Yunnan could not afford to pay its employees for half a year. Yet it managed to take a bank loan for its chief to make an "observation" tour in Southeast Asia. Such overseas tours cost Y2.5 billion nationwide in 1992. In some cities, overseas tours mean hundreds of tour groups or thousands of travelers each year. Since their travel details are unfamiliar to accountants at home, irregular and fraudulent receipts are routinely reimbursed. A delegation that is supposed to visit one city may bring back receipts from several cities.[46] Even for domestic travels, excess expenses are reimbursed through bloated or fictitious claims. Not surprisingly, domestic travel costs amount to a third of administrative expenses at some local government agencies.[47]

Commemorative events have persisted and gained a new life since the 1990s. To cite a few extreme examples, 44.4 percent of the eighty-one public institutions in one county, including county government agencies, held elaborate celebrations in one year. Even a small agency received almost a hundred invitations each year. In another county, twenty of its public organizations, including agencies of the county government, had invited more than two thousand counterparts for celebrations in the first eight months of a year. On average, this county hosted more than one thousand guests and 230 agencies per month. Not only is such frequency burdensome for hosts and guests alike, more so are the costs. Well-to-do visitors often bring along thousands of *yuan* in gift money, which sometimes more than make up for the costs of the occasions. This, in turn, acts as an incentive to hold more ceremonies,

[46] "Private Consumption of Public Funds: An Immeasurable Black Hole," DFLZWZ 6 (1995): 10–12.
[47] "Corruption in Travel Receipts," DFLZWZ 7 (1997): 22–23.

which then burden all invitees, especially the less affluent. At the opening ceremony for a new village (*xiang*) police station, two poor villages had to contribute "IOU" slips at Y1000 for each village.[48]

Bureaucratic Negligence: Oversight of Fraud and Mismanagement

At first look, bureaucratic negligence may not seem a deliberate misdeed, since it denotes a failure to perform official duties properly because of laxity, not dishonesty. Chinese policies and the public treat this misstep as corruption for two reasons. One is that negligence is caused by failure to perform one's official duties responsibly, competently, or prudently. In the reform era, such failure is often due to the profit motive. The second reason is that negligence harms public interests. Though selfish motives may not be directly involved, the common assumption is that were it in the private sector, an executive would be more careful to avoid obvious blunders.

Throughout the 1980s, negligence occurred commonly in the form of officials being defrauded in business deals due to a lack of experience in a commercial economy. Typically an official would enter into a business agreement with another party over sale and purchase, investments and loans, collaboration and joint ventures, or equipment and technology. The official usually represented the side that made the ordering, paying, lending, and investing on behalf of a state firm. Because of the official's failure to conduct background checks and his poor understanding of business, the other party bilked the state by fleeing with capital, defrauding loans, breaching contracts, canceling orders, or supplying inferior products. The latter was often a self-employed, collective, or TVE business. Often the problems occurred because the official was inexperienced with the mechanisms of contractual and legal protections and gullible before appealing deals and dealmakers. Seemingly rich businessmen from Hong Kong and Taiwan were a frequent source of the problem in the 1980s. Since mainland officials had little knowledge of an overseas company or its contractual terms, they could be goaded into signing a contract with all sorts of unfavorable obligations for the Chinese side. In my data for the 1980s, many such cases involved heavily indebted and unsuccessful overseas Chinese seeking a new life or a new prey on the mainland. But fundamentally, an official's poor judgment was the culprit. His eagerness to make quick profits, his light regard for public funds, and his obsequious attitude toward overseas businessmen all contributed to his laxity.[49]

---

[48] "Worrying Thoughts on Commemorative Events," DFLZWZ 1 (1995): 6.
[49] Casebook #3, 143–77 and Casebook #4, 95–141.

Many examples bear out these features, with dismaying details. During 1988–1989, Mr. Luo Qinzhang, CEO of Hunan Machinery Industry Company, approved purchase of overpriced and underweighed products from Hong Kong, including steel, synthetic and chemical materials. Out of eagerness to please "old suppliers," he ignored fallen prices and falling demands in the domestic market. Some of the imports had to be sold at heavy discounts, while most lay wasted. The total loss to the state neared Y5 million.[50] During 1981–1986, the director of the Bureau for the Management of Overseas Chinese Farms of Guangdong, who also headed the province' Overseas Chinese Enterprise Company, provided loan guarantees and collateral for a Hong Kong businessman, all on behalf of his state bureau but without official approval. He even used his state company to borrow loans from a Chicago bank to help pay off debts he owned in Hong Kong. The businessman was supposed to invest the loans in local farms. No investment was ever made, but the Chinese side had to shoulder HK Y50.83 million in losses.[51] In another egregious case, the International Trading Company of Shanxi Province entered into agreement with a Hong Kong businessman to build a joint steel plant in 1986. Without any feasibility study or communication with the Ministry of Economy and Trade in Beijing, Shanxi failed to discover that the same individual had backed out of a hotel project in Shenzhen earlier and possessed few assets. Plunging ahead blindly, Shanxi willingly provided loans, loan guarantees, and collateral for a mere 20 percent of the project. If the plant profited, the businessman would reap most of the profits. But if it failed, Shanxi would bear most of the liabilities. In the end, the phony investor fled, defrauding the Shanxi company of HK Y55.6 million.[52]

Another common occurrence in the 1980s was the failure to prevent and deter the manufacturing of counterfeit products, particularly when they resulted in serious material and human damages. It was not always negligence that led to an official's neglect of such activities. Profit incentives and regionalism also played a role. The latter factors were particularly important in poorer regions where profit-making opportunities were limited. Regardless of intentions, indulgence of counterfeit production is classified under negligence because of the failure to follow regulations and exercise supervision. During the 1980s, common counterfeits included fake fertilizers, pesticides, crop seeds, liquors, medicine, and equipment. Increased demand for fertilizers and other chemical products by farmers had resulted from the liberalization of agriculture since 1978. The shortage and rationing of those products,

---

[50] Casebook #4, 133–35.
[51] Ibid., 133–39.
[52] Casebook #3, 173–79.

in turn, stimulated counterfeit production on a massive scale. Proliferation of village and self-owned businesses, further, made counterfeiting widely possible. Two examples are illuminating.

From 1983 to 1987, eighteen pesticide plants popped up in Miluo, a remote city in Hunan. Mostly run by villages and without technical credentials, they produced large quantities of fake pesticides and sold them to 131 counties in 17 provinces, causing huge damages to the agriculture of these regions. In 1986, twelve of the plants were closed down by various central ministries, including those in charge of chemical engineering, trade, agriculture, and commercial regulation. Yet a year later, Miluo's mayor ordered several plants to be relicensed without inspection or approval from the city's Bureau of Chemical Engineering or the Bureau of Quality Control. Many resumed the production of fake pesticides. The Ministry of Oversight from Beijing issued orders to the mayor to implement tough measures against counterfeiting, but he all but ignored them. For these missteps, he was convicted on criminal negligence, along with officials at the city's bureaus of commercial regulation and TVE administration as well as village officials.[53]

In the second case, Wanrong County of Shanxi was a major site for producing fake pesticide and rat poison during 1986–1988. Using mixtures of sand, sulfur, lime, coloring, and gasoline as ingredients, twenty-one TVEs in nine villages, along with some self-employed businesses, produced ten brands of poison at a volume of 1241.19 tons in 1988. Fourteen state firms, under the jurisdiction of the county's Economic Commission, also joined the counterfeiting. Sold to thirteen provinces and even Beijing, their products failed to protect crops everywhere. Yet the central government's prompt response had little effect locally. In the first year alone, four ministries—of agriculture, industrial and commercial regulation, health, and trade—sent down teams to inspect and discipline the counterfeiters. But on their departure, local officials no longer bothered with the matter. Without deterrence, many plants restored production and new ones opened. Legitimate firms joined them by assisting with product labels, bank accounts, business seals, and packaging materials. Some credit unions continued to supply loans. The deputy county governor himself helped to sneak fake pesticides out of the county. For unknown reasons the penalties were light for this case. The county's party secretary and governor received only an "intraparty warning," while the deputy governor lost his post but not his employment.[54]

Like other types of corrupt behavior, negligence has worsened after 1992.

[53] Casebook #5, 49–50.
[54] Casebook #4, 107–10.

Being defrauded in business deals remains the major misdeed, but now this occurs through formal contracts and with high financial stakes. Though the use of contracts marks a major progress from the earlier practice of agreements, some officials continue to be lax. Frequent blunders include signing contracts without carefully verifying information, failing to discover contractual traps, carelessly agreeing to contractual changes, and importing investment and equipment without checking credentials.[55] The worst case involved the deputy mayor of Chongqing, who headed delegations of electronic executives and technical experts on several overseas trips to shop for a LCD and CCD manufacturing line. After spending a total U.S. $8 million in various costs over several years and two trips to the United States, they brought home an outdated manufacturing line in 1998, with an actual value of no more than $40,000. The sellers, a Chinese-American couple near Boston, had originally purchased the line for $800,000. Needless to say, they entertained their visitors well, showering them with, among other things, two paid trips to Las Vegas.[56] Even President Jiang Zemin's own plane could not avoid a similar fate of negligence during its makeover in the United States. The Chinese crew reportedly went on sightseeing tours and thus did not detect the installation of spying devices by the American crew.

Mismanagement of public firms and projects is another common negligence in the 1990s. One reason for this is that managers are faced with new situations after being freed from state plans. Without state dictates or a grasp of market forces, some managers make wrong purchases, decisions, or investments. Others pick wrong partners and cultivate business relationships in costly ways. Still others leave factory equipment idle, output unaccounted for, and employees and thieves colluding to steal from the plant.[57] What makes these actions negligence is that in all cases, managers failed to do background checks, feasibility studies, or follow regulations and procedures, which would have easily prevented their blunders. In one case, three consecutive directors of the Jingshan Grain Bureau in Hubei lost nearly Y1 billion from 1989 to 1999, all from mismanagement in administering grain procurement and retailing.[58]

Other forms of mismanagement arise from a general corrosive climate, which helps to erode professional morale and the responsibility ethic. Many construction officials, while not taking bribes themselves, close their eyes to

[55] Zhang, "Reflections on Establishing," 6–7; Zhang, "How State Assets are Lost," 16–17.
[56] Ju Zhi, "A Billion *Yuan* Imports a Pile of Scrap Metal—The Top Economic Crime Case since Chongqing Became a Centrally Administered Metropolis," DFLZ 8 (2000): 10–13.
[57] Zhang, "Reflections on Establishing," 6–7; Zhang, "How State Assets Are Lost," 16–17.
[58] Qing Wen, "An Overview of Corruption Cases in 1999," DFLZ 3 (2000): 22–25.

those who do and keep silent about problems caused by poor contractors. It is precisely this professional and moral failure that caused the nation's worst construction accident. On January 4, 1999, the entire Qijiang Rainbow Bridge collapsed in the outskirts of Chongqing, killing forty people and injuring fourteen. What shocked the public the most was its completion date of less than a year before the accident and its Y6.3 million cost. The chief culprit turned out to be the deputy magistrate cum director of urban and rural construction in Qijiang County, who, after taking bribes, allowed the contractor to go ahead without a permit and ignored numerous violations of building codes during the construction. With his abetting at the top, middle-level officials in charge of project supervision and quality control chose to overlook visible problems, such as unsafe components, low-grade materials, and poor job quality. For these failures, the latter officials were convicted on negligence charges, with jail sentences between three to five years. (A five-year term is the maximum for negligence.) The deputy magistrate received the death penalty for bribe taking and negligence.[59]

Negligence has also reached into the capital-intensive arenas after 1992. With the new developmental frenzy, one approach many localities resort to, in the name of stimulating fast and massive investment, is to attract financial deposits—from within the work unit and from the public—with high interest rates. The deposits are then turned around as business loans for still higher returns. The approach, employed by urban banks and workplace credit unions, was widely popular in the mid-1990s. The enticing prospects were often attractive to eager and inexperienced depositors. But the rash injection of capital flows often caused an overheated economy and excess capacity. The heavy debts incurred by businesses, in turn, proved to be less than efficient and overly burdensome. Nonperforming loans resulted. Yet the public had either to be paid at further losses to the fund-raisers, or see their deposits frozen, the latter at great risk to social stability. The most notorious case involved the party secretary of En'ping County in Guangdong, Li Guang-hui. Under the rhetoric of "encouraging economic development," Li directed the city's financial institutions to attract deposits with high interest rates in 1994. For two years, more than Y11 billion was raised, leading to more than Y6 billion in high-interest loans. By the end of 1996, more than Y4 billion of those loans, or two-thirds, became nonperforming, with unpaid interests totaling Y1.2223 billion. To meet with payments for depositors, the city had to borrow "assistance funds" from higher-level banks. The Y5 billion in additional

---

[59] "Trial of the Qijiang Bridge Case Ends, 13 Sentenced," DFLZ 6 (1999): 8; "Belated Remorse," DFLZ 6 (1999): 7; Zhang Qing, "Uncover the Dark Case of the Bridge Collapse," DFLZ 6 (1999): 10–19.

loans cost the city Y522.79 million in interest payments alone. Li's policies
caused other serious problems. The initial failure to pay depositors led to public riots. The debt problem triggered a financial crisis in the city. Li and the
deputy mayor were eventually convicted on negligence charges and each received a four-year sentence.[60]

Corruption and Reform: What Beneficiaries and Costs

Many forms and outcomes (if not always the original intentions) of nontransaction corruption, as discussed above, fall under the theft of the public
coffer. As Andrew Wedeman argues, such theft, or looting, is more devastat-
ing on economic growth than the other two forms of corruption that he
groups under "rent scrapping" and "dividend collecting." The latter two usually describe transaction-type corruption. The destination of the black-mar-
ket gain makes an important difference on its consequence: because of the
secretive nature of looting and the precarious business environment it creates, looted money is rarely directed back into the domestic economy.
Looting thus depletes resources for economic development and entails absolute loss for an economy.[61] In contrast to some more productive forms of
transaction-type corruption, looting also involves nefarious motives. Revisionist arguments about economic efficiency and social integration, thus, are
not relevant to nontransaction corruption. From these perspectives, two pos-
tulates may be made about the possible effects of nontransaction corruption.
One is its greater financial and fiscal impact and the other is its function as a
disincentive against more productive activities.

Both consequences are unequivocal yet complex in the Chinese context,
varying according to the type of looting, the reform period, and whether the
organization or the individual is the main culprit. In the pre-1992 period,
looting was limited at the individual level, both in arrogated amounts and offenders' ranks. The organizational forms, that is, accounting violation and
squandering, were largely redistributional in nature, since funds often went
to workplace welfare functions. The beneficiaries were usually firms and their
employees, while the "loser" was the state coffer. This diversion of public resources may be seen to have a "positive" impact in the sense that it allowed
managers and workers to taste the rewards of managerial and fiscal flexibility. Moreover, SOE appropriation did not yet act as a serious disincentive
against productive behavior, since the plan quotas still had to be filled and

[60] "Former Party Secretary of En'ping City Sentenced for Negligence," DFLZ 6 (2000): 23 and
"Former Deputy Mayor of Jiang Men Sentenced for Negligence," DFLZ 3 (2000): 19.
[61] Andrew Wedeman, "Looters, Rent-scrappers, and Dividend-collectors: Corruption and Growth
in Zaire, South Korea, and the Philippines," *Journal of Developing Areas* 31 (Summer 1997): 457–78.

above-quota production had to be profitable. Although the extra incomes could have been better spent on productive investment and business expansion, they at least offered a direct incentive for supporting such reforms as greater financial accountability, firm autonomy, and performance-linked remuneration. Because managers could not yet set up their own businesses or "stockify" (*gufen hua*) state firms, and because they still depended on workers to fulfill production orders, they had incentives to direct funds to collective welfare rather than siphoning them off to private accounts.

However, the post-1992 period has seen a surge of looting at both individual and organizational levels, and in more detrimental ways. Organizational actors become more prominent and exert greater harms than individual ones. The beneficiaries and destinations of organizational looting in the form of accounting violations and squandering are no longer the workplace and its collective welfare. Several reasons account for this change. First, each stage of ownership reforms separates managers further from both the state above and the workers below, allowing managers near autonomy over firm finance and expenditure. Second, policies that allow massive downsizing and the use of migrant workers enable managers to ignore workers' well-being, not to mention welfare. Third, the imperatives of market competition and business relations provide both an occasion and pretext for managers and other officials to spend excessively on entertaining, gift giving, amenities, and other kinds of perks. Finally, squandering provides a way out of the risks of individual looting. As a result, SOE managers, along with heads of other public organizations capable of extracting public funds, have become the primary beneficiaries of accounting violations since the 1990s. Concurrently, squandering, rather than benefit distribution, becomes the primary means of those violations.

Both the beneficiaries of collective looting and the destination of squandering are not only unproductive but often counterproductive. By some estimates, industries across the country spent over Y150 billion annually in the mid-1990s on just two functions, feasting and gift giving, also the two leading destinations of accounting violations. This amount was equivalent to 40 percent of the annual output value of all SOEs' fixed assets and 20 percent of all self-governing village industries' annual revenues. The impact on reform was often direct. In one city, city officials spent the Y1.5 million earmarked for price reform on feasting and gift giving. As a result the public was left with no subsidies to cushion the hit of price liberalization, feeding tremendous public resentment for the city government.[62] Massive diversion of firm funds and evasion of taxes otherwise due to the state, progressively depress

---

[62] "The Annoying Convention."

government revenues. The fiscal shortage in part contributes to notorious problems of meager allocation for local governments, leading to illicit levies by the latter to solve their own fiscal problems. These burdens, in turn, fall hardest on those SOEs and farmers least able to pay. The fiscal shortage has also been responsible for meager social programs to safeguard those displaced by market reforms. The other side of financial violation and speculation by local governments and other public organizations is the depletion of finance for private-sector businesses and the pervasive use of informal finance by private entrepreneurs.[63]

Equally counterproductive, as well as arbitrary and onerous, have been the levies and fines frequently imposed by agencies as sources of extra income. While they overburden the public, especially firms and farmers, the levies are often squandered as entertaining expenses for a few agencies and their cadre. In the notorious case of Guluo, a relatively poor city in Hunan Province, firms and farmers were levied 295 different fees totaling Y6.7 million annually in the two years between 1992 and 1994. A considerable part of this revenue paid for city officials' feasting and travels, while the rest were split among themselves. After a 1994 reform took away city agencies' powers to enact levies, payments went down by 20 percent for farmers and 10 percent for enterprises. The city's revenues increased by Y10 million while firms saved Y4 million in the two years since.[64] In another egregious case, the Police Bureau of Bao'an borough, Shenzhen, netted Y5.13 million from levies between 1993 and 1995. Using various pretexts, they imposed charges on the borough's lucrative and vulnerable sources: "sponsorship dues" from the self-employed, contractors, disco and bar owners; "temporary residence fees" from migrant workers; "security levies" from neighborhoods and residents; "insurance payments" from businesses; hiked rates from license applicants; and arbitrary fines on prostitutes, gamblers, and drug users. To facilitate exaction, the bureau printed its own levy and fine slips, so that the revenues could be kept off official records and used internally at will. In all, 380 pads of such slips were used in less than one year, reaping Y359,000 in illegal earnings. In 1995 alone, this branch spent Y800,000 on feasting, another several hundreds of thousands of *yuan* on a luxury model of Mercedes-Benz for its chief, and the rest on generous bonuses and subsidies for the staff. When the case was exposed in late 1995, 80 percent of the levies had been consumed.[65]

[63] I thank Kellee Tsai for bringing this point to my attention. See her *Back-Alley Banking: Private Entrepreneurs in China* (Ithaca: Cornell University Press, 2002).

[64] Cited in "Anticorruption Efforts Should Be Focused on Institutional Building—Comments by CCPDC Standing Committee Member Qi Peiwen on How to Halt Corruption," DFLZWZ 5 (1997): 15–16.

[65] "One Police Station in Shenzhen Levied Y5 Million Illegally," DFLZWZ 4 (1996): 16.

The typical intertwining of accounting violation and squandering, shown in the foregoing cases, has fed a cycle that consumes firms and managers at the detriment of productive activities and genuine reforms. To receive administrators or inspection teams from above becomes a routine headache for subordinate work units, be they factories or villages. If businesses offered to entertain the visitors in the 1980s, now they feel obliged because the outcome of inspections depend on the quality of entertainment. The same feeling goes for the outcome of other business transactions such as a contract bidding and a loan applications. The demands of entertaining, thus, becomes a new kind of administrative intervention in the market economy. Like previous deference to administrators, few are now willing to scale down entertaining, even while everyone condemns the diversion of resources from pressing social needs. So continues the cycle of more squandering and more accounting violation to finance it. The effort to woo Chen Xiaotong, son of Chen Xitong, shows the dilemma for businesses. The head of the building firm had to chase Chen around with brain-racking arrangements for entertainment. Since the princeling was used to dainties of all kind and could be impressed by little, the builder had to be more imaginative. After offering rounds of feasts averaging Y20,000 (U.S. $2,500) each meal, he topped it all with an exquisite dinner of all snake delicacies, complete with a seductive snake dancer. The expenses came from his firm, factored as part of necessary costs. The generosity finally convinced Chen of the firm's "sincerity." The entertaining, in other words, was an annoying but unavoidable cost.[66]

Blatant accounting violations and squandering, committed by local governments and public institutions, have broader encouraging and sanctioning effects on individual cadre and the general public. For they embolden gray behaviors to lapse into dark ones. If employee bonuses funded by diverted money are fine, extra expenses and amenities for officials become legitimate. If collective cheating by public institutions is acceptable, illegal ventures such as organized smuggling by other groups and individuals seem justifiable. If concealing profits is commonplace for public firms, individual officials find it comfortable to covertly transfer profits and assets out of firms into private pockets. If tax evasion is universal, more audacious moves follow.[67] Collective frauds, moreover, play a role in encouraging frauds everywhere, not least by lesser firms and players in the economy. From accounting reports to statistics, from achievement awards to professional titles, and from advertisements to product brands, fraud seems to permeate society. They give a special

---

[66] Zhong Shi, *Nie Hai Chen Zhou,* passim.
[67] "A Look into Violations by Directors and Managers," DFLZWZ 4 (1995): 17–18.

meaning to the new "free" economy and undermine the very principles of open competition that market reform is supposed to foster.

An extreme example of the spin-off effects on individual behavior is the case of Yuan Jinjin, whose abuse single-handedly impaired a key reform program in his city. As deputy director of the Labor Department in Tianjin between January 1996 and March 1997, Yuan was in charge of personnel and employment matters for workers, especially the masses of workers downsized by SOEs. But the state funding under his control, intended for such programs as unemployment and reemployment assistance, became the sources of a brave new life-style. Overwhelmed by an office much prized and courted, Yuan learned to appreciate the ostentation of the nouveau riches. Armed with an expensive briefcase, a beeper, a cell phone, and the company of a few staffers—all at official expense—he spent evenings in discos and bars, with nightly feasts, wines, and entertainers. Within a year he had visited every upscale restaurant in the city and devoured fine dishes of every kind, averaging one visit every other day and over Y2000 each visit. His dining receipts, itemized as conference expenditure and business meals, were duly reimbursed at work, where his own signature was required and where his main purpose for showing up was to cash receipts. In his fourteen months on the job, Yuan was reimbursed 206 times totaling more than half a million *yuan*. Thanks to the egregiousness of the case, he was convicted of embezzlement and given a suspended death sentence.[68] Had the amounts been not so outrageous, Yuan would have likely been disciplined for "squandering," usually not an indictable offense.

Among the major forms of looting that result from individual misconduct—misappropriation, embezzlement and negligence—the size of the loot has also got significantly larger since the 1990s and with more costly effects. Whether the officials or private businesses are the beneficiaries, looting does not generate the kind of incentive mechanisms for, or efficiency effects on, economic reform as is sometimes seen in bribery.

Misappropriation may be the least costly because of the usage of appropriated funds. These usually head for three destinations, all of which are less damaging to reform than other forms of expropriation. The majority is used as startup or working funds for the business activities of corrupt officials. In the Chengdu survey cited earlier, 73 percent of the investigated cases fell into this category. The rest usually went into the business activities of relatives and friends, or speculation in the stock and property market.[69] From a functional

---

[68] "Deputy Director Dined Himself onto the Death Roll," *Xinhua Yuebao* 12 (December 1998): 62–64.

[69] Rong and Gu, "How Are State Resources Appropriated," 17–18.

point of view, these destinations may be "positive" if they contribute to private enterprise and the expansion of the private sector, a key goal of market reforms. In fact, sometimes the illegitimacy of the funds places pressure on the violators to make their businesses more profitable so that they can return the money before exposure. Yet other times the effortless origin of the funds removes any incentives to be responsible. For all three destinations, so long as the funds are returned, the losses would not be total. But often, de facto looting occurs because the original funds are locked or lost in speculative or business activities. In only about 15–30 percent of exposed cases were diverted funds partially or fully retrieved.[70] The overall loss to the public coffer, thus, may not compensate for the efficiency of private accumulation.

Embezzlement has yet graver consequences in financial and functional terms. According to the government's Bureau of State Assets Management, the total loss of state assets due to embezzlement, misappropriation, and mismanagement (in that order) exceeded Y500 billion in the decade from 1982–1992, or a rate of Y50 billion per year. This is equivalent to one-fifth of the country's total fixed state assets of Y2.6 trillion in 1992, and Y80 billion more than the country's total revenues of Y418.8 billion in 1992.[71] Because there is no intention to pay back, most embezzled funds are not reinvested to generate additional profits. Other major destinations of nontransaction corruption—hoarding, consumption, and capital flight—drain resources away from domestic investment and worsen the overall environment for economic activities. According to the Chinese Economic Times (*Zhongguo jingji shibao*), illegal flight of Chinese capital to overseas destinations had accumulated to U.S. $65–$85 billion from the beginning of the reform period to the mid-1990s. In more recent years, the rate of capital flight to overseas destinations alone is estimated at U.S. $10 billion a year.[72] To put it in perspective, bribe money, tabulated from the more than 210,000 cases investigated by prosecutors' offices nationwide, totaled Y2.58 billion in five years from 1988 to 1993. That is a rate of Y500 million per year, or one-twentieth of overseas capital flight rate.[73] None of these figures reflect the true extent of losses, of course, for the real scale of embezzlement will never be known.

Finally, embezzlement by firm managers is always at the expense of SOEs. As such it exerts critical damage on firms by depleting their resources, impoverishing workers, stalemating reforms, and bankrupting firms. These dam-

---

[70] Based on Casebooks #1–10, especially Casebook #1, January 1996–Dec. 2002.

[71] Cited in He Qinglian, *Xiandaihua de xianjing* (Trappings of Modernization) (Beijing: Jinri Zhongguo Chubanshe, 1998): 106.

[72] Gong Chengxiang, "An Analysis of the Phenomenon of Book-keeping by Close Kinship," DFLZWZ 6 (1998): 13–15.

[73] "A Worrisome Report on Crimes Committed by Legal Entities," DFLZWZ 3 (1995): 8–9.

ages also have special distributional consequences because they amount to informal privatization of SOEs. In fact, one scholar already employs "spontaneous insider privatization," a term commonly used to characterize the process of post-Soviet privatization, to describe recent erosion of state property rights in Chinese SOEs.[74] Other scholars observe a comparable phenomenon in the context of TVEs being converted into shareholding cooperatives.[75] This chapter finds insider privatization frequent at some local small- and medium-size SOEs. Unlike the type of redistributional effects before 1992, the negative distributional effects of embezzlement at SOEs in the later period do not generate popular support for reform. On the contrary, they have contributed to cynicism and hostility among workers about shareholding reforms and managerial autonomy.

Negligence, perhaps the least selfishly motivated of all corrupt acts, can do greater harms than the other types. One comparative figure is illustrative. From 1988 to 1990, the city of Beijing disciplined 2,135 cases of embezzlement and bribery, and only 95 cases of bureaucratic negligence. The ratio of the former group to the latter is 22:1. However, actual financial losses show a different picture. The bribery and embezzlement cases resulted in Y34.39 million in total loss for the city, but the negligence cases contributed Y154.1 million in total loss, or 4.4 times more. The average loss per case, moreover, is Y16,000 for the former group, and Y1.62 million (or ten times) for the latter group.[76] Nationwide, 3,189 cases of bureaucratic negligence were prosecuted in 1991, with a total loss of Y830 million, or more than a quarter of Y1 million per case. In the same year, 3,339 additional cadre were sanctioned by disciplinary agencies for lesser forms of negligence, with another few hundreds of millions of *yuan* in losses. Further, partial losses can often be recovered in bribery and embezzlement cases, as bribe money and stolen funds are retrieved from involved felons. But losses caused by negligence are almost never recovered.[77] Bureaucratic negligence has also indirectly contributed to the overall crime

[74] Ding Xueliang, "The Illicit Asset Stripping of Chinese State Firms," *The China Journal* 43 (January 2000): 1–28; "Who Gets What, How?" *Problems of Post-Communism* 46:3 (May–June 1999): 32–41; and "Informal Privatization through Internationalization: The Rise of Nomenklature Capitalism in China's Offshore Business," *British Journal of Political Science* 30 (Part 1) (January 2000): 121–46.

[75] Sally Sargeson and Zhang Jian, "Reassessing the Role of the Local State: A Case Study of Local Government Intervention in Property Rights Reform in a Hangzhou District," *The China Journal* 42 (July 1999): 77–99; and Susan Whiting, "The Regional Evolution of Ownership Forms: Share-holding Cooperatives and Rural Industries in Shanghai and Wenzhou," in Jean Oi and Andrew Walder, eds., *Property Rights and Economic Reform in China* (Stanford: Calif. Stanford University Press, 1999): 171–202.

[76] Liu Jinghuai and Wei Yunheng, "Heavy Tuition: Investigation and Reflection on Serious Bureaucratic Negligence and Malfeasance Cases," *Liao Wang* 4 (1992); and "Negligence Is No Light Crime," DFLZWZ, 2 (1994): 21–22.

[77] "Negligence Is No Light Crime," 21–22.

rate. Thanks in part to the ease of defrauding negligent officials, contract defrauding has become one of the top crimes in the country, ranking third among all crimes by the late 1980s.[78] Losses from failed and defrauded importation of foreign investment and technology, apart from the exorbitant financial costs, are long term and developmentally detrimental.

Only tax fraud has some ironically mixed consequences for the economy. On one hand, widespread evasion has dwindled the tax base as the main source of government revenues. This has not only hurt the state and the public generally, but also firms and their reform agendas more specifically. The reduction of fiscal revenues has forced the government to relinquish many social services, especially those critical to SOE reforms, for instance, welfare provision for downsized and retired workers. Local state agencies, in turn, have resorted to levying illegitimate and erratic fees to make up for fiscal shortfalls. State firms often end up shouldering many social services, such as welfare and medical provisions, as well as local levies.[79] However, the efforts by state and nonstate firms to dodge taxes often end up stimulating the consumer market. In trying to write off nonbusiness expenses as business costs to reduce tax payments, many scramble to spend lavishly on construction projects, consumer goods, and entertaining. Private owners of entertainment facilities, in fact, complain that each round of anticorruption campaigns ends up hurting them by driving away big-pocket consumers.[80] Private distribution, in other words, in part substitutes for public redistribution.

CONCLUSION

By examining five types of nontransaction corruption over two reform periods, this chapter has demonstrated that, first, each of the five nontransaction types has evolved in accordance with changing incentives or declining restraints occasioned by market reforms, progressively worsening in quantity, quality, and impact; and that second, the nontransaction types, often neglected by leading theories and empirical discussions of corruption, can have more widespread and detrimental consequences.

The evolution of nontransaction corruption over the two periods is best reflected in the changing types of violators, mechanisms, and destinations for diverted and looted funds. In the early reform period, the perpetrators of

[78] Wang Yuxing, "A Black Specter in the Market Economy: Fraud through Contracts," DFLZ 6 (2000): 14–15.
[79] See "Anticorruption Efforts," 15–16
[80] The author's interviews and firsthand observations.

nontransaction corruption moved from clerical staff and petty officials in the prereform economy to the lower and middle management levels since reform. They were the grass-roots decision-makers or executors in the day-to-day activities of SOEs: those in charge of purchase, marketing, treasure, and accounting, as well as those in charge of individual departments within the firm. During this period, violators were largely managerial personnel of lesser SOEs and contracted SOEs. Nonbusiness public organizations such as local government agencies, judiciary and law enforcement agencies, and social/cultural/educational institutions were not major violators. As for mechanisms for predation, it was no longer exclusively state property that was the target of various appropriations, as in the prereform era. Rather, the mechanisms diverged: resources from the state's allocation on one hand, and from firm's revenues on the other. The destinations of diverted funds, finally, began to move away from the largely personal uses of the prereform period and into an mixture of personal/workplace/business goals: personal accumulation, business funds for family members and friends, workplace benefits, workplace entertainment, among others.

The type of violators, mechanisms of violation, and usage of arrogated funds has greatly diversified in the post-1992 period. The scope of violators has broadened to the top tier of SOE management, larger SOEs, local government agencies/agents, as well as nonbusiness and nongovernment public organizations. These are no longer just public organizations with income from state allocation or firm production but also those with rights to appraise SOEs assets and transform their ownership, power to extract income from the public, and access to the capital of financial institutions and funds for developmental assistance. The mechanisms of violation, likewise, have diverged to a variety of new sources: SOE shares and assets, administrative budgets and welfare expenditures, developmental assistance, levies and fines, loans and contracts, underground contracting, domestic and overseas profits, bank deposits and investor funds, tax rebates, and even educational funds. The destinations of diverted funds have moved into more daring areas: large quantities of private deposits and overseas flight, sizable businesses outside SOEs, organized speculative activities, modern amenities, lavish private and collective entertainment, and defrauded projects.

There are several reasons why nontransaction types of corruption, especially those in the second period, can have graver consequences than transaction-based bribery discussed in the previous chapter. Above all, the sources of black money differ. The five types examined in this chapter directly invade the public coffer rather than profiting from "rents" (in the sense of the rent literature), namely the legitimate or illegitimate profits of nonstate actors. As

such, they have fiscal and financial consequences that seriously affect the reform of the state sector at the macrolevel and the reform of individual SOEs
at the microlevel. Many enterprise, fiscal, and social welfare reforms, as well
as short-term priorities and the long-term development of the country, depend on the health of the state coffer. Yet widespread accounting violations
and squandering have not only diverted resources away from pressing social
agendas but also subject them to frivolous pursuits. At the enterprise level,
appropriation, embezzlement, or negligence by officials can deprive a firm
of its life support in the worse cases and create financial chaos and employee
resentment even in the best cases.

Second, the scale of financial losses in each type of looting is on average
larger than bribery cases, especially since the 1990s. This is not just because
the public coffer is much larger than the pocket of private bribers, but also
because the sources of public funds have diversified and expanded, especially
after 1992. The anonymity of nontransaction appropriation further impels
large-scale, audacious takes. At the same time, the openness of organizational
violations encourages similar psychological drives. Third, the destinations of
looted funds are socially unproductive and generally counterproductive, as
they usually do not head for productive activities and its beneficiaries are not
the sort of unprivileged entrepreneurial groups sometimes seen in bribery
cases. Even for the looted funds that did go into business activities, on balance this has occurred at the expense of SOE reforms and the well-being of
SOEs. In addition, accounting violations and squandering, usually committed by public organizations, have widespread moral and political consequences. Because they are more openly practiced and omnipresent, they exert
broad predatory and exemplary effects on society, are hard to prosecute and
discipline, and cost the regime much needed political legitimacy and support
in a difficult time of economic transition.

4

BETWEEN THE STATE AND LOCALITIES

The Regional Dynamics of Corruption

In this chapter, I examine interactions between reform and corruption by looking horizontally at regional patterns of post-Mao corruption. As shown in chapters 2 and 3, decentralization and the progressive transition to the market have effected the forms and outcomes of transaction and nontransaction corruption across two reform periods. Likewise, differences in structural incentives across localities and sectors should also affect corrupt behavior horizontally. Characteristics of post-Mao corruption may be locality specific and path dependent on local reform and developmental experiences. Using the differences between the relatively less corrupt first reform period and the more corrupt second period as a model, we can ask, "Do more 'market-affected' and 'state-weakened' regions experience more corruption than the less market-oriented ones?" Has that corruption exerted more harmful effects on local development and reform outcomes, much as corruption in the second reform period has been more detrimental than in the first? Or are different dynamics at work?

Horizontally across localities, much as synchronically across reform periods, dominant patterns and outcomes of corruption have been largely shaped by the larger "structural features" that drive corruption elsewhere. "Marketized" forms of reform-era corruption are more dominant in more developed regions, while intensified forms of socialist-era corruption are more prominent in underdeveloped and remote regions. This intensification, however, has been due to similar structural mechanisms elsewhere that have rendered cadre more ready to commit abuses since reform. Locality-specific features intervene in the type of opportunities available for rent seeking as well as in the configuration of local patterns of abuse. In this connection, the chapter will examine three regional models: independent kingdoms and local corruption chains, coastal regions and organized smuggling, underdeveloped regions and poverty-derived schemes. A central analytical framework for organizing the discussion will be the relative strength of the state and the extent of market opportunities in a locality. The "state" here refers to the authority of higher administrative and disciplinary agencies over a local government. This framework will be laid out in the discussion of the first regional phenomenon below. It also guides the discussion of the other two regional trends later in the chapter.

INDEPENDENT KINGDOMS AND LOCAL CORRUPTION CHAINS

Local corruption chains and rings refer to the phenomenon in which almost an entire local government, or a large number of its officials, engage in violations. A case can involve many local government officials simultaneously, which is known as *wo an* (a "burrow case"). Or large groups of officials outside the government (i.e., in SOEs) and societal groups are closely tied to the misdeeds of local officialdom. Here we have situations where corruption is no longer a matter of individual behavior or local sectarian interests, but an epidemic within the locality and even a local pattern of governance. Such tendencies have become more common since the 1990s. Specifically, three regional trends may be observed, which form a useful framework of analysis for this chapter.

The Top-Down Pattern

Where the strength of the central state and market opportunities are both meager, corruption chains tend to be top down in a locality. Corruption starts from the top with ripple effects down the chain of the administrative command. This "top" is often the very top in a local administration: the magistrate or party secretary of a county; the mayor, deputy mayor, or party secretary of a city; and occasionally, the provincial governor. Usually found in less developed and more remote counties, cities, or provinces, this pattern is mainly due to three factors. One is the greater likelihood of "office-for-sale" practices in these regions. At the very least, there is a greater tendency for *ren ren wei qin* (favoritism and nepotism). As a result, local administrations tend to be filled with like-minded and self-seeking officials, who overlook or indulge one another's misdeeds and even collude in misconduct. Second, the prominence of office for sale in such regions is related more to the lack of alternative opportunities for profiteering than the continuance of the old administrative system. In fact, it is the weakening of the old administrative system, with its more rigid supervision and control mechanisms, that has exacerbated the problem. Finally, officials of remote regions are more likely to have *su zhi* problems, as the Chinese often put it, referring to the quality, personal character, and educational level of the cadre corps. The poor attributes of top officials, in turn, have immeasurable exemplary effects on other cadre. In short, the top-down model is likely to spring from relatively independent kingdoms dominated by local officials in remote, rural, and underdeveloped regions. The top-down pattern here resonates with what Kevin O'Brien calls "paralyzed villages" and what Thomas Bernstein and Xiaobo Lu refer to as "agricultural China."[1]

The best example of multilayered, top-down chains of local corruption is Guangxi Autonomous Region. Its far-flung location on the southern border, relative ethnic autonomy, and recent development combined to create auspicious opportunities. As an underdeveloped region, Guangxi became a magnet of government development programs since the 1990s. Typical of poor localities, such programs brought in ample pubic resources for cadre enrichment. Between 1999 and 2001, Guangxi earned the distinction of uncovering one corrupt official at the *chu* rank and above bimonthly, the highest rate in the country. Among the better known are former governor and later deputy chairman of the National People's Congress, Cheng Kejie, executed in 2001 for bribery; former deputy governors Xu Bingsong, sentenced to life for bribery, and Liu Zhibing, sentenced to fifteen years in prison for bribery; three former heads of provincial departments (treasury, transportation, and communications) and a former deputy head of the Police Department, all convicted on bribery; former mayor of Guigang city and former head of the bank of Yuling city, both executed for bribery; former head of the Zhongshan County bank, sentenced to twelve years in jail for writing an unauthorized check of Y1.2 billion; and former party secretary of Qinzhou city and former deputy secretary-general of the regional government, both convicted on bribery.

[1] Kevin O'Brien, "Implementing Political Reform in China's Villages," *Australian Journal of Chinese Affairs* 32 (July 1994): 33–59; and Thomas Bernstein and Xiaobo Lu, *Taxation without Representation in Rural China* (London: Cambridge University Press, 2003). I thank Kellee Tsai for bringing these parallels to my attention.

At the top, Cheng Kejie was the highest ranking official ever executed in the history of the PRC. Several other deputy provincial governors have been convicted for corruption, but Cheng and Li Jiating, both of ethnic provinces, supply the two cases where the chief executive received the death sentence (Li's was reprieved). Cheng took in Y40 million for helping bribe payers acquire loans, land, contracts, and promotions. Guangxi is also the only region where two other provincial-level governors received prison sentences, all in the last few years. Xu Bingsong, deputy governor from 1993–1998, received Y555,000 from businessmen, while Liu Zhibing, deputy governor since 1999, took Y866,322 for loan guarantees and intervening in smuggling investigations. To trace the chain further, Xu's corrupt career started while serving as party secretary of Yuling region of Guangxi, where his two successors—or three party secretaries in a row—were all brought down by corruption. Before their downfall, one of those two successors had risen to head another Guangxi city, and the other to head the party disciplinary committee of Guangxi and even to join the central disciplinary committee.[2] Under each of the three officials' reign in the Yuling region, yet another one of Guangxi's greediest officials, Li Chenglong, flourished and served as the nexus of the local corruption network.

Li, then party secretary of Yuling County and later mayor of Guigang city, was executed in 1999 for Y16 million in bribe taking and other illegal income. The web of Guangxi's corruption networks first became known during the investigation of Li, when a mysterious senior official intervened to limit the investigations, intimidated witnesses, and passed information to the detained Li. Only when central prosecutors arrived and relocated the investigation to nearby Guangdong, were investigators able to go on. (The mysterious official turned out to be deputy governor Xu Bingsong.) To avoid the death penalty, Li offered information on Governor Cheng, linking the province's corrupt networks to the very top. Besides his superiors, Li's case also dragged out a trail of subordinates who engaged in wide-ranging abuse. A list of his bribe payers appears in table 2.2 in chapter 2. All of the bureau chiefs and mayoral aids promoted by Li, as shown on the table, engaged in wanton graft during Li's tenure in Yuling. With such individuals around him, it was little surprise that Li's own lawyer complained in court: "Li Chenglong's power in Yuling was monitored by no one at the time. As everyone knows, the People's Congress has no real effects in this regard. His power was absolute and absolute power breeds absolute corruption." Outside the offi-

---

[2] "Former Deputy Governor of Guangxi Sentenced to Life in Prison," DFLZ 1 (2000): 17; Yin Hongwei and Lo Nanhua, "A Mayor Who Takes in Tens of Thousands of *Yuan* Daily," DFLZ 7 (2000): 25–27.

cialdom, Li forged close ties with the province's "ten business kings" (*shi da wang*), who were his major briber payers. Li arranged for them not only favorable business deals but also political offices.[3]

Equally rampant was abuse in another Guangxi County, Hepu under Nanning city. Its party secretary, He Jianling, later to head the coastal city of Beihai, collected Y240,000 for arranging twenty-four job placements and promotions in the late 1990s. These included some of the most important and lucrative posts in the two localities he served: directors or deputy directors of the bureaus of construction, trade, customs, treasury, state assets management, land, taxes, industrial and commercial regulation, special economic zones, personnel, legal affairs, and others. Three of the office buyers and a deputy county governor also joined twelve others to build an infamous "corrupt street" in 1993–1994.[4] The fancy houses, built on public land and partially at public expenses, were conspicuous oddities in a county too poor to pay its public employees. Ten of the twelve officials on the street were top officials from the city's Construction Bureau, while the remaining two headed the Utilities Bureau and the Land Resources Bureau respectively. One other "corrupt street" has been known since reform, in Suiqi County of Guangdong. In this case too, public land and funds were used by top county officials to build an exclusive residential area in an impoverished region.[5]

More cases of top-down corruption will be seen in a later section on underdeveloped regions.

The Bottom-Up Pattern

The second model of a local corruption chain is the bottom-up pattern. This usually occurs in regions where societal and market forces are strong even while the central or the local state may not be particularly weak. Here, the vibrant activities of societal groups can engulf local officials, or alternatively, offer enticing inducements for the latter. Expectedly, this pattern is likely to be found in more developed and less remote regions.

Two main dynamics are usually at work in this model. On one end are strong societal initiatives in these localities, where commercial and developmental opportunities create intense incentives for business interests to compete for official advantages. These groups also possess greater financial and

---

[3] Yin and Lo, "A Mayor," 26.

[4] "Crackdown on Corruption," DFLZ 3 (1999): 31; and Zhong Wu, "A Ring of Greedy Officials Caught on the Corrupt Street," DFLZ 5 (1999): 22–24.

[5] Lu Ping, "Here Is a 'Cadre Street,'" *Dangjian Wenhui* 4 (April 1991): 14–15. Huang Hai and Li Dahong, "Reflection on the Violations and Transgressions of Leading Officials," DFLZWZ 1 (1997): 23–24.

organizational resources to influence local power. As a deputy head of Henan's Supreme Court commented, "Why were a particular large group of officials involved in economic crimes in Gong Yi city? The reason is that TVEs are particularly vibrant in that city, with intense interests in snatching projects and supplies. They compete by smothering state agencies and officials with bribes, so much so that one finds it hard to dodge and resist." After hearing a case involving one municipal government, the head of another provincial supreme court observed that the mayor did not solicit bribes but bribers eagerly showered him with gifts. Bank officials also report profuse unsolicited bribes from loan seekers each year. On the other end of societal initiatives are rent-seeking pressures on individual officials. While market-oriented officials help to promote private-sector development, the process also creates multiple incentives. Well aware of business dependence on official services and support, officials easily succumb to private-sector inducements. Even when local officials initiate bribe taking and other profit-sharing schemes with the private sector, however, the key difference with the top-down model is that local officials rely on the business sector, rather than the public coffer, as the key source of self-enrichment. The bottom-up model here does not correspond to the Sunan model or Wenzhou model in the recent literature.[6] It encompasses not only localities on the eastern and southern coasts, but also those in any province where business activities provide the main target of official predation. In short the bottom-up model is likely to exist in relatively independent kingdoms dominated by market-supporting local officials and assertive local entrepreneurs.

Several dramatic cases in recent years illustrate the bottom-up pattern. Most notable is the Yuanhua case of Xiamen, where a private smuggler almost brought an entire city government. The case will be detailed in a later section on smuggling. In another notable case involving Wuxi, a vibrant medium-size city in the affluent province of Jiangsu, a retired factory worker was able to run a large pyramid scheme with complicit officials. During 1992–1994, her operation raised Y3.2 billion and caused a direct loss of more than Y1.2 billion to firms and individuals. More than three hundred organizations in twelve provinces were swindled and became intricately indebted. The case brought criminal convictions to ninety-nine officials who accepted gift shares. Among them were a deputy mayor, who allocated Y10.5 million in city funds to help her operation; the city's prosecutor general, whose wife helped promote the fund; and a deputy chair of the city's CPPCC.[7] The case

[6] I thank Kellee Tsai for raising this point.
[7] Reporters from *Xinhua* News Agency, *Renmin Ribao,* and *Xinhua Ribao,* "An Illegal Investment Fund that Calls for Deep Reflection," DFLZWZ 3 (1996): 16–19; "Who Caught Chen Xitong's

helped to uncover eighty-five related instances of abuse implicating ninety-four more individuals and was to touch off the exposure of corruption rings in Beijing in the mid-1990s. A less dramatic but more conventional case is Jianyang city of Sichuan. Because of its proximity to the provincial capital and the Chengdu-Chongqing highway, Jianyang became a darling of investors after winning special economic rights in 1991. But its developmental drive made city officials vulnerable to building contractors and land buyers. Eight of the eleven members of the city government's standing committee became involved in a chain of bribery scandals, including the mayor and three deputy mayors, the party secretary and three deputy party secretaries.[8] Two cases in chapter 2, involving the head of a Zhejiang village (who asked lumber contractors for bribes) and the female head of an ICMB outside Shanghai (who pressured private businessmen to defray costs of her son's wedding), provide good examples of the bottom-up model at the rural level.

For more scrupulous officials, the incessant swamping of gifts from an aggressive private sector is a perennial source of frustration. Aware that these gifts always mean requests for favors later and possible exposure one day, they avoid them like infectious diseases. Concerned wives and mothers also worry constantly about the ability of their husbands or sons to resist the kaleidoscopic offers from favor seekers. But refusal to take gifts can be equally perilous, as such a reputation threatens colleagues and superiors, who often collude to destroy the career prospects of reluctant bribe takers. In Lixin County of An'hui, the party secretary was even given repeated death threats for rejecting Y600,000 in bribes during his tenure there from 1999 to 2001. He had to be promoted to a different location against his will.[9] The survival strategy of such officials is usually to accept small and noncash gifts, which are safe from both disciplinary agencies and peer estrangement.

The Top-Bottom Interactive Pattern

In between the two models just described is a third pattern. Where the local state and market forces are well matched, the corrupt activities of officials and societal groups tend to interact with and reinforce one another. The likely candidates are provincial capitals and metropolitan centers where the reach of the central state may be close, but the strength of the local government

---

Tail?" DFLZWZ 1 (1998): 4; and Xinhua News Agency, "The Completion of the Trial of the Largest Illegal Fund-raising Case in the Country," DFLZWZ 2 (1996): 14.

[8] Mao Hao and Yang Shuren, "The Sacrificial Altar to Power," DFLZWZ 1 (1996): 18–19.

[9] Wu Xiaofeng and Jiang Niao, "Repeated Threats against a County Party Secretary Who Rejected Y600,000 in Bribes," DFLZ 8 (2001): 38–40.

and market forces can be just as strong. One result, as found in the case of Chen Xitong in Beijing, is that local chieftains may be entrenched and strong-headed enough to run their terrains like independent kingdoms in defiance of the center. Such independence breeds the promotion and protection of cronies, as Chen's patronage of Wang Baosheng and others demonstrate. It also insulates the local administration from monitoring by outside forces, further enhancing a fertile ground for favoritism and cronyism. But such independent kingdoms differ from those in the top-bottom model in that they tend to be in urban centers, where business forces are likely to be strong as well, thus competitive and aggressive in seeking official patronage. All these factors contribute to a pattern of corruption marked by active official and societal interaction. In contrast to the other two models, both the state and the business sector provide significant targets of official predation in this third model.

A case in point is Shenyang, capital of Liaoning Province. A major industrial base in the socialist era, the city has been plagued by ailing SOEs and massive layoffs in the recent decade. Adding to its slow economic progress was a contingent of corrupt officials who controlled all key branches of the city government and who milked the city dry with wide-ranging abuses in the 1990s. At the top, Mayor Mu Suixin traded public offices, land, contracts, and protection for organized crime for kickbacks. Ma Xiangdong, executive deputy mayor in charge of foreign investment, used city funds—designated as bonus for investors—to gamble in Macau and set up a private company in Hong Kong. The chief of the Tax Bureau harvested Y200,000 to Y300,000 in cash gifts for each Lunar New Year since the late 1990s and kept stacks of envelopes filled with cash bribes in his office. The chief of the Price Control Bureau stashed away Y40 million in slush funds and purchased six residences with public funds. The head of the municipal court sheltered half a dozen mistresses with public funds and bribe money. The chief of the State Assets Bureau dropped Y10,000 at a time on escort ladies. The chief of the Finance Bureau used city funds for frequent overseas travels. The list goes on: head of the city Prosecutor's Office, head of the Land Resource Bureau, head of the Tobacco Bureau, and head of the Construction Bureau. The entire municipal government fell in 2001.[10]

At the societal end, one of the major bribers of the mayor and other city officials was Xia Renfan, chief executive of the city's bus company. A nationwide model reformer in the 1980s, few could recognize him as the same

---

[10] Gui Wei, "Looking into the Case of Mu Suixin and Ma Xiangdong," DFLZ 10 (2001): 29–30; and Zhong Tian, "Ma Xiangdong's Path to Self-destruction," DFLZ 12 (2000): 12–13.

person a decade later. With bribes, Xia contracted all five transportation companies from the city to form a conglomerate in 1992, achieving a monopoly over Shenyang's mass transit system. However, his company chronically reported deficits and received tens of millions in city subsidies each year, the latter secured again with bribes. While Xia sold off more and more of the assets he contracted to manage, he kept the annual salary of his employees at around Y3000 for six years. Without bonuses or benefits, this wage level was extremely low at a time when the combined average income was several times higher for workers in the country. Despite such a record, after receiving tens of thousands of *yuan* in bribes Mayor Mu agreed to appoint Xia to head of the city's Transportation Bureau. Only a collective protest from the bureau's staff stalled off his appointment. The state of Xia's transportation company looked all the more suspect when concurrent with its visible demise, Xia poured tens of millions to build a lavish private manor the size of a large village. Greenhouses alone numbered twenty-seven, all equipped with latest sprinkler systems.[11]

The other major societal player was Liu Yong, who rose from a street peddler to being a major business operator in Shenyang. By 1995, his company had twenty-six subsidiaries covering a variety of retail trades, with twenty-five hundred employees and Y700 million in fixed assts. But it was a company, according to Shenyang's Police Department, built on gangster tactics: "violence, ruthlessness, lawlessness, cold-bloodedness, murder, tax resistance, and ferocious revenge." With a doctored resume that concealed his background as a fugitive out on bail, Liu managed to become a model entrepreneur and a representative to the municipal People's Congress. Behind him, not surprisingly, was an array of official patrons bought off with handsome bribes: executive deputy mayor Ma Xiangdong, who went on his Macau trips with bodyguards supplied by Liu Yong; chief prosecutor of the city's Prosecutor's Office, also Liu's "Godfather"; a Labor Bureau official, Liu's "Godmother"; and a deputy head of the city's Intermediate Court, Liu's mistress. Liu's arrest in December 2000 brought down eight Shenyang officials. In a further testimony to the grip of local corruption chains, Shenyang's officials had to be transported to Jiangsu and handled by the court system in the latter province.[12]

It is notable that Shenyang was a second provincial capital to succumb to citywide corruption among the Northeast's three provinces. In Heilongjiang, a series of cases were prosecuted five years earlier. The Guomao Trading Town

---

[11] Cheng Gang, "The Big, Rotten Manor of Shenyang," DFLZ 3 (2002): 31–33.
[12] Gao Yu, "Deputy Mayor and the Gang Leader," DFLZ 6 (2001): 37–38.

Company, contractor of the largest and centrally located shopping mall in Ha'erbin, had not paid a penny of taxes two years after its opening since 1992. Some of the Y14 million in evaded taxes were used to buy off city officials, who in turn granted the contractor tax exemptions as a joint project of the city. In 1997, more than two hundred individuals, including twenty-five city officials, were found guilty of bribery in connection with the scheme, among them the head of the city's national Tax Bureau and two deputy mayors.[13] During the same period, three other large SOEs and one city agency were also found guilty of abuse on a similar scale. In all, Ha'erbin was able to recover Y150 million in booty and losses from the four cases.[14] As in Shenyang, local residents felt profoundly betrayed by the exposure of the corruption ring, especially by its link to the plight of their local economy.

Beijing, under Mayor Chen Xitong, provided the most dramatic example of the top-down interactive pattern of local corruption. As the seat of the nation's capital, Beijing lived under the nose of the central government, so to speak. All mechanisms of central command and discipline, and the most sophisticated media and opinion forums, were nearby and any information of misconduct could easily filter out and up. Yet the city was plagued by complex webs of corruption that matched the worst regions in the country. Fittingly, these webs of corrupt ties started to form during the height of the first reform period in 1986 and culminated in the height of the second reform period in 1997. The unfolding of these webs first began with the seemingly unrelated case of Wuxi's pyramid scheme in 1995, when the name Li Min emerged during investigations. Li, a deputy chief of Beijing's Police Department, was revealed to be a key backer of the Wuxi scheme and a former assistant to Mayor Chen Xitong. Li was also closely linked to Chen's current assistant, Chen Jian. The investigation of Chen Jian, in turn, uncovered new scandals at the Capital Steel Company, where Deputy CEO Zhou Beifang was a major bribe payer to Chen Jian and another mayoral assistant, Yan Zhenli. The latter was an assistant to deputy mayor Wang Baosheng.

At the Capital Steel Company, a major state conglomerate that employed 240,000 plus people, Zhou Beifang's case was the latest in a series of scandals unfolding among the top management since 1990. These included Guan Zhicheng, party secretary and deputy CEO, sentenced to death in 1991; his mistress, sentenced to life in prison in 1991; two deputy CEOs appointed as Guan's successors, sentenced to suspended death and fifteen years in prison

[13] "Disclosing the Exchange of Money and Power—The Guomao Town Case of Ha'erbin," DFLZWZ 4 (1998): 19–22; "Yu Xinhua Risked her Life for Two Years to Expose Corruption," DFLZWZ 5 (1998): 3–4.
[14] "Ha'erbin's Deputy Mayor and Others Disciplined for Violations," DFLZWZ 11 (1997): 14.

respectively in 1994; CEO of the company's shipping branch, sentenced to suspended death in 1995; and Zhou Beifang, deputy CEO, sentenced to suspended death in 1996. Convicted on bribe taking and/or embezzlement charges, these individuals had taken booty ranging between Y1.5 million to Y9.28 million each. The last official, Zhou Beifang, generously bribed mayoral assistants Chen Jian and Yan Zhenli. Zhou was also a business partner of the mayor's son, Chen Xiaotong.[15] These assistants and offspring of top officials, with unchecked power and omnipotent connections, acted as key links between the supply and demand ends of local corruption chains.[16]

At Beijing's city government, investigations of his assistants panicked deputy mayor Wang Baosheng, who committed suicide in mid-1995. Postmortem investigations drew out twenty-two additional offenders among his current assistants and former subordinates from the Treasury Bureau, previously headed by Wang. Among his cronies were the bureau's deputy chief and its chief of staff, who allowed Wang to dispose of the city coffer at will. Wang Baosheng alone appropriated Y100 million and U.S. $25 million, and embezzled over Y260,000. Wang and his protégé Chen Xitong also concealed Y18.3 billion in city revenues, built lavish villas, and sheltered mistresses with city funds.[17] By the end of 1996, two additional provincial-level officials and ten additional bureau-level officials in Beijing's municipal government were found guilty of corruption, including the secretary general of the city government cum deputy chair of the People's Congress of Beijing, head of the city Administration Bureau cum deputy chair of the city CPPCC, head of the Housing Transformation Bureau, a deputy secretary general of the city party committee cum one of Chen Xitong's aide, and eventually Mayor Chen Xitong himself.[18] Given the scale of violations at the core of the capital city, it is not difficult to see why such a chain of corruption needed to be broken from its top, no matter what the real intentions of Jiang Zhemin were in bringing down the mayor.

The pattern of entrenched local chieftains and bureaucratic abuse bore itself out again in Beijing during the initial outbreak of SARS in the spring of 2003. For weeks the municipal government kept information about the

[15] Liu Jusheng, "An Analysis of the Five Major Economic Crime Cases in the Capital Steel Co.," DFLZWZ 8 (1996): 17–21; and Wang Hongfeng and Wang Jianzhong, "Capital Steel's Major Bribe-taking Case," DFLZWZ 12 (1995), 21.
[16] Feng Yi, "The Symptoms, Causes and Remedies for the Violations by the Assistants of Leading Officials," DFLZ 10 (1998): 8–9.
[17] Shen Hezhong, "The Origin and Development of Chen Xitong's Case," DFLZWZ 3 (1998): 22–24; "Who Caught Chen Xitong's Tail," 4.
[18] Xu Jiangshan and Xia Junsheng, "The Progress in Anticorruption Work in Beijing and Some Reflections," Liao Wang 45 (1996); Shen, "The Origin and Development," 22–24.

scope of the problem from the central government, so as to minimize political losses. Central government officials complained that they received more cooperation from the province of Guangdong, which for decades had a reputation for unruliness, than from Beijing.[19] "Cheating the above and the below," indeed, appears to afflict most seriously "independent kingdoms" like Beijing.

COASTAL REGIONS AND ORGANIZED SMUGGLING

Coastal regions have produced all major organized smuggling cases in recent years: Guangdong, Guangxi, Hainan, and Fujian in the South, linked to the South China Sea; Zhejiang and Jiangsu in the East, adjacent to the East China Sea; and Shandong and Liaoning in the North, adjoined with the Yellow Sea. The dynamics of smuggling within each locality is affected by commonalities as well as differences in their geographical and structural features. The southern coastal region enjoys advantages in infrastructure, level of development, and historical ties to the outside world. Proximity to overseas influences and investors, liberal policies, and distance from Beijing, moreover, have afforded these provinces a more open and flexible environment. But the successful external examples do not just offer incentives to emulate, but also urges to traffic imports. In the southern coastal localities, the bottom–up model often characterizes the pattern of smuggling activities. For less-developed coastal regions, as in the North, the top–down pattern is more typical. For internal provinces, import smuggling is usually done through liaison offices based in the coastal regions and on a smaller scale than local groups in coastal towns.

Besides geographic and structural factors, another dynamic is the tension between local and central interests, which makes smuggling an easily thriving activity at the local level but a hard-to-stamp-out plague for the center. As a *New York Times* reporter writes, "In places such as Shantou, where the smuggling of diesel oil, cars, cell phones, and much more has long underpinned the economy, there is a vast ripple effect when police get tough with smugglers: Lime-green luxury flats sit empty on Jinsha Road, taxi drivers queue for hours to get a fare, factories that used cheap smuggled cloth now teeter on the brink of bankruptcy."[20] Or as the head of the Antismuggling Office of Shantou city remarked, "We've had to educate local grass-roots

[19] "China's Crisis Has a Political Edge," *Washington Post*, April 27, 2003, p. A3.
[20] Elizabeth Rosenthal, "Smuggling War Rippling through China," *New York Times*, March 6, 2000.

cadres who held mistaken notions, such as 'smuggling does not do any harm' or 'smuggling helps economic growth.' . . . They do not understand that smuggling harms the entire national economy."[21] From the central government's point of view, import smuggling threatens the country's growth targets, robs Beijing of badly needed customs revenues, and squeezes the profits of some of the country's most important state-owned industries. Moreover, the type of corruption that goes hand in hand with smuggling has eaten into the civil service, customs authorities, and law enforcement forces.

Not surprisingly, organized smuggling became a key target of Beijing's anticorruption offensive in the late 1990s. The CCP central committee convened a work conference on smuggling in September 1999. The shocking unfolding of Zhanjiang's case in 1998 and Xiamen's in 1999, involving hundreds of officials and tens of billions of *yuan* in smuggled goods, heightened national attention to rampant and large-scale organized smuggling. Across localities, organized smuggling has exhibited interregional and intraregional patterns. To differentiate these, three types of smuggling may be classified.

Smuggling by Legal Entities

"Legal entities," or *fa ren,* usually refer to public firms, otherwise known as *danwei* (work unit). Because of the central role of the work unit, this type of smuggling is part of institutional corruption, or corruption by organizations.

Foreign trade (*wai mao*) corporations, go-between firms licensed with rights to import and export on behalf of local businesses, were once the foremost "legal entity" smugglers before their disintegration in the late 1990s. Reforms in the 1980s transferred foreign trade rights directly to some manufacturers, but many smaller firms still needed to go through trade corporations. Taking advantage of this, the latter found ways to creatively import goods on behalf of local businesses: concocting contracts, obtaining unmerited permits, misrepresenting items and destinations, and claiming undue tax relief. They may prepare the necessary paper work to import items on behalf of a legal manufacturer eligible for tariff advantages. Together they imported entirely different items at different quantities and prices, and resold them in the domestic market. Work units in special economic zones (SEZ) have been another group of prominent "legal entity" smugglers. As part of policy incentives for SEZs, favorable tariff rates are allowed for imported inputs and equipment, if manufactures are destined for exporting. This may be manip-

---

[21] Michael Kramer, "In China, Smuggling Is a Daytime Job," *The Financial Express,* November 6, 1998.

ulated to import any goods with the same methods used by trade corporations. Nonbusiness organizations eligible for import rights make up yet another group of legal organized smugglers. Law enforcement agencies and army-affiliated corporations can legally import military-related equipment. These rights too may be used to smuggle commercial imports.

Being a "legal entity" itself offers incentives. Organizational status helps to cover up the criminality of smuggling. Organizations can easily use public assets (company funds and bank loans) for smuggling operations. Legal entities are seldom brought to criminal prosecution for smuggling. In 1998, the Customs Office of Xiamen city, Fujian, investigated twenty-two cases classified as "large and major" (da an yao an), with monetary values totaling Y147 million. Yet thanks to their organizational status, the offenders received merely light fines and confiscation of imported goods.[22]

Smuggling by Local State Agencies

This type of smuggling falls under the top-down model of local corruption. Here a local state agency takes the initiative and receives support from the highest level of the local government. Sometimes the local government itself may initiate and coordinate the undertaking. The initial motive is not private profiteering, but the interests of local state agencies or the local economy. This type of smuggling has mainly occurred in relatively underdeveloped coastal regions or (later rich) regions in their earlier development

Late learners would often point to Shenzhen, Shandou, Zhuhai, and Foshan, all coastal cities in Guangdong and now among the most developed in the country, as early examples to emulate. From their origin as poor fishing towns, these localities were seen as having utilized preferential policies to accumulate huge initial capital through imports speculation. As SEZs, they could import controlled goods at favorable tariff rates, as long as these were justified by local developmental needs. Once imported, few looked closely as to where the goods ended, allowing the imports to head elsewhere in the country and making them technically smuggled goods. After layers of speculators, prices could go many times higher. The early smugglers were "fortunate" in that Beijing had not quite caught up with the schemes in the 1980s and that organized smuggling was still scanty.[23]

When Hainan earned its special economic zone status in the late 1980s,

---

[22] Li Jun, "A Comprehensive Look at the Phenomenon of Corruption in Smuggling Activities," DFLZ 2 (1999): 11–12.

[23] Lan Bo, Zai Zousi Kuangchao de Beihou (Behind the Maddening Wave of Smuggling) (Beijing: Gaige Chubanshe, 1999): 18–22.

Governor Lei Yu explicitly sought to emulate the practice of vehicle smuggling. A scantily developed island at the time, Hainan lacked the capital base and infrastructure to attract overseas investment. Lei's heavy lobbying helped to win some projects from Beijing, but he was impatient with the pace of local growth. With his ultimate endorsement, local agencies set out to approve the importing of vehicles and color TV sets for speculation. Smuggling soon exploded to uncontrollable scales and became practically the main business of the new province. In the last few years of the 1980s, various local agencies approved the importation of eighty-nine thousand vehicles, most of which were involved in speculative sales in or out of the island. Hainan was both "fortunate" and "unfortunate" to have caught the last train. In the wake of the 1989 Tiananmen protests, Hainan and Governor Lei Yu became the most visible casualties of the post-Tiananmen anticorruption campaign. From the chief executive of a provincial government, Lei was downgraded to a deputy party secretary for a rural county.

The post-1992 market drive would soon draw other officials to emulate Hainan, an unsurprising turn of events given that Lei Yu's own fortune was reversed with his new appointment as Guangxi's deputy governor in 1993. Most notorious in the immediate post-1992 period were two citywide cases involving Rushan in Shandong and Dandong in Liaoning, both coastal cities in northern provinces. The two cities shared some features with their southern counterparts in the latter's earlier days: relatively underdeveloped, and a lack of commercial or investment activities locally.

Rushan's new director of the Commerce Bureau, Liu Qishan, had difficulties generating commercial activities since assuming office in 1992. Eager to show accomplishments, he turned his hope on smuggling. After numerous trials by his subordinates and seizures by the coastal police, he became acquainted with coastal police officers and befriended a few of them through small gifts. The officers helped to coach a safe scheme for Liu's bureau: to voluntarily give up smuggled goods, pay symbolic fines, and recover the goods from the Customs Office. But the central government caught up with the new wave of smuggling more quickly this time. By late 1993, there were signs of an imminent crackdown. Liu's deputies and police collaborators tried to seize a last chance by trafficking over ninety-nine hundred cargo boxes of cigarettes. When the ship was stopped by the Qingdao coastal police (a major port nearby), Liu turned to his mayor for help. Concerned more with his city's financial losses than violation of law, Mayor Wang Jianzi intervened to recover the cargo on the pretext that the case would be handled back home. But instead of letting his Police Department confiscate the goods as procedures required, he let them loose. The case soon drew national attention amid the antismuggling campaign in late 1993. In connection with this case and additional bribery charges related to this and other instances of smuggling, three individuals received the death sentence, including Director Liu and two police officials. For his role, the mayor received a suspended death sentence. Six other members of the police or the Commerce Bureau received prison terms.[24]

In the other explosive case of the same period, Mayor Chang Yi of Dandong was an active supporter of smuggling from the beginning. Since taking office in 1992, he had tried futilely to halt the city's economic slide. So when the head of his Supply Bureau complained about financial difficulties and suggested smuggling South Korean cars to turn the city around, the mayor decided to give it a try. His reasoning was that "didn't all those southern coastal cities get rich this way?" and "I am not doing this for myself." Thereafter, the city government coordinated smuggling efforts among its agencies—trade, transportation, police, and customs. Even local banks were convened to provide loans. Four shipments and 150 cars later, the Supply Bureau was a very rich agency. Its success inspired other city bureaus and corporations to follow suit. To avoid suspicion, they operated the shipping through the distant Shanghai port. But the frequent shuttling of a mysterious, out-of-town vessel led the Shanghai patrol to stop it in late 1993. This single inspection uncovered more than one hundred smuggled cars. Though striking in its size and scale, bribery played no role throughout in this case, in contrast to Rushan where the police and the customs received bribes. As a result, Dandong's mayor and other key individuals received relatively light punishments: fourteen years for the mayor and two to thirteen years for twelve other officials.[25]

Local interests also motivate those localities without favorable geographic access to attempt *indirect* smuggling, that is, to purchase imports from smugglers and speculate back home. In a remote township in Jiansu, local leaders decided on smuggling as a way to jump start the local economy after receiving a reproach from the city government for its lackluster economic performance. At a meeting of township leaders to debate the matter, members agreed on "indirect smuggling" as a safe and feasible method, and picked specific local companies to "experiment" with the new "reform policy."[26]

[24] Zhang Shuotang, "A Report of Rushan's July 16th Smuggling Case," DFLZWZ 7 (1994): 29–30; and "Four Main Culprits in Two Major Smuggling Cases Executed," ibid., 24.

[25] Zhang Chunling, "Issuing an Arrest Warrant to the Mayor," DFLZWZ 11 (1994): 21–22; and Sun Shouchun, "The Anti-Corruption Work Report of 1994," DFLZWZ 3 (1995): 11.

[26] Lan Bo, *Zai Zousi Kuangchao*, 150–155.

Smuggling by Private Parties and Individual Officials

The third type of smuggling falls under either the top-bottom interactive model or the bottom-up model of local corruption, depending on the circumstances. It often occurs in coastal locations where societal and market forces are strong even though the central state may not be particularly weak. The smuggling activities of aggressive societal groups rely on the collusion of individual officials from key branches of the local government. When organized crime groups actively corrode the integrity of officials, the bottom-up model best describes the local patterns. When local officials and agencies actively collaborate with private smugglers, the top-bottom interactive model better applies.

Many nationally known cases fall into the top-bottom interactive pattern. In Dongguan city of Guangdong, a magnet of overseas investment, the head of its Antismuggling Office led a secret life of gambling in Macau by receiving bribes from private car smugglers. Those bribes totaled over Y1 million in two years from 1996–1998 and secured him a life sentence.[27] In Zhuhai city, adjoining Macau, the head of the antismuggling section in one coastal police branch helped to guard private smugglers. Twenty-three hundred cargo boxes of cigarettes later, he received a death sentence.[28] In Lianyungang of Jiangsu, a port city in East China, a former police officer ran a police-affiliated corporation to smuggle automobiles. With the help of his former bosses and bribes, he brought the head of the city's port Customs Office aboard his operation.[29] The list of key officials abetting smugglers is a longer one: deputy minister of the Public Security Ministry, head of the Central Customs Commission, mayors and deputy mayors in Zhanjiang and Xiamen; directors or deputy directors of municipal customs offices in Zhanjiang, Xiamen, Shenzhen, Shantou, Beihai, Shanya (Hainan), Zhoushan (Zhejiang), Hangzhou (Zhejiang), and Jinan (Shandong). All are coastally located, major cities. Some of the municipal customs offices have seen their chief executives fall repeatedly.

Zhanjiang's infamous case illustrates the intricacies of the interactive model. Initially, the city's situation bore some resemblance to the two northern cases. From the 1950s to the 1970s, the city ranked second, after Guangzhou, in the economy of Guangdong. But in the twenty years since, thanks to sluggish reforms and leadership errors, the city lapsed to the last place in

---

[27] Jiao Huidong, "Antismuggling Official Protects Smuggling Criminals," DFLZ 11 (1999): 29–31.

[28] Sun, "The Anticorruption Work Report of 1994," 11.

[29] Li, "A Comprehensive Look," 11–12.

the province's economy. By 1994, it had only a sugar industry to speak of, with a meager Y2 billion in annual revenues for a city of 6 million people (or Y300 per capita). The city offered little to attract outside talent or investment. Under such circumstances, municipal officials turned a blind eye to the smuggling boom in the city, hoping that it would help invigorate the local economy. But the mayor was also to play an important role in intensifying the criminal activities.

Zhanjiang's smugglers started moderately in 1991 with cigarettes. By 1994, smuggling became rampant along the city's fifteen hundred kilometers of coastline, covering all five counties and stretching to sugar, vehicles, and household electronics. From 1994 to 1998 smuggled imports not only displaced local products but also plagued markets nationwide. The growth of smuggling and protective networks intensified the criminality of the city in general. Organized crime groups grew, bought weapons to protect their activities, killed law enforcement officers, and terrorized the city. Rather than reviving the economy, smuggling enriched a few well-connected individuals, corrupted a host of government officials, and contributed to a distorted economy that combined "power and organized crime."[30] The tip of the criminal ring involved three organized groups. One was headed by the mayor's own son, locally known as the "king of vehicle smuggling." The second was led by a "king of petroleum smuggling," who controlled 85 percent of the city's oil supply and contributed to 10 percent of China's imported oil in 1997. The third was operated by two Chinese-born Hong Kong residents, who practically ran a parallel Customs Office that taxed all smuggled imports into the city. The three groups collaborated with one another and with corrupt city officials. Together they dominated the smuggling trade in Zhanjiang.

Although it was never the city's official policy to assist smuggling, Mayor Chen Tongqing's public tolerance and private appetites helped reinforce a favorable climate for smugglers. Chen not only failed to restrain his own son but gave him assistance in securing financing and markets for smuggled cargo. Chen also nurtured an army of corrupt officials through the sale of cadre appointments and promotions, netting Y1.1 million in four years from 1994 to 1998.[31] The circle of self-seeking and poorly qualified cadre, in turn, prolonged the city's economic stagnation and worsened smuggling. Chen's conduct also set a negative example for other officials. Among the latter, a deputy

[30] Huang He and Hu Weiming, "A Report on Combating Smuggling in Zhanjiang," DFLZ 2 (1999): 23–24; Liu Ziwu, "A Shocking Case of Smuggling, Over Y10 billion Involved," DFLZ 4 (1999): 22–23.
[31] "How Many Offices Did Chen Tongqing Sell?" DFLZ 10 (1999): 20.

mayor participated in smuggling, the head of the Antismuggling Office intervened on behalf of smugglers, a borough Tax Bureau joined in a business with smugglers to sell smuggled petroleum, the head of the Customs Office granted special import and tariff rights to the two Chinese-born Hong Kong smugglers (one being his mistress); and finally, the head of the investigative section of the Customs Office and the head of its Hong Kong section supplied inside information to smugglers. Officials in other city agencies, including the coastal patrol, port authority, shipping services, commercial inspection, and police also provided assistance after taking bribes.

Scrutiny of Zhanjiang began after the CCP's antismuggling conference in September 1998, since it was a case only central and provincial investigators dared to touch. It is estimated that the three major organized groups in this case had smuggled over Y10 billion in goods and evaded another Y6 billion in tariffs between 1995 and 1998, making it the largest case of smuggling in China at the time. The case eventually implicated more than three hundred people, including more than two hundred government officials (twelve at the *ting-ju level*, forty-five at the *chu* level, and fifty-three at the *ke* level). In the final sentencing, four smugglers and two officials received the death sentence, three smugglers and five officials a suspended death sentence, and seventeen others life or lesser sentences.[32]

The smuggling rampage in Xiamen during the latter half of the 1990s shared many features with Zhanjiang's. But the most notorious case of Xiamen, the Yuanhua Company, can be better seen through the bottom-up model. Unlike in Zhanjiang, the locality or the state of the local economy did not contribute directly to the rise of Yuanhua and its chief operator, Lai Cangxing. Rather, Lai's dogged efforts to take prisoners of all useful officials were critical to the success of his operation. And unlike the major operators in Zhanjiang's case, Lai had no family ties to top city leaders nor romantic liaison with customs officials. In fact, Lai first started his small operation as a poor farmer from the countryside. Material lures and shrewd schemes, thus, played critical roles.[33]

[32] Zhao Ziwen et. al., "Law Does Not Allow the Exchange of Power and Money—Details of the Uncovering of the Extraordinary Smuggling and Bribery Case in Zhanjiang, Guangdong," RMRB (overseas edition), June 8, 1999; Wang Jianzhang, "The Randy Party Secretary," DFLZ 9 (1999): 25–26; Zheng Yi, "Using Sex to Go through the Customs," DFLZ 12 (1999): 27–28; and "Six Principal Defendants Dealt the Death Penalty in the Extraordinary Smuggling and Bribery Case of Zhanjiang," DFLZ 8 (1999): 23–24.

[33] "Unveiling the Yuanhua Smuggling Case of Xiamen," DFLZ 12 (2000): 23–24; Qing Wen, "Lai Cangxing and the Extraordinary Smuggling Case of Yuanhua, Xiamen," DFLZ 2 (2001): 37–40; Yu Yingrui, "A Portrait of the Official Scoundrels in the Yuanhua Case," DFLZ 11 (2001): 26–30; "First Sentencing in Xiamen's Smuggling Case," DFLZ 1 (2001), 37; "Second Sentencing in Xiamen's Smuggling Case," 4 (2001): 26; and Liu Ning and Tian Huiming, *Zhongguo zhi Tong* (China's Agony) (Beijing: Wenhua Yishu Chubanshe, 2001): 1–22.

One key strategy of Lai was the use of an army of highly paid "public re-lations" employees to court the right connections. These were often the off-spring of officials in all key branches of the city government. Their job was to obtain the surrender of the targeted officials through all possible tempta-tions. The "desired" branches included the offices of mayors, law enforce-ment, customs, import inspection, and commercial regulation, as well as banks, at provincial (Fujian) and city (Xiamen, Fuzhou, Tanzhou, Quanzhou, and Putian) levels. A second strategy was Lai's extremely generous induce-ments, based on his firm belief that anyone could be bought by the right type of temptations. For one birthday party, he let two hundred "important guests" leave with a goodie bag of Y10,000 in cash each. Such occasions were many. For those uninterested in money, Lai found female seducers to be just as lethal. In the famed "Red Chamber," a sumptuous seven-floor palace of dis-cos and saunas, Lai entertained his important guests with lavish feasts, cou-ple suites, and sultry beauties. A third strategy was a watertight operation. From public relations employees to potential bribees, Lai's targets were care-fully chosen and focused. From customs and inspections to packaging and shipping, Lai's arrangements to get through regulatory hurdles were system-atic and "professionally" carried out.

With such elaborate efforts, Lai came to control all local government branches key to his smuggling trade. Customs chiefs gave authorization to his illegal imports. Customs officers prepared all proper documents, or sim-ply treated his goods as duty-free inputs destined for reexporting after local processing. It was futile for any honest agent to complain, since Lai had bought off key officials at all local levels. In fact, it was impossible for such an agent to keep his job or even to refuse bribes. Law enforcement officials made sure that no one interfered with Lai's vessels and trucks. Even a deputy min-ister of the Public Security Ministry in Beijing, Li Jizhou, intervened in an investigation of Lai's smuggling ship in Hainan without allegedly realizing that the Y1 million Lai had earlier given his wife to support her business or the U.S. $500,000 to support his daughter's overseas study were in fact bribes. Deputy mayors and deputy party secretaries of Xiamen helped him push out competitors from state firms, secure favorable land deals, and obtain bank loans. Bank chiefs helped him with monetary transactions. Port authorities assisted at the docks. The list goes on. Even on the eve of Yuanhua's down-fall, when investigators were closing in on him in August 1999, the chief of Fuzhou Metropolis Police cum deputy chief of Fujian Province Police tele-phoned Lai with tips for him to flee. The cell phone and precharged chips had been provided by Lai earlier.

The magnitude of Lai's operations was as expansive and complex as his efforts to seduce officials. His imports included consumer goods, computer chips, vehicles, chemical and construction materials, and above all, petroleum. His investments extended to petroleum-related industries, real estate, and recreational services. Lai's financial prowess allowed him to become a symbol of reform in Xiamen and the city's most sought-after investor. Local agencies allowed him to pick projects, locations, and lines of credits. His omnipresent sponsorships and commercial logos lent legitimacy to his illegal business. In all, Lai had smuggled Y53 billion in goods and evaded Y30 billion in tariffs, or five times larger than Zhanjiang's case. The enormity of the case is reflected in the multiple trials across five cities in Fujian and Beijing since 2000. By the end of 2001, 213 officials had been sentenced, including deputy minister Li Jizhou of the Public Security Ministry, 3 deputy mayors, 3 deputy (city-level) party secretaries, 6 bank chiefs and deputy chiefs, 2 Customs Office chiefs, and 2 deputy police chiefs at city (Xiamen) and provincial (Fujian) levels. The trials resulted in 18 death sentences, 1 suspended death sentence, 18 life sentences, and 177 long-term sentences. Investigations and trials of lesser officials and business associates continued, while Lai remains sheltered in Canada as a political refuge candidate.

UNDERDEVELOPED REGIONS AND POVERTY-DERIVED SCHEMES

It may seem contrary to the thesis of this study to suggest that underdeveloped regions have also experienced a significant surge in corruption since reform. Indeed, a different dynamic is at work in regions where development lags behind. This dynamic is typical of the top-down model of local corruption. Limited market activities offer few opportunities for self-enrichment such as those in booming regions, so that cadres fall back on the state as the main source of private gain. And the government has remained a good source for several reasons. First, poor regions tend to be targets of government developmental programs, rather than magnets for outside investment. In poor regions with meager local revenues, state funds are either a major source for local development or, alternatively, a windfall for cadre enrichment. Second, traditional sources of cadre power—power over personnel matters, military conscription, teacher recruitment, residential status, and family planning—remain more important in poor regions, except now these may be cashed in the marketplace. Third, new fiscal autonomy has given poor regions greater incentives and mechanisms to commit *san luan,* or unruly exaction of fees, contributions, and fines from the local populace.

Structural characteristics also contribute to rising abuse in underdeveloped regions. Physical and administrative remoteness, compounded by expanding devolution, leaves them isolated from the higher administrative apparatuses of the state. Village officials believe that anticorruption drives will usually reach the county level, not the "sesames and peas" of the village level.[34] As one village head, in an outskirt of Tai'an in Shandong, shouted into a loudspeaker in front of his villagers, "This place is far away from the emperor. The district disciplinary committee does not come here. The Prosecutors' Office does not come here. I am in control. As long as I am still in charge, the sun rotates around me!"[35] Legal deterrence is also weak in poor regions. Although plundered amounts may be large relative to the local economy, aggregate totals can be small enough to evade legal sanctions. In addition, disciplinary officials in rural communities concurrently serve in other official functions (usually as deputy party secretary of the village) and lack the independent power and resources to look into wrongdoings.[36] Finally, underdeveloped regions are seldom subject to the sanction of public censure. The media seldom bothers to report on remote rural communities. Ordinary farmers in such regions tend to have less education and political competence, not to mention greater trepidation toward officials.[37]

This section discusses some prominent forms of abuse in poor regions in recent years: misappropriation of antipoverty funds, office for sale, and organized tax frauds. Compared with *san luan,* these schemes have received little attention in recent studies.

Misappropriation of Government Aid

As the government shifted away from central planning in the early 1990s, it has turned its attention to public investment projects with developmental objectives. The central state now administers four major "special project funds" (*zhuan xiang ji jing*), designated for poverty alleviation, government bonds, infrastructure construction, and higher education. Poor regions benefit especially from the first three programs, covering poverty reduction, economic assistance, infrastructure building (utilities, irrigation, and energy), population resettlement, and frontier development. In addition, the government provides welfare benefits and disaster relief for distressed regions and populations.

---

[34] Hu Hongli and Chen Yuelian, "Monitoring of Cadres in Underdeveloped Regions Should Be Strengthened," DFLZWZ 10 (1998): 10; Zheng Haixiong and Guan'er, "Worrisome Reflections on the Multitudes of Village Administrative Agencies," DFLZWZ 9 (1996): 10.

[35] Li Yamin, "Tai'an's New Party Secretary," DFLZWZ 12 (1996): 12.

[36] Liu Xiangyun, "Disciplinary Committees at Villages and Townships Need to Resolve Six Problems," DFLZ 11 (1999): 8.

[37] Hu and Chen, "Monitoring of Cadres," 10; Zheng and Guan, "Worrisome Reflections," 10.

Available statistics about the abuse of antipoverty funds tell a revealing story. From 1997 to the first half of 1999, central and local governments spent a total of Y48.8 billion in antipoverty funds. In an inspection by the State Auditing Bureau in late 1999, Y4.343 billion of that total was audited. Of these, 20.43 percent were found misappropriated, diverted to other use, or put in slush funds. The breakdown is as follows. First, Y1.318 billion was diverted to residential construction and vehicle purchase for local agencies. To give an example, Hebei's Antipoverty Office "borrowed" Y7.15 million from nineteen poor counties and two state firms in the name of setting up an antipoverty economic zone. But Y1.83 million was used to construct new housing for the office's own employees. Next, Y1.26 billion was used to make up for local fiscal shortages and deficits. Of nine recipient counties in Liaoning, seven put aside a total of Y12.49 million for their budgetary needs. One county in Inner Mongolia spent Y1 million on renovating the county guesthouse. In Guizhou, agencies at the two administrative levels of district (*di*) and county (*xian*) appropriated a total of Y110 million to balance their books. Third, ignoring the central regulations and intended goals of aid programs, Y1.266 billion was used as commercial loans by local agencies. The Treasury Department of Sichuan Province used Y64.98 million as small loans to individuals. But the criterion for the loans was high-interest returns, not the type of investment projects. Finally, a total of Y478 million was found fictitiously spent, transferred away, deposited privately, put aside in slush funds, or used to pay IOU slips. In Shanxi, Y7.03 million was uncovered from the personal bank accounts of local officials. In Ningxia, Y970,000 went to the private pockets of thirty-six officials at the county, township, and village levels. In Sichuan, the provincial Antipoverty Office put aside Y920,000 for vehicle purchase and staff bonuses.[38]

Similar violations abound in the use of government hydraulic funds. In the same auditing in late 1999, the State Auditing Bureau inspected the usage of centrally allocated hydraulic funds. Ten percent of the audited funds, or Y3 billion, were found diverted to other uses. Most commonly, hydraulic funds paid for new buildings, investment projects, and administrative expenses. The Yangzi River Hydraulic Commission received Y9 million to build fishing reservoirs, but commercial hotels were built instead. The Songhuajiang River Commission of Liaoning received Y4 million to treat endangered embankments, but an antiflood headquarters was constructed. The Administrative Bureau for the Taihu Lake Valley, in rural Jiangsu, put all of its Y20 mil-

---

[38] "Work Report of the State Accounting Agency Shows Violations by 36 of 55 Central Agencies Audited," DFLZ 12 (2000): 18–19.

lion hydraulic funds in the Shanghai stock exchange. In the same nationwide auditing, state auditors also inspected major hydraulic construction projects administered by the central state. Of the fifty-eight projects inspected, Y1.78 billion were found misappropriated and another Y3.32 billion wasted in fictitious claims, bloated expenditure, and squandering. A typical case was the Feilai Valley Water Control Project in Qingyuan, a county-level city in Guangdong. Here, 20 percent of the resettlement allowance for dislocated populations, or Y314 million, was spent on real estate investments, two money-losing cement factories, staff apartment buildings, golf club memberships (Y1.8 million) for top officials, and overseas sight-seeing trips. Another Y132 million were deposited in the project's credit union, whose insolvency almost wiped out the account.[39]

Transportation facilities, private deposits, and investment shares are also common destinations of diverted funds. With little bearing on poverty reduction, they are rationalized as official perks. During its 1993 inspection, the State Auditing Bureau found that nearly 50 percent of audited counties in poor regions bought vehicles for key officials. One county used Y1.5 million on a Rolls-Royce. A village government spent its teachers' two months salaries, allocated by the county treasury, on a new car.[40] Sometimes relief goods were resold for profits, rather than delivered to localities and populations in need. Or the funds, often involving hundreds of thousands of *yuan* per allocation, were deposited in banks in the name of local agencies. Funds were also used to purchase shares in investments nominally held by local government agencies. The gains were shared by agency members. At higher levels, officials who approve or allocate relief funds may seek a share of the resources allocated to a locality through a commission or "thank-you" fee. These violations were largely reported in poor counties of Shaanxi, Shanxi, Hunan, Henan, Sichuan, Fujian, and Guangdong provinces. The absence of other poor provinces in these investigations, such as Qinghai or Ningxia, may not be a testimony to their honesty, but more likely, the inability of investigators to uncover wrongdoings.

Along with hydraulic funds, resettlement funds—for relocating displaced or impoverished villagers to more productive locations—are also vulnerable to misuse. A case in point is the Three Gorges Project, the largest hydraulic project in the world. Beginning in 1997, the government scheduled investments of Y2.67 billion over five years on the resettlement and rebuilding of Fengjie County, a region that will be submerged under water by the project.

[39] Ibid., 19.
[40] Ma Zixin, *Quanli de Heidong* (The Black Hole of Power) (Beijing: Gaige Chubanshe, 1999): 218.

Fengjie's resettlement involves eighteen townships and more than 120,000 residents. A report of fund usage in this county found frequent small abuses. For instance, a firm specializing in transportation goods used 13 percent of its relocation funds on cell phones, beepers, phone installation, and a truck, plus salaries for employees and retirees. A village spent 80 percent of its funds, earmarked to treat sliding slopes, on installing a telecommunication system. Some relocation projects (construction, transportation, land improvement) went to unqualified contractors. Other projects claimed undue reimbursements. Still others were approved by dishonest inspectors.[41] Other counties have had it worse. In the largest embezzlement case involving the Three Gorges Project, Huang Fangxiang, who headed both the Bureau of State Land Assets and the Bureau of Land Requisition in Fengdu County of Chongqing, embezzled Y16 million in resettlement funds and land requisition payments from displaced families. In another testimony to the weakness of state control in remote regions, Huang colluded with his subordinate agencies and enjoyed further protection from his wife, a deputy county governor. Only when auditors arrived from Chongqing did the accounting irregularities become exposed.[42] In Wanzhou County, resettlement officials lost more than Y1 million at the mahjongg table. Even a township head in Yunyan County was able to receive over Y28,000 in bribes from contractors.[43]

Most of the reported resettlement violations involve collusion among officials, a core feature of the top-down model of local corruption. An entire body of cadre at an administrative level colludes to bilk aid funds. This further testifies to the weak control of the state over its agents and agencies in remote and underdeveloped regions. In Shaanxi Province, seven officials from its Department of Civilian Affairs, including the chief, exhausted all means to embezzle Y11 million from relief, welfare, resettlement, and poverty funds. In Baoji city of Shaanxi, four members of the Bureau of Civilian Affairs, including its head, split Y250,000 in poverty and relief funds among themselves. In an old revolutionary region (lao qu) of Hunan, a deputy governor deposited funds privately with a few other colleagues. Together they shared the interests on the Y500,000 principal. In Foshan County of Guangdong, a

---

[41] Ma Hongping and Tian Jiaquan, "Strengthening Law Enforcement and Monitoring in the Relocation Arena," DFLZ 8 (1999): 20–21.

[42] Lu Hua and Deng Ke, "Head of State Land Assets Swallowed Tens of Millions Yuan in Resettlement Funds," DFLZ 4 (2000): 19–22; Lu Tianqing and Wang Qian, "Strengthen Monitoring, Exercise Good Control over Resettlement Funds," DFLZ 7 (2000): 23–24;

Lu Tianqing and Wang Yong, "Major Case Broken, Gigantic Thief Speedily Caught," DFLZ 9 (2000): 8–10.

[43] Lin Mu, "A Township Party Secretary Stumbled over the Resettlement Project," DFLZ 2 (2000): 27–28.

deputy county governor bought his office a Toyota jeep with Y500,000 in flood relief funds.[44] In Shanghang County of Fujian, a deputy county governor in charge of resettlement doled out contracts, purchase orders, and personnel appointments according to bribes, assisted by the entire crew of the county's resettlement office—its director, two deputy directors, and five *ke* rank officials. While the county suffered losses from overpayments to contractors and suppliers, the deputy governor pocketed Y200,000 herself.[45]

Diversion of resettlement funds for commercial activities is another common abuse. In Jiaozhuo city of Henan, one of the poorest regions in the country, a deputy head of the Hydraulic Works Department and concurrently the Relocation Department, "loaned" Y3 million of relocation funds to a private businessman. The official claimed that he had intended for the profits to go to his agency, rather than himself, having been lured by the promise of an 11 percent interest rate. But the harm was done nonetheless: a third of the funds failed to return when the borrower fled the country.[46] In all, the patterns of abuse in antipoverty, hydraulic, and resettlements funds are fundamentally similar.

Office for Sale

Carried out by key officials and frequently in poor regions, office for sale fits neatly into the model of top-down corruption. Personnel promotion and placement was a basic mechanism of control and advancement in the prereform system. It has remained a key path for individual betterment after reform in poorer regions. *Shi quan,* or substantive power, has special appeal in the market economy, as it means authority over tangible and cashable resources and projects. Career moves also bring improvements in salaries and material comforts, in terms of job location, rank category, and residential and transportation amenities. These perks and benefits are especially important for officials in poor regions. Finally, the relative lack of bribes from a weak business sector leaves office for sale as the main source of extra income for local officials.

Not surprisingly, there has been a sharp rise in the occurrence and size of bribes in office-for-sale cases. Moreover, of all reported cases surveyed by this

[44] See case reports in DFLZWZ 7 (1997): 24; 8 (1997): 19; 11 (1997): 14; 12 (1997): 11; and 1 (1998): 16. See also Li Hua, Lu Jian, and Zhang Jiying, "The Downfall of Seven *Chu*-ranked Officials," DFLZWZ 1 (1998): 18–22.

[45] Zhong Minyuan and Fan Bo, "A Female County Governor whose Faith is Money," DFLZ 11 (2000): 25–26.

[46] Bi Ming, "A Nouveau Riches who Swallowed Huge Amounts of Relief Funds," DFLZ 4 (2000): 22–23.

study, almost all occurred in relatively poor provinces or poor regions within well-to-do ones: Shanxi, Hebei, Jiangxi, Henan, Ningxia, Shandong, Guangxi, and Guangdong. With the exception of Zhanjiang in Guangdong and Tai'an in Shandong, they all occurred in rural counties. Even Tai'an is a largely rural, county-level city. And with no exception, they all involved the top executive of local governments, especially at the county level, and those in charge of personnel departments. Compared with bribe taking in exchange for resources or projects, it should be pointed out, bribe taking for personnel appointments is quite cumbersome. Promotions are decided collectively at top-level meet-ings—be they county, municipal, or provincial levels—and usually require fur-ther approval at the next level of state/party administration. Job transfers and placements depend much on the needs and the moods of prospective employ-ers. So when officials choose to accept bribes to push for promotion or place-ment, it is a strong testimony to the lack of alternative means of enrichment and to the fact that political institutions are weak vis-à-vis personal politics.

The link between office for sale and the lack of alternative avenues to en-richment is well illustrated in a rather extreme example below. Tongxin County of Ningxia is a mountainous region known for its severe climate and impoverishment. Thus, instead of passing to their relatives and friends the sort of lucrative contracts and deals elsewhere, county officials chose the logical way: getting them on the government payroll. Between 1991 and 1998, the county added 357 cadre-status individuals to its payroll in violation of pro-cedures, including 140 with doctored resumes and counterfeit official seals. A hiring at or a promotion to the cadre status (*gan bu*) entails better salaries and material benefits. Of those 357 cases, 217 managed to get approval from higher personnel agencies, that is, the Personnel Department at the district (*ti*) and provincial (*qu* for Ningxia) levels. Among those 217, 18 were school-age children (the youngest being five years old), 4 were farmers, 39 were fac-tory workers, and 156 were clerical staff in local state agencies. As many as 95 county officials at the *ke* rank and above participated in the promotion schemes, including 4 at the *ting* level and 25 at the *chu* level. Needless to say, such abuse greatly bloated the county government, draining its already mea-ger revenues and depriving local populace of urgent developmental funds.[47]

Indeed, when political institutions of a county or city are so weakened by the corruption of an entire governing body, the latter would not even bother to put on an appearance of going through the regular procedures of person-nel matters. Tai'an of Shandong is a case in point. A mountainous, poor city

[47] Zhang Jianru, "A Personnel Corruption Case in an Impoverished County," DFLZ 1 (2000): 14–16.

lagging well behind the province's coastal regions, Tai'an offered few opportunities for personal enrichment for its top officials in the early 1990s: a few Hong Kong investors (who eventually cheated the city out of more money than investing in it) and one state-owned petrochemical plant. So Hu Xuejian, mayor from 1990 to 1992 and party secretary from 1992 to 1995, found his main take from a crop of eager office climbers. Some of them rose to become members of his inner circle, including a deputy party secretary of the city, secretary general of the city government, two deputy mayors, head of the city's Communications Department, and chief of the city police. Of the mayor's forty bribe givers, Y610,000 in total take and nearly one hundred counts of bribes, most came from the layers of cadre within the city. With such people filling the ranks of the city government, there was little deterrence to stop Hu from making appointments at will. When he was finally brought down by corruption scandals, not surprisingly, so was the inner circle of officials he had promoted.[48]

Even when the political setting remains institutionalized in a remote and poor region, it is often not enough to overwhelm a willful chief executive. From 1991 to 1994 Zheng Yuansheng was the party secretary for Guangfeng, a large county in northeastern Jiangxi known for its poverty. The county's party committee was large, so that a few officials would always raise some objections when Zheng tried to push his favored nominees through promotion meetings. At the same time, promotions were numerous, sometimes nearly a hundred positions discussed at a meeting, so that attendees did not always have enough time or information to weigh everyone carefully. Such meetings often became ceremonial and Zheng's decisions dominated ultimately. In one case, Zheng had to convene extended meetings to secure a promotion satisfactory to one bribe giver, a township party secretary desiring a "substantive" post at the county level. After three meetings, the briber was still not happy with the position offered him each time. Finally, those attending the fourth meetings grew impatient, being still up at 2:00 a.m., and asked Zheng to make a decision himself. Thereafter the briber fulfilled his wish of becoming a deputy chief of the county's Commerce Bureau, for a total price of Y10,000.[49] In all, Zheng accepted Y140,000 for fifty-three positions during his three-year tenure, a high figure for a poor county. Officials from eighteen out of its thirty townships paid for their placements. Ninety-one percent of these were *ke* ranked or higher, and almost all used public funds.[50]

[48] Li Yamin, "Hu Xuejian's Last Words," DFLZWZ 12 (1996): 23–26; and Li Yamin, "Hu Xuejian's Last Statements," DFLZWZ 1 (1997): 18–20.

[49] Xu Jiangshan et. Al., "A Rare Case of 'Office for Sale," DFLZWZ 11 (1996): 18–20.

[50] "Crackdown on Corruption," DFLZWZ 7 (1997): 23.

The cycle of corruption and poor job performance feeds on itself, further stunting local development. Not surprisingly, the nation's worst cases of office for sale have occurred in the less-developed regions (see appendix 4).

Organized Tax Fraud

As discussed in the previous chapter, tax fraud is almost universal among SOEs and nonstate firms. So what is special about underdeveloped regions in this regard? As it turns out, some poor counties have played a special role in one of the worse organized tax fraud in recent periods. What makes this a regional phenomenon is that collusion of local officials or even an entire local government is often present. In these cases, tax fraud is organized and pervasive as a local phenomenon and enjoys a local "support system." These features are characteristic of the top-down model of regional corruption. The reasons are not unlike those for organized smuggling in poor coastal regions: bilking resources from the state can be easy alternatives when there are no other local major income sources. Organized tax schemes also become a regional phenomenon in poor regions because of the more predatory nature of the offenders. Elsewhere, tax fraud usually involves illegitimate reductions and exemptions or inflated rebates. But poor regions often cheat refunds for taxes that are never paid and on things that are never produced. These regions even serve as national centers for massive tax frauds.

One of the most utilized tax fraud involved the value-added tax (VAT). At 17 percent, it was levied, until late 2002, on manufactured goods but could be refunded by a rebate for exported goods. The rebate was intended to make exports more competitive. But the pre-1994 tax code, effective since 1985, contained a major loophole: while VATs were levied by the local government, the rebates were given by the central government. The two different sources of tax authority made it possible for schemers to fabricate tax filings locally and cheat the central government out of rebates. The concocting of false claims was almost impossible for a single individual or even a single agency without an elaborate support system. A normal process to claim VAT rebates included documentation of (1) VAT filings by producers at local tax bureaus, (2) export licenses, (3) purchase orders from foreign buyers, (4) customs declarations of actual exports, and (5) foreign currency transactions through banks. Elaborate and organized efforts were thus needed among several local agencies, sometimes the entire local government: from falsifying sales and tax receipts to fabricating export licenses and orders, and from forging customs documents and bank transactions to faking export occurrence.

This is precisely why collusion by local agencies is more likely in less-developed regions, where state monitoring is weak horizontally and vertically.[51]

The most harmful type of fraud occurred when rebates were claimed while neither exporting nor tax filing, nor even production, ever occurred. It constituted absolute theft from the state coffer, in contrast to the partial losses from tax evasion or reduction. It is not surprising that some poor regions would find rebate fraud appealing. A case in point was Xianning, a poor county-level city in Hubei. From August to November of 1992, five enterprises conspired with local authorities to claim Y12 million in rebates from the central government, all with forged documents and the backing of the mayor and the head of the local Tax Bureau. Neither exports nor production had ever taken place.[52] In another prominent case, five counties and one city (Ruicang) in the backward province of Jiangxi engaged in similar fraud with the support of local leadership. In Ruicang's case, the mayor even convened a meeting to assign tasks to various city agencies and talked with or phoned their chief executives to coordinate intracity cooperation. Between February 1992 and June 1993, local agencies in the six localities supplied firms with 70 phony tax receipts and 304 phony sales receipts, at a monetary value of Y237,466 million. A total of Y15,494 million in rebates was claimed from the state as a result.[53]

Tax reforms in 1994 sought to close the loopholes by introducing a uniform national tax system. Reductions, exemptions, and rebates would no longer be determined by local governments. Nationally standardized seals and serial numbers, printed by the central government, would appear on the receipts for tax payments, in place of local ones. However, the Central Tax Bureau was still represented by its branch offices at the local level, leaving the latter to local abuse. Across the country, firms quickly found out that in some regions, local tax branches or agents were willing to supply VAT receipts, illegitimately filled out for a fee; or even blank receipts, officially declared "lost" or "stolen." In fact, blank tax receipts printed by the central government became more "precious than gold" in the black market and a major target of theft since 1994. On the buyers' side, the new VAT system gave small firms a special incentive to engage in fraud. For the new system only issued

---

[51] Jing Si, "An Analysis of Major Types of Corruption in Recent Years," *Dangjian Wenhui* 2 (February 1994): 34–35; Li Jihua, "An Analysis of VAT Rebate Frauds and Related Schemes," *Zhengzhi yu Falu* 1 (February 1995): 54–55; and Mo Kaiqin and Zhu Jianhua, "An Analysis of VAT Rebate Frauds," *Jingji yu Fa* 6 (June 1993): 20–21.

[52] Fang Mo, "A Crime of Collusion—A Report of a Major VAT Fraud Case from Xianning, Hubei Province," *Dangjian Wenhui* 8 (1993): 18–19.

[53] Jing Si, "An analysis of major types," 35.

VAT receipts to manufacturers with revenues greater than Y1 million and retailers with wholesale revenues greater than Y1.8 million (smaller producers and retailers are unlikely to export). This code put small businesses at a disadvantage when competitors could claim rebates to offset production costs. Small firms were thus motivated to fabricate VAT receipts to maintain competitive advantages.[54]

Here again, some poor regions found a thriving business. In fact, the largest cases of tax fraud in the country since 1994 all involved the organized sale of VAT receipts in poor regions. The most notorious involved Jinhua County of Zhejiang. Though located in one of the most-developed provinces, Jinhua failed to develop the type of bustling TVEs and private businesses that decorate much of the semirural scenery in Southeast China. Ninety-five percent of Jinhua's population remained agrarian in the mid-1990s. In 1994 the county government initiated a policy of encouraging investors with the promise of exempting VAT for the first three years and halving it in the next three years, even though local governments no longer had such authority under the new tax code. Before long, 218 real or shell companies emerged locally to take advantage of the new local tax incentives. Instead of actual investment or production, they acquired blank VAT receipts through swindle and peddled them to buyers across thirty provinces. In three years, they sold 65,536 receipts, at a monetary worth of Y6.31 billion in tax payments and a loss of Y750 million in tax revenues for the state, making it the largest case of tax fraud in the history of the PRC. Eleven local offices of the Central Tax Bureau participated in supplying blank receipts. The county's Tax Bureau itself, a local state agency, also participated, selling 17,587 receipts to buyers nationwide, defrauding the state of Y137 million in tax revenues. The county's party secretary, tax bureau chief, and communications bureau chief also actively tried to cover up the schemes. In all, eight local officials, including the bureau's head and deputy head, were found guilty in criminal trials.[55]

Other nationally known cases of VAT fraud invariably involved poor regions. Most notably are Nangong city of Hebei, where the local Tax Bureau initiated fraud against its own national tax authority from 1994 to 1999, selling 17,587 receipts to thirty-five provinces, at a monetary value of Y1.065 billion in tax payments and Y137 million in rebate claims; Jixian county of

[54] Research Office of the Disciplinary Commission of Hunan Province, "New problems Faced by the Party's Anticorruption Work," DFLZWZ 8 (1994): 6–7.
[55] "Defying Law Will Not Be Tolerated—A Report on the Largest Tax Fraud Case in the Country," RMRB, November 6, 1998; Ping Yi, "Life and Death Battles behind China's Number One Case of Tax Fraud," Zuojia Wenzhai, March 21, 2000; Wang Jiyuan, "How Was the Country's Number One Case of Tax Fraud Uncovered?" DFLZ 1 (1999): 19.

Tianjin, where the Tax Bureau saw ten of its fifteen branches writing phony VAT receipts between 1997 and 1999, selling 8,293 receipts at a monetary value of Y220 million in tax payments and Y20.48 million in undue rebate claims;[56] and Liuzhou of Guangxi, where a major VAT scheme was led by the daughter of a deputy governor, who intervened to protect her from exposure.

CORRUPTION AND REFORM: WHAT BENEFICIARIES AND COSTS

Have the regional peculiarities of corruption impacted local paths of economic reform and development in ways similar to the effects of pre-1992 and post-1992 corruption discussed in chapters 2 and 3? The situation seems to vary with each dominant pattern locally.

The top-down pattern, often emanating from local officialdom in under-developed regions, disproportionately benefit key local officials, particularly in the cases of office for sale, misappropriation of government funds, and local corruption rings. Short-term benefits from graft, in turn, act as disincentives to effective reforms or efforts to improve local economies. When local officials participate in or indulged in illicit ventures, they are obviously not concerned about genuine reforms, nor the right course of local development. Worse yet, their behaviors betray little concern on their part for the adverse effects of their actions on effective governance and economic performance in their districts. And their extra incomes make them blind to the poverty around them. In the impoverished county of Jingyu, Liaoning, annual income averaged less than Y3000 per capita in 1999. But its party secretary, Li Tiecheng, amassed Y440,000 from 165 counts of office for sale during the same year. This amounted to 80 percent of the combined income of the county's more than two hundred officials at the *ke* rank and up, and 2.29 percent of the county's total revenues of Y19.2 millions for that year. Li's family wealth increased from Y30,000 to over Y2.7 million between 1992 and 1999, including six real estate properties across the province. By Li's own admission, he had become too accustomed to bribes to wonder how officials with an average annual salary of Y10,000 in a poor county could afford to pay him a few thousand *yuan* during each major holiday?[57]

A particularly harmful consequence is that office for sale entails giving de-

---

[56] "Looking Back at Cases Investigated and Disciplined in 1999," DFLZ 3 (2000): 22–25.

[57] "Bribe Giving in Jingyu, Liaoning: No Exceptions in Any County Agency," *Zuojia Wenzhai,* March 2003, 7; and "Over One Hundred *Ke*- and *Ju*-ranked Officials Pay Bribes to the County Party Secretary," DFLZ 5 (2003): 21–22.

cision powers to unqualified and unscrupulous individuals. Those motivated
to purchase office, in turn, are likely to abuse it for personal gains. At the same
time, office sellers usually have to protect the poor job performance of their
clients. Bribe-based appointments also help the patron to build a chain of
cronies inclined to yield to one another's influence peddling, as the fall of the
entire city hall in Tai'an and Shenyang showed. In poor regions where office
for sale is prevalent, bribe money tends to come from relief, developmental,
and educational funds. Diversion of such funds, for this and other purposes,
drain away critical capital for reform projects and deprive impoverished lo-
cals of their only developmental opportunities and resources. Even among
those corruption forms designed to improve the local economy, for instance,
officially organized smuggling and tax fraud, are generally unproductive and
counterproductive for poor regions. For short-term profits thwart attention
to productive ventures and stunt long-term optimal growth. Protection of illicit activities creates a precarious environment for governance and business
generally.

The cycle of top–down corruption and poor cadre performance also feed
on each other, further impeding local development. Tai'an, with its famed
mountain and great tourism potential, is a case in point. Lack of reform had
left the local economy stagnating and deprived the city of surplus revenues
in the early and mid-1990s. To showcase the city's "progress" under reform,
Mayor Hu Xuejian imposed mandatory levies on the already hard-pressed
boroughs and residents, so he could build a few "white elephant" projects.
The mayor himself profited, nonetheless, from frequent bribes offered by office buyers, usually paid for with the "blood and sweat" of the local populace. His take from the city's police chief originally came from a kickback
from a branch police chief, who had in turn appropriated the fund from the
revenues of his traffic police squad. Such revenues often came from arbitrary
traffic fines. Another client of the mayor, a township party secretary, assem-
bled his bribe money from a village head, who in turn appropriated it from
farmers' dues. After Mayor Hu's downfall, the new mayor of Tai'an received
three big sacks of complaint letters, two of them from farmers complaining
about arbitrary and excessive levies. Within a year, the new city government
managed to arrest eighteen "village bullies" responsible for unbearable
levies.[58] In cases such as these where bribe money come from citizens, rather
than the private business sector, bribery becomes looting, or the most detrimental form of corruption.

Shenyang is another case. The end of its corrupt administration in 1999

[58] Li, "Hu Xuejian's Last Words," 23–26; and Li, "Tai'an's New Party Secretary," 12.

has since resulted in remarkable economic growth. The city's domestic production revenues rose by 10.1 percent in 2001 and another 13.1 percent in
2002. Its fiscal revenues grew by 34.3 percent in 2001, and its overall industrial revenues increased by 18 percent in 2002. Revenues from the lease of
public land grew by 15 percent in 2001 and more than 30 percent in 2002.
The new city administration instituted various reforms in the personnel and
recruitment system. It took off 74 percent of the items on the list of things
requiring regulatory approval. It addressed problems important to the daily
livelihood of the city's residents that had been pushed aside for years by the
previous corrupt administration: residential utilities, public transportation,
residential relocation, road construction, and reemployment.[59] The end of
corruption, in short, has visibly reversed the fortune of the city.

Top-down corruption has special exemplary effects on low-level cadre and
on local society in general. As one Chinese analyst comments on Guangxi's
case, "The gang of greedy officials just looks at one another. If you do it, I
will do it. In this culture, 'monitoring' and 'control' fall by the wayside."[60] In
Tai'an's case, the secretary general of the city government, promoted by the
mayor after paying bribes, eventually became the largest embezzler in Shandong's postrevolution history. Expectedly, he blamed his downfall on the
mayor's example and indulgence.[61] In the organized smuggling cases of Dandong and Rushan (and some southern coastal cities earlier), the example of
one agency often inspired many followers. In the organized tax fraud of Xianning, Jinhua, and many others, the acquiescence of local authorities encouraged social groups to engage in illicit activities with little fear of sanction.
By the same token, top-down corruption has special demoralizing effects on
local entrepreneurship and the business environment. Failure to build infrastructure, improve governance, or limit predatory behavior, among other
things, deter outside investors while driving away local talent. Neglected or
poor public works, such as hydraulic and highway projects, further dampen
developmental opportunities (see appendix 3). Most of all, the paucity of financial and technical assistance, reform initiatives, and leadership, especially
in isolated and remote villages of underdeveloped regions, has disadvantaged
one of most burdened and least-helped groups under the country's economic
reform: poor farmers.

In the bottom-up model, local officials and private business interests can

[59] Zheng Youyi, "The Shenyang Phenomenon in the Battle against Corruption," DFLZ 4 (2003):
17–18.
[60] Yin and Lo, "A Mayor Who Takes," 25–27.
[61] Li, "Hu Xuejian's Last Words," 23; and Lu Tai and Ji Shan, "The Evil Man of Tai'an, Lu Jiao-
qing," DFLZWZ 11 (1997): 15–17.

be both initiators and beneficiaries of corrupt exchanges.[62] Market-oriented officials help spur private business development, whose reliance on local official service and support in turn create rent-seeking opportunities for the former. This situation presents mixed outcomes for reform. If the aim of business groups is to get things done smoothly when having to deal with local officials, the initiatives and aggressiveness of these groups attest to the vitality of new economic forces and of local market reforms. And material interests at least partially sustain local cadre's support for private-sector activities. However, when bribers' aim is to avoid regulatory burdens, sabotage fair competition, violate laws, and harm public interests, then it undermines the goals of reform. In Xiamen and Zhanjiang, the dominance of private smugglers exerted far worse damages on the local and national economy than any other type of smuggling. Lai Cangxing came to dominate a third of the nation's petroleum market and Fujian's entire rubber market, while Zhanjiang's "king of petroleum" controlled 85 percent of the city's oil supply and 10 percent of China's imported oil in 1997. Their aggressive tactics seduced entire local administrative apparatuses. The scale of their activities contributed to powerful criminal business cartels. The huge profits propped up a twisted new economy, destroying the legitimate economy and delaying and derailing any genuine reform efforts. The net losses from tariff revenues and income taxes, finally, dwindled the resource base of both local and central governments. According to Prime Minister Zhu Rongji, after cracking down on the two smuggling rings in Zhanjiang and Xiamen, nationwide customs revenues increased enough in 1999 for Beijing to give a raise to the 80 million members of the country's civil service.[63]

Illegal businesses also learn from examples of legal businesses, whether public or private, which can set off a chain of illegal activities at the grassroots level. A case in point is organized smuggling. Along major highways in the Pearl River Delta Basin, tens of thousands of small plants have mushroomed in the spaces between cities and villages. Most claim to engage in *lai liao jia gong,* or "foreign materials, Chinese processing." Finished products are supposed to be reexported. By local and central preferential policies, imported inputs for this type of manufacturing are exempt from tariffs, as are finished products from value-added taxes. Ninety percent of such local processing is done in Guangdong province, especially around the Shenzhen delta

---

[62] I thank Kellee Tsai's input on this point. The orientation of the local government makes a huge difference on private sector behavior. See her *Back-Alley Banking: Private Entrepreneurs in China* (Cornell University Press, 2002); Jon Unger, *The Rural Transformation of China* (M. E. Sharpe, 2002); and Susan Whiting, *Power and Wealth in Rural China* (Cambridge University Press, 2001).

[63] Prime Minister Zhu Rongji, press conference on March 15, 2000.

region. The related trade accounts for more than half of all freight passing through the city's ports. Therein arises what the Chinese customs authorities call *fei liao zhou si,* the smuggling of input materials in the name of local processing. In one Shenzhen locality, dozens of new plants appeared overnight on paper to claim tax benefits, but when customs officials arrived to verify physical capacities, none was to be found. The shell plants had registered for the sole purpose of smuggling materials for speculation.[64] The impact is deeply felt on the factory floors and streets of coastal as well as interior regions. Imported fabrics, ubiquitous on store shelves and peddler stands, have rendered idle domestic producers and workers.

In the top-bottom interactive model, the mixture of strong local states and vibrant business sectors counteracts and balances the effects of the other two models to produce mixed outcomes. Within the officialdom, corruption is likely bred by the nepotistic networks among fellow officials on the one hand and by favor seeking from social groups on the other. Proximity to political centers renders outright office for sale more difficult and retardation of reform unlikely. But the independent kingdom built by unruly local leaders fosters favoritism in personnel arrangements. Weakened accountability and transparency, in turn, encourage arbitrary and self-serving decision making, even in the face of close proximity to political centers. As seen in Beijing's case, mayoral offices carried out numerous misappropriations and transgressions without apparent political repercussions before Wang Baosheng's suicide. Moreover, officials in such localities often have a large reservoir of public resources at their disposal, ready for preferential allocation or misappropriation. What all of this means—the presence of corrupt official corps and lucrative public projects and resources—is the ready availability of official largess for societal groups to exploit. The latter are likely to benefit from ties with officials, fostering the type of strong alliances represented by the close relations between Beijing's top officials and those at Capital Steel Company. But when the business activities of private groups are themselves destructive, as in Shenyang, Zhanjiang, Xiamen, or Jinhua, the close interaction between such groups and the local officialdom can be fatal to real local development.

Institutional learning and response may be one positive outcome out of the many outrageous cases that occur beyond the far reach of the central government. In late 2002, the government decided to halt the VAT rebates for exporters. Manufacturers no longer have to pay VATs, but nor can they claim rebates for exports.

---

[64] Lan, *Zai Zousi Kuangchao,* 171–82.

CONCLUSION

The chapter has demonstrated linkages among regional and structural features of localities, levels of development, and local patterns and consequences of corruption. Broadly we may characterize three general patterns of these linkages.

First, in more remote and less-developed regions, corruption is more likely to be initiated by officials, more traditionally based, and with top-down ripple effects. Many factors account for this pattern. Thanks to the weak reach of both state agencies and market forces, individual officials and local governments are more likely to engage in illicit schemes for private or local sectarian interests. This pattern is characteristic of the northern smuggling rings, the organized rebate fraud, the misuse of relief funds, and the sale-of-office cases. Second, thanks to the dearth of market opportunities and private sources of graft, local officials are more likely to target state resources for self-enrichment. This is typical of misappropriation, office-for-sale, tax fraud, and organized smuggling cases for poor regions. Third, more traditional sources of cadre power (power over personnel matters) remain important for private enrichment in poorer regions, while greater materialistic urges and local autonomy have also made abuse in those areas worse and more frequent than before. Finally, the combined effects of the preceding three factors help create a local epidemic that can accumulate into top-down chains of corruption within a locality, as illustrated by Guangxi and Tai'an in the 1990s.

Second, in moderately to highly commercialized regions where market forces are strong even while the reach of the state is not particularly far or weak, corruption is more likely to be initiated by social groups, with bottom-up ripple effects. Business interests have ample incentives to seek advantage or protection from local officials for their legal or illegal activities. Further, business groups possess financial and organizational resources to engage in corrupt practices, sometimes on massive scales. These features are magnified in Xiamen's Yuanhua case and Wuxi's pyramid scheme. At the same time, officials are likely to profit from nonstate rather than state sources of income, or dividends from the legal or illegal undertakings of societal groups. Because market channels are far more lucrative here, nontraditional sources of power—power over regulatory rules—are more important for officials' private enrichment. Finally, the combined effects of the above factors can sometimes engulf entire local governments or individual agencies and contribute to bottom-up chains of local corruption.

Third, in localities where the local government can be strong vis-à-vis both a vibrant society *and* a nearby central state, thanks to strong local leaders or the political and economic strength of key municipalities, corruption is likely to be incubated in a climate of local fiefdom, favoritism, and patronage. Local officials can be audacious and independent enough to sponsor or protect corrupt practices, even while private initiatives and central strengths may be well matched. Further, since both public and private resources provide lucrative avenues for private accumulation, officials are likely to target both sources for predation. Likewise, both traditional mechanisms of official power (power over personnel matters) and market mechanism of cadre power (power over regulatory matters) remain important for extracting rents and booty. Finally, the combined effects of the foregoing factors can produce complex webs of protective networks for both corrupt officials and societal groups. Beijing, Zhanjiang, and Shenyang have all born out these characteristics.

In all, the regional dynamics of corruption has once again confirmed strong linkages between economic reform and corruption. Despite rich local variations, the basic incentives and mechanisms of corruption across diverse regions have been created or enhanced by the context of economic liberalization, administrative decentralization, and local flexibility.

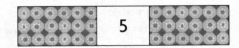

5

BETWEEN THE STATE AND OFFICIALS

The Decline of Disincentives against Corruption

Chapters 2–4 elaborated on the many incentives and opportunities for corruption across reform periods and localities. Yet disincentives—checking mechanisms—are just as important in shaping cadre conduct.[1] The question is in essence one of state capacities: if corruption has become progressively worse and more rampant, where have the state's deterrents gone? Why have they not been more effective at controlling the party's rank and file? Here, in terms of its capacity to act against cadre abuse, the Chinese state appears to suffer most in the administrative dimension of its capacity. State capacity remains relatively potent in the other two dimensions, institutional and political. In the institutional dimension, the Chinese system has enjoyed regime continuity, along with its capacity to make political and economic rules. In the political dimension, the autonomy of national elites from societal pressures and concern with regime legitimacy/survival, in fact, motivate national elites to devote political capital and state resources to building state capacity in the anticorruption arena. However, in the administrative dimension, the state's ability to enforce compliance and organizational coherence from its bureaucratic ranks has been cast in doubt by the pervasive abuse documented in the preceding chapters.

In this chapter I address the question of interactions between reform and

[1] I thank professors Elizabeth Remick and Tom Bernstein for these insights.

corruption with regard to disincentives against cadre abuse. I demonstrate that while the incentives and opportunities for corruption have multiplied over time, the disincentives against it have progressively weakened over the course of economic liberalization and administrative decentralization. In contrast to those who see the Chinese state as having progressively adapted or even strengthened more recently,[2] I argue that the opposite is certainly closer to reality with regard to the state's checking mechanisms. I examine the state of these mechanisms from four angles: structurally, at the chain of bureaucratic command, the cadre recruitment system, and the monitoring system; policywise, at the autonomy of sectarian policy making by localities; ideologically/morally, at the restraints and motives "internal" to individual officials; and administratively, at the enforcement of anticorruption rules.

MODERATE PHASE

Before the early 1990s, the lingering plan track, along with its command hierarchy, limited the powers of lower agencies and agents. While plan guidelines no longer dominated decision making at lower agencies and firms, the latter had discretionary power only over the above-plan portions of output and revenues. While routine decision powers were devolved to local governments and firms, the latter still depended on higher state agencies for material, financial, personnel, and institutional support. This reliance also meant they had limited space to make and implement local policies in defiance of central directives and high agencies. Further, while the separation of the party and the state at local levels proceeded at the expense of the party, routine appointments and promotions still required the formal approval of party organizations. DIC offices survived in most public institutions—in part because the latter still existed and party branches were not yet seriously sidelined by management. Finally, budgetary and fiscal matters remained under the purview of central planning. Established procedures and practices of accounting, auditing, purchase, expenditure, allocation, supply, distribution, and extraction were not yet outpaced by the growth of financial and economic autonomy of state agencies and firms. If mechanisms and reputation for discipline are crucial in maintaining links of hierarchical authority, they largely existed and persisted in the first reform phase. But all these changed dramatically since the 1990s.

[2] I thank Professor Tom Bernstein for suggesting this point.

THE TYRANNY OF THE NEW "FIRST-IN-COMMAND"

The foremost change, resulting from the demise of the hierarchy of the command economy, is what Chinese analysts widely refer to as "the absolute power of the first-in-command" (*diyibashou juedui quanli*) at lower levels.[3] This new "first-in-command" is no longer the party secretary, but the head of a local government, state agency, or public firm. This individual may thus be called the chief executive. The rise of the chief executive at local levels in the wake of the state's retreat has become the primary source of weakening checks against cadre deviance. This is true of all administrative ranks at the subnational level, from lower to higher levels. Of the officials investigated at the *di-ting* rank in 1998, for example, 42.1 percent were chief executives at the equivalent level of the mayor of a sizeable city, the head of a department in a provincial government, the commissioner of a district above counties, or the CEO of a large state firm.[4]

The foremost reason for the new "first-in-command" is the handover of central planners' job to localities, firms, and markets, thereby passing unprecedented discretionary power onto the hands of local chiefs while simultaneously removing checks against them. Most local economic decisions no longer require higher-level approvals. Except for centrally funded investments, local chief executives have taken over the approving power for critical factors of the local economy, at the firm, county, municipal, or provincial levels. With hierarchical relations of the plan system gone, upper administrative echelons are left with few reliable channels to learn about routine violations by lower agencies. From land privatization to public projects, from financing to public levies, and from SOE reforms to development assistance, local chiefs can sign off approvals at the stroke of the pen. Though collective decisions are formally required at an administrative level where an approval is to be given, an overbearing and unruly local chief can make willful decisions without informing peers or subordinates. Governor Cheng Kejie of Guangxi easily overruled a provincial decision that allocated a piece of land for an ethnic theme hall. He reallocated the site to a mall developer and provided cheap financing. Shenyang's executive deputy mayor, Ma Xiangdong, not only approved but waived payments for a choice piece of land for Liu Yong, a gang leader, to develop a billion-*yuan* mall in a location where "every inch is gold."[5]

---

[3] "Expert from the Chinese Academy of Social Sciences Sees Rising Corruption Caused by Revival of Patriarchalism," DFLZ 6 (2002): 25.

[4] Shao Daosheng, "Two Problems that Need to Be Addressed Urgently in Today's Anticorruption Work," DFLZ 10 (2002): 16–18.

[5] Gao Xing, "Deputy Mayor and the Mafia Boss," DFLZ 6 (2001): 37–38.

With local autonomy and decentralization, "the first-in-command" also means that the local chief no longer needs to report to anyone or be accountable to anyone. Except for important personnel matters and investments involving central funding, the hierarchical structures and requirements for reporting to higher authorities have disappeared. By offenders' own admissions, this near autonomy has removed any structural disincentive against arbitrary decisions in local matters. In the words of a bureau head in Chongqing city, the prerogative of being the number one was not having to report his work to anyone, or to ask for approval for anything; his words would be rules and laws, and must be followed if even wrong. Five years later, in 2002, this official received a sixteen-year prison sentence for bribe taking, embezzlement, and misuse of power.[6] The lack of control is even truer of chief executives at higher ranks. Hu Xuejian, former mayor of Tai'an, used to marvel, "When one reaches my rank, there is nobody to check me." Li Chenglong, former mayor of Yuling, Guangxi, agreed: "I have too much power. My power can easily be changed to money. Supervisory agencies have no real meaning for me." Mu Suixin, former mayor of Shenyang, put it more bluntly: "Central decrees and regulations will have to be adapted once they reach me. I implement the ones I approve, and I do not implement the ones I disapprove." Hu Changqing, former deputy governor of Jiangxi, made several trips to Hong Kong and Macau over the course of a year and half for gambling and illicit entertainment. Yet nobody ever seemed to have paid attention to his whereabouts or to his absence, often days at a time. Hu compared himself to "a horse let go off its reins" and "a cat that moves freely in and out of a cattle pen."[7]

Reforms to balance (but not check) the power of the chief executive, especially at SOEs, have yet to work effectively. In place of the higher administrative agencies of the past, a new leadership structure has emerged as the "modern management style" in SOEs that have become shareholding companies. The new system has two parallel structures, designed explicitly to balance managerial power. On one side, the business leadership consists of the managerial executives, the board of directors, and the shareholders' meetings. On the other side, the monitoring leadership consists of the party committee, the trade union, and the supervisory council (*jian shi hui*). The double tripartite system, however, remains little more than a pair of formal structures. One problem is the personnel arrangement at the top. In a majority of situations, there are indeed two parallel leaders at the top, the CEO and the party

[6] Shen Yi, Han Hongfang and Chen Yong, "The Chief Executive Position Does not Mean A Free License to Abuse Power and Big Money," DFLZ 8 (2002): 25–26.
[7] Shao Daosheng, "Two Problems," 16; and Li Xueqin, "New Thinking on Fighting Corruption: Democracy and Reform," DFLZ 7 (2000): 17.

secretary, with each at the helm of one of the two structures. But just as often, the party secretary is also the chair of the board of directors, thus crossing over to the business side. Rather than serving to constrain the CEO by questioning him, he usually concurs with him in business matters. In the remainder of situations, things can be worse: the same person often concurrently holds all three top positions at the enterprise—the CEO, the party secretary, and the board of directors. He can simply monopolize all decisions at the firm.

In another sign of weakening checks, members of the new monitoring structure at SOEs—the supervisory council, the DIC office (as part of the party committee), and the trade union—do not get to participate in board meetings or other decision processes. The head of these offices may participate if he happens to hold the party secretary position or a managerial position. In the latter capacity, however, his independent voice as a supervisory agent is weak and has little bearing on the firm's decision making. Ultimately it is the management that decides on all business matters. If a CEO chooses to distort or hide financial and business information from the party and supervisory personnel, he can do so easily.[8] Members of the party branch and the supervisory council, moreover, can be threatened with layoffs. And this has become a common concern among them, especially in less-developed and unruly regions. In one Henan firm, the party committee reached a collecive decision to give the CEO a disciplinary warning over his financial violations. In return, the CEO fired the party secretary from the plant.[9] Shareholders, often long-term employees of the SOE, are easily threatened with layoffs as well. As one Chinese analyst observes, a CEO nowadays can be a free despot, about whose violations higher officials have little knowledge, peer-level officials have little courage to speak against, and ordinary workers have little chance of finding out.[10]

Holding multiple official positions, simultaneously in local state agencies and firms, seemed an inconceivable arrangement before. But local flexibility has made such cross-over a frequent occurrence, resulting in another source of weakening checks against the chief executive. Such concurrent positions, expectedly, enhances the authority one already has as the chief executive of either a SOE or a local state agency. This is especially true of situations where

[8] Luo Shan, "Looking into Violations by State Enterprises," DFLZ, 1 (2002): 13–15; Xiao Zhen, "New Issues Facing the Construction of Party Ethics and Administrative Integrity in State Enterprises," DFLZ 2 (2002): 17–18; Ju Qinghui, "Some Thoughts on Perfecting the Supervisory System in SEOs," DFLZ 12 (2001): 19–20.

[9] Zhang Yan, "Reflection on Building and Perfecting Mechanisms to Supervise Managers of State Enterprises," DFLZ 3 (2000): 6.

[10] Cheng Gang, "The Rotten Mansion of Shenyang," DFLZ 3 (2002): 31–33.

the state agency he heads also has jurisdiction over the SOE he heads, not so much in routine decisions but in the areas of regulatory decisions. A case in point is the tobacco industry, where abuse has been frequent. In An'hui Province, one individual headed three state and business organizations with six titles: CEO and party secretary of the Tobacco and Cigarette Company of Bengbu city, manager and party secretary of the Bengbu Branch of the Anhui Tobacco Company, and CEO and party secretary of the Tobacco Bureau of Bengbu city. In Hebei Province, an individual also had six official titles simultaneously in and out of the government: CEO and party secretary of the Zhangjiakou Cigarette Factory, manager and party secretary of the Zhangjiakou Tobacco Company, and director and party secretary of the Tobacco Bureau of Zhangjiakou city. In each case, the official profiteered from speculating on the price of tobacco at a cost of millions to the state in lost revenues.[11] In Shenyang, Xia Renfan headed the mass transit sector, while trying to purchase the position of the chief of the city's transportation bureau. Had he succeeded, he would have had a still easier time raising fares, dismissing workers, cutting wages and benefits, and plundering more.

THE DISARRAY OF THE CADRE RECRUITMENT SYSTEM

How did so many corrupt officials climb to the chief executive position in the first place? This is the inevitable question asked by the public after the exposure of each major case. The cadre recruitment system is obviously an important source of the problem. The current system is twofold. One is the appointment and promotion of cadres to key positions at an administrative level—the head or deputy heads of a SOE, a law enforcement agency, a local government or one of its agencies at the county, municipal, or provincial level. The recruitment of cadre for such leading positions is the prerogative of party committees and branches. The second component of the recruitment system is the appointment and promotion of medium-level cadres and below, within an administrative level. The recruitment here is often the prerogative of the local "first-in-command."

The first system is supposed to involve several procedures, each designed as a structural check. It starts with *minzhu tuijian* (democratic nomination), or the nomination of candidates for promotion after grass-roots consultation. This consultation, if it does take place, is organized by the party branch at the grass-roots level. The next step is *kaocha* (scrutinizing) by the personnel de-

---

[11] "The Key to Anticorruption Work Is to Stop at the Source," DFLZ 1 (2001): 13–15.

partment of this party branch, or a thorough checking of the candidates, from their performance records, backgrounds, to peer support. This is followed by collective *taolun* (discussion) by the grass-roots party branch, or whatever the equivalent party organization to which the candidates are subordinate. The successful nominees are then *shangbao,* or reported to the next higher party authority. The fourth step is further scrutinizing by the higher party authority and finally, a formal submission of the nominees to the party committee at this level for final approval.[12] For candidates who are already chief executives, for example, a mayor, a county magistrate, or a CEO, it is the party organization at the next higher level that conducts the above set of procedures. The multiple steps here, however, have frequently failed to filter out errant nominees, including some with well-known notoriety at the grass-roots level. The problems are many, some intrinsic to the selection system, others arising out of recent liberalization. Together, they have failed to provide effective checks through the appointment and promotion system, once a major mechanism of the center to control its rank and file.

One new problem is that the traditional methods of nominating and scrutinizing can no longer meet with the complexity of the changing times. In the days when party strengths were strong, grass-roots cadres and employees were more forthcoming about voicing opinions about nominees during the nominating and consulting stages. The simpler routines of the old days allowed co-workers to have better knowledge of and closer access to the nominees. But grass-roots colleagues and subordinates now have greater fear of revenge by nominees if they speak up about anything negative. Nominees are also more likely to be clever operators adept at maneuvering political networks and putting on good appearances. Moreover, the candidates have usually been decided by a few key officials before the personnel department starts the consulting and scrutinizing process. Sometimes personnel staff may simply want to please their superiors by rubber stamping their favorites. Other times they may just want to avoid displeasing their superiors. Scrutiny by personnel staff can also be superficial and one-sided, since they are no longer required to scrutinize the personal life of candidates. Yet it is personal life that often betrays cadres' corrupt side nowadays, as will be discussed later. In remote regions, party organizations from above rarely make visits to grass-roots branches and are not familiar with real situations at the ground level. Worse yet, even if the personnel department uncovers a nominee's problems, its recommendations may not be taken seriously by those chief executives bent on promoting their cronies.[13]

---

[12] Sheng Quanyong, "Promotion Despite Corruption: A Problem not to Be Ignored," DFLZ 1 (2001): 21–22.

[13] Li Ying, "An Analysis of Violations by the Chief Executive," DFLZ 3 (2001): 31–32.

Another new problem is the orientation of "economics in command" in the selection and promotion of cadres. Individuals who can apparently generate economic growth, bring in projects and funds, and find investors and revenues are considered as "competent individuals" (*nengren*) to be promoted and championed. Noneconomic issues such as personal integrity and political orientation are brushed aside. Yet such "competent individuals" are also the ones who may be bold with bribery and other "creative" practices. This is especially true of individuals who have their eyes set on quick ascension. Moreover, some of them may not have genuinely promoted development, but have been skillful at showy speeches and projects.[14] Such projects have become known as *zhengji gongcheng,* or "political achievements projects," typically important for officials who have little real achievements to show. In economically depressed Shenyang, Mayor Mu Suixin spent millions to build a fancy square downtown, complete with waterfalls. In the poor county of Luxian, Henan, officials showered funds on a "mountain ranch" where no cattle would later roam, a "ten-thousand-pig farm" where only a few hundred pigs since lived, and a "ten-thousand-*mu* walnut trees orchard" where few nuts are seen five years later. The feat was outdone by Fuyang of northern An'hui, where Y380 million was spent to build a "Grand International Airport" in a poor city (until recently a county) where not only international but domestic travel would be scanty. The airfield remains a refuge for wild birds.[15] Such expedient showiness has spread from poor cities to poor counties and down to poor villages. In one western county, government reviewers audited the accounting records of all villages before a personnel reshuffle. Ninety percent of the villages turned out to have deficits accruing from showcase projects. The projects were often big, time consuming, and unpractical.[16] Nonetheless, many localities champion the selection and promotion of "competent individuals" and espouse this as a new personnel policy in their reform efforts. With this criterion, even individuals with known records of misconduct may be promoted to important positions.

The practice of preselecting candidates for promotion, often by a few officials at the same or next administrative level, encourages potential nominees to curry favors with key officials, and sometimes just the one top official. And the enhanced autonomy of this top official now ensures such favor currying of real outcomes. Rather than focusing on the quality of their work, some aspiring candidates are motivated to pay more attention to building

[14] Liu Shude, "Analysis and Reflection on Fighting Corruption in the Financial Sector," DFLZ 7 (2001): 25.

[15] "Sale of Office Hidden in 'Normal Procedures,'" *Zuojia Wenzhai,* April 29, 2003.

[16] Sheng Xiaoping, "Deficit Spending for Political Achievements: An Alternative Form of Corruption," *Shidai Chao* 8 (2003).

connections, finding patrons, and catering to the idiosyncrasies of key superiors. The latter, not surprisingly, show a special preference for compliant followers. The de facto system of "a few people selecting cadres, and the
selection of cadres among a few people," furthermore, encourages the sale of
office, since both the "buyer" and "seller" can be certain of the outcome.[17]
As shown in many office-for-sale cases in chapter 4, an unruly chief can decide whom to nominate and for what position. He can advance or hinder a
nominee, doctor a resume, cover up a nominee's bad record, or push through
totally unqualified candidates.

The result of such an exclusive and elusive selection process, in turn, contributes to a phenomenon known as *bianfu biansheng*, or "promotion while
engaging in corruption." Such cases are many and seem quite inconceivable.
To cite just a few of the highest-ranking offenders, Cheng Kejie accepted all
of his Y40 million of bribes while serving as deputy governor and governor
of Guangxi. Yet he was promoted to the deputy chairmanship of the National
People's Congress (reportedly with Li Peng's backing). Hu Changqing took
most of his ninety bribes (Y5.44 million) during his tenures as deputy director of the Religious Affairs Bureau in the central government, as gubernatorial aide, and then as deputy governor of Jiangxi during 1995–1999,
before he became governor of Jiangxi. Xu Bingsong sold numerous offices
and other favors for huge bribes while serving as deputy party secretary and
commissioner of Yuling District of Guangxi. Yet despite continuous complaints from citizens, he became a deputy governor of Guangxi. Meng Qingping kept numerous mistresses with bribe incomes while serving as CEO of
the Hainan Iron Mine and party secretary of Hainan (later a province).
Nonetheless he climbed quickly to become a deputy governor of Hubei.[18]

The party's campaign to "youthify" its officialdom does not seem in itself
able to screen out such candidates. Instead, younger offenders have been on
the rise. According to Jing Dali, head of the Department for the Prevention
of Office-Related Crimes (*zhiwu fanzui*) at the Supreme People's Procuratorate, 19.28 percent of registered embezzlement and bribery cases in 2002
involved officials below the age of thirty-five (7331 out of 38,022); and 29.14
percent of the negligence cases involved the same age group. The Prosecutor's Office of Guangzhou reported a similar scale: of its closed corruption
cases from 1997 to early 2003, 20 percent (or 364) involved officials under
thirty-five. In another new trend, the educational level of younger offenders
is getting higher. Of the 364 offenders in Guangzhou, 62.9 percent, or 229,

---

[17] "The Key to Fighting Corruption Is to Stop It at the Source," DFLZ 1 (2001): 13–15; Chu
Zhengkun, "Reflections on Major Corruption Cases," DFLZ 10 (2001): 17–19.
[18] Sheng Quanyong, "Promotion despite Corruption," 21.

completed three years of college and above, and 17 had graduate degrees. These ratios were far higher than was the case for other age groups. These developments show that the promotion of better educated, younger people would not likely in itself reduce corruption. In fact, the size of younger officials' loot is often larger. Two explanations are possible. One, since younger officials have not reached chief executive positions where bribe taking is easier, they often engage in nontransaction type corruption, which tends to involve larger loot. Second, officials under thirty-five came of age in the era of reform, with scanty memory of a far more stringent CCP. They grew up not only in a different political environment, but also a social environment of ever expanding stimulus and validation for material acquisitions. In fact, the same qualities that make themselves likely candidates for promotion can also make them vulnerable to corruption: eagerness for instant grandiosity and immediate utility.[19]

While increased local autonomy makes it easier for the unscrupulous to win nominations and offices, however, it is difficult to remove top officials at an administrative level once they are appointed. Since their appointment and promotion have been approved by the party organization at the next higher level, the grass-roots organization has no power to remove or demote those appointees. For example, neither a mayor nor the city council or the local people's congress can recall an errant deputy mayor. Complaints have to be filed with the provincial party committee, which then meets to discuss the case. The control of the higher authority here is designed as a checking mechanism, but it actually becomes a loophole that encourages wayward officials to seek protectors both locally (so that complaints will not be filed to the higher level), and at the higher level (so that filed complaints will be ignored). This is exactly the reason for the phenomenon of "promotion while engaging in corruption," and for local corruption rings such as those of Guangxi and Shenyang. In the case of Shenyang's deputy mayor, Ma Xiangdong, many complaints had been filed about him from below over the years. But as a crony of the mayor, he won promotions almost as quickly as he took graft. If he had not been accidentally discovered by security agents while gambling in Macau, Ma might well have kept climbing the official ladder for years to come.

The second part of the cadre recruitment system, the appointment and promotion of medium-level cadres and below within an administrative unit, allows ample local autonomy. Decisions are only to be made at that admin-

[19] "Four Characteristics of Violations by Young Officials," from *Liao Wang* (August 2003), cited in *Shidai Wenzhai,* August 6, 2003.

istrative level, usually by the chief executive and with nominal approval of the party branch. An ever-expanding prerogative since economic reform, such autonomy is supposed to enhance managerial flexibility and market criteria. But it has also become a key source of corruption in personnel matters. At SOEs, in particular, the CEO has an almost completely free hand in selecting his own appointees, especially if he also concurrently heads the party committee and the board of directors. Such a CEO can make a formality of consulting the latter two bodies. He can appoint his relatives and cronies to key positions so as to ease the way for plundering firm assets. He also has the autonomy to lay off whomever he finds undesirable, even disciplinary officials. At local state agencies, chief executives face more structural barriers, as most appointments and promotions still require collective decisions at the same administrative level. In remote regions and counties where the central state is weak, however, such a collective process may be only nominal.

THE DEPENDENCE OF MONITORING AGENCIES

This section looks at the state's monitoring mechanisms. The major components of the system have shown to be weak in some aspects and outdated in others, serving to weaken disincentives against misconduct through supervision and discipline.

The monitoring and disciplinary system is threefold, consisting of the Party's Discipline Inspection Commission (DIC), the State's Ministry of Supervision, and the criminal justice system. The first two are parallel to each other, one based in the party apparatuses and the other the state bureaucracies. Each also has its own parallel organizations down the hierarchy of the party and state structures. The function of a dual system is that the party is responsible for routine monitoring and discipline within its ranks, while the state within its administrative hierarchies. Violators who are both party members and administrative officials, thus, must go through both mechanisms (the party channel first), while nonparty members only go through the state's supervisory mechanism. If violations are serious, the cases are then transferred to the Prosecutors' Office and further processed by the criminal justice system.[20]

Yet what appears to be a "double checking" or even a "triple checking"

---

[20] This and the following paragraphs are based on Hou Shaowen and Zhang Xinbin, *Lianzheng jianshe sixiang baoku* (Reference Materials for Building Honest Government) (Shandong: Jinan Chubanshe, 1995): 347–56.

system is not always effective in reality. Originated in 1949 and suspended since 1959, the state supervisory system was restored in December 1986. The reinstatement marked recognition of major changes since reform: the increasing presence of nonparty members in administrative and managerial positions and the increasing "separation between the party and the state" that results in more violations in the administrative ranks. Like the overall Chinese political system, the dual party-state checking systems have parallel structures at the central, local (provincial, city, and county), and work unit level. Yet it is not a vertical command system accountable to the authority at the next higher level. Rather, both systems are based on "dual leadership." As the CCP Charter stipulates, "Disciplinary commissions at local and grassroots levels should carry out their work under the *dual leadership* of the party committees at the same level and the disciplinary commissions at higher levels" (emphasis added). But the charter prioritizes local party control by stating that "when disciplinary agencies at various levels discover violations by members of the party committees at the same level, they should report to the party committees at that level and seek approval before proceeding to open investigations." The same principles apply to the state supervisory structures. Supervisory agencies at local and grass-roots levels are under the dual leadership of the local government at the same level as well as of supervisory agencies at the next higher level. Administratively, disciplinary and supervisory agencies depend on party committees and local governments at their corresponding levels for staff size, budget allocation, and personnel decisions.

Several problems result from this dual system. Above all, disciplinary and supervisory mechanisms at each level are subordinate to local party and state agencies. Yet they are supposed to monitor the behavior of their nominally parallel, but effectively higher authorities. Although the head of the local DIC is a member of the local party committee, he often ranks last in its internal pecking order. It is equally hard for disciplinary or supervisory agencies at higher levels to control the lower ranks, since the latter are also under the jurisdiction of local party committees. As for the local branch of the Ministry of Supervision, its head is appointed by the local chief executive and sometimes known as a "hearing-impaired" person. Essentially, local chief executives have a veto over who may be investigated and how far. As noted earlier, the "economic worth" of errant officials and the economic impact of full exposures can be a major consideration in their decisions, as are nepotistic ties and local cover-ups. At SOEs, the subordinate position of disciplinary officials has an additional meaning. As one DIC official complained, "The CEO is the legal representative of the firm. If we supervise them today, they may take away our job tomorrow."[21] At small SOEs, the DIC office is usually not present. In rural areas, disciplinary and supervisory branches are located at no further than the county level. Officials at township and village levels, like those at small SOEs, are thus outside the scope of the formal monitoring system. Here deputy chief executives often serve as disciplinary and supervisory officials. In other words, they are supposed to supervise themselves and their immediate chiefs.

The following case provides a dramatic illustration of the frailty of the dual monitoring system. In Henan, three consecutive heads of the province's Department of Transportation were brought down by corruption in four years between 1997 and 2002: the first received fifteen years in prison, the second a life sentence, and the third a likely lengthy term as well. The reasons for failing to stop not just one, but three errant officials in a row, offer textbook lessons on the problems of the monitoring system. Although a DIC office was present in that particular transportation department, it did not have the power to authorize investigations of the department's head. The DIC office would need to first report to the provincial DIC and seek its approval. Yet the decision on whether or not to report to the provincial DIC resided with the party branch of the transportation department. As is usually the case, the departmental head also concurrently headed the party branch. The DIC office was thus incapacitated: it was impossible for the department head to agree to having himself reported to the higher DIC office. When the provincial government was forced to deal with the three cases, it chose to limit its investigations to the transportation chiefs only. Concerned about the negative fallout for local development and about institutional stability, it did not seek to uproot the cronies of the three officials' from the department. Nor did it attempt to conduct structural reforms. The repeated misconduct of three consecutive executives, thus, was almost inevitable.[22]

Additionally, uneven sanctions weaken deterrence and control. Chief executives are often unafraid of monitoring and can influence the decisions of those who would monitor them. Party members may often be at an advantage, because after receiving penalties from the DIC, minor offenders are not likely to suffer double or triple jeopardy in the hands of the other two checking systems. DIC penalties, however, are often inconsequential: even the most serious penalty, dismissal from party posts and revocation of party membership, do not cause reductions in salary or rank status, as would penalties from the state's supervisory agencies, such as demotion or dismissal from office.

---

[21] Zhang Yan, "Reflections on Building and Perfecting the Mechanisms to Supervise Managers at SOES," DFLZ 3 (2000): 6–7.

[22] "Three Bureau Heads, One after Another," *Zuojia Wenzhai*, April 18, 2003.

The highest administrative penalty, termination of employment, can only be given by higher party and state agencies, not DICs. Finally, the legal system gets most of its corruption cases from the referral of the first two agencies. Thus it is not by itself a strong deterrence against misconduct. All these problems help render monitoring mechanisms ineffective, subservient, or haphazard.

To its credit, the DIC system has carried out its restructuring over the past two decades. Two major reforms have been tried locally. One was started in Zhangjiagang, a city in Jiangsu Province, in 1991, where the city's DIC would choose and send disciplinary officials to head county DICs. Known as the Zhangjiagang model, its contribution is the elevation of the status of the DIC: it is to be headed by an official from a higher administrative level. The second reform was started by the DIC of Jiangsu Province in 1992, where the DIC head would concurrently serve as a deputy party secretary of the province's party committee. Known as the Jiangsu model, the improvement here is the elevation of the status of the DIC head: he is a key member of the party committee to which the DIC subordinates. Easier to implement in reality, the second model has been promoted by DICs across the country. More and more DIC heads have become a member the local party committee, a member of its standing committee, or even a deputy party secretary. That is, the DIC head has moved from a nonparticipant to a full voting participant in the highest party organization at a given level.[23] This presence allows the DIC head to be present at decision meetings of those whom he is supposed to supervise. But this is only a first step. The DIC head is still in no position to prevail over the chief executive in economic and most personnel decisions.[24]

THE ARBITRARINESS OF SECTARIAN POLICY MAKING

The growing autonomy to make local policies is another development that has weakened the center's capacity to control local agencies and agents. This autonomy allows localities to legally and literally make policies in violation of central regulations and decrees. The foremost of such local policies, according to the head of a provincial DIC, is the ability of local agencies to

[23] Li Yongzhong, "Fighting Corruption from the Perspective of the System," DFLZ 5 (2003): 19–21.

[24] CCPDIC Office of Public Promulgation and Education, ed., *Fanfu Changlian Jianghua* (Topics on Fighting Corruption and Promoting Honest Administration) (Beijing: Zhonggong Zhongyang Dangxiao Chubanshe, 1994): 131–33.

"levy and spend" (*zi shou zi zhi*) and to "levy and split" (*zi shou zi feng*).[25]
That is, to spend what they levy on the small collective and to split what they
levy among staff members. Local levy power is tolerated because higher agencies do not have sufficient revenues to meet the needs of local development
or even local administration. Not surprisingly, the worst reported cases tend
to be from poorer regions.

If state agencies are permitted to spend the incomes they raise, they have
obvious incentives to raise them arbitrarily and illicitly. Between 20 percent
to 40 percent of local levy categories run contrary to central policies, and the
rates are often arbitrary. Rather than development, the extra levies are often
driven by a ubiquitous climate to earn extra income for the small collective.
Almost all government agencies, from the chief executive office to subordinate departments, utilize their jurisdictional authority to create levies. As one
Chinese analyst puts it, the official seal of every agency is its "money tree":
business licenses are the "money tree" of Industry and Commerce Management Bureaus, hygiene certificates that of sanitation departments, drivers'
licenses that of police departments, and marriage certificates that of neighborhood committees. Many fees are normally uncalled for, such as application for the construction of new roads, bridges, and the like; or a request for
salary adjustments, personnel transfers, and award nominations. Other fees
may be legitimate but deliberately excessive, as in the case of business licenses,
car registration, legal arbitration, filing of lawsuits, utilities installation, fines
for petty violations, or marriage and birth certificates. The fees range from
under Y100 to tens of thousands of *yuan*. Some local governments even set
up numerical targets for levies (*chuangshou zhibiao*) for subordinate agencies.
The targets must be fulfilled before full allocation of local state funding will
be made.[26]

The methods of levying come close to extortion sometimes. In the case
of car registration, a Beijing resident has to clear eleven hurdles and pay the
same number of fees before going on the road. Beside the usual sales tax, insurance premium, and a driver's license, there are also charges for a parking
permit, a moving permit, a verification certificate, a user tax, vehicle testing,
an identification plate, an information file, and a highway tax. For imported
cars, one also needs to visit the customs office for a certificate. The entire
process takes three painstaking months. A parking permit alone costs Y1700,
the monthly salary of a middle-income earner. Across the country, there are

[25] Li Xueqin, "Democracy and Reform: New Thinking on Fighting Corruption," DFLZ 7 (2000):
17.
[26] Kong Zhijian, "An Analysis of Creative Levies by Local Agencies," DFLZ 5 (2000): 23–24.

more than fifteen hundred kinds of charges and levies related to transportation and vehicles.[27] Other agencies are just as creative in soliciting fees, depending on the localities. To receive the mandatory personal ID card, one may
have to take a photo at the local police department for a fee. To get a marriage license, a couple may have to pay fees for family planning insurance,
mother and newborn protection, child immunization, premarriage counsel-
ing, physical checkups, and a procreation certificate. To pass an annual inspection, a car owner may have to become a member of the drivers' association
and subscribe to its publication on traffic security. To pass a site inspection, a
builder may have to order building materials from sellers assigned by the in-
specting agency. To have salary adjustments approved, a SOE may have to subscribe to the publication of the labor bureau. To have electricity connected,
one may have to buy equipment from stores run by the utility bureau. To pass
sanitation standards, a restaurant may have to buy supplies from contractors
associated with the hygiene bureau.[28] The list goes on and on.

Rather than using levies as a means to serve the public, some local agencies can turn them into an end in itself, moving yet further from the real purposes of local policy flexibility. Police departments, for example, use fines to
"punish" prostitutes and their patrons. But the real purpose may often be the
money supply rather than law enforcement. In fact, more prostitution means
more revenues and rooting out prostitution would actually end that supply.
Likewise, violation of family planning policies has become a source of revenues for some rural administrations. In villages where violations are common, some village chiefs even use fines as their main source of revenues. Such
fines amounted to a quarter of budgeted revenues for some village and township governments. In localities where counterfeiting and smuggling are rampant, fines have become the "money tree" for local governments as well.
The city of Huizhou in Guangdong took in millions by letting go smugglers
after fines were paid. For localities lacking such "special resources," natural
resources can offer an opportunity. One township in Hunan encouraged villagers to build private houses on farmland, a practice banned by central decrees, so the township could collect fines. In Chongqing, one township defied
a long-standing central ban by allowing land burials, after Y5000 were paid.
In Xining of Qinhai, the public parks department briefly opened the city's
martyrs mausoleum for public burials.[29] For agencies without opportunities

[27] Cai Engze, "A Power-based Economy Is a Natural Enemy of the Market Economy," DFLZ 8
(2001): 25.
[28] Kong Zhijian, "An Analysis of Creative Levies," 23.
[29] Ibid., 23.

to levy fees and create revenues (e.g., a party branch office, a women's association), organizing conferences, seminars, and training sessions are among the
ways to "level" the playing field.

In extreme cases, the financial incentive can turn into gross miscarriage of
justice. Some local agencies, including law enforcement agencies, may use
abusive measures to force citizens to pay fines or, worse, to set them up for
fines. In Siping city of Liaoning, several prosecutors lured two leather manufactures to make counterfeit leather goods, so that the latter could be caught
and fined. After arresting the two and their family members on charges of
counterfeiting, the prosecutor's office was able to collect Y350,000 in confiscated profits and Y600,000 in penal fines. In Xinjiang Autonomous Region, one county police department arrested four innocent young women
and forced them to admit to prostitution. To avoid harassment and possibly
torture, the women gave the police officers the names of seventy-four male
acquaintances. Twenty-five of the men were arrested and asked to pay Y5000
each if they were to be set free. Ten people paid before the case was exposed.[30]
In one city, the natural gas company collaborated with the safety inspection
department to squeeze consumers. They demanded inspection of gas tanks
before their due date, proclaimed them unsafe, and mandated purchase of
new ones. Those who resisted would see their gas supply cut off. In north
Jiangsu, the poor half of this well-to-do province, one highway toll station
waived tolls for vehicles of local party and state officials. Given the high tolls
levied across China (three hours' drive can require Y300 in payments or
more), the waiver means huge savings. Station staff, in turn, is showered with
handsome New Year's gifts from local officials, paid certainly not out of their
own pockets. Paying fines in lieu of spending prison time has also become a
"local policy" in some regions. Even felons on the death roll occasionally get
a sentence reduction by paying a fine.

The extra levies are often intended for the sectarian interests—workplace
improvement and employee bonuses—of the levying agencies. While the degree of violations may differ, the practice of using levy revenues for sectarian
interests appears to be universal. The police department of one municipality
vividly summed up how they managed to build a new office building: fre-
quenters of brothels paid for the foundation, prostitutes paid for the concrete
mixture, gamblers paid for the walls, and thieves paid for the roof beams. In
setting up the leather counterfeiter so that fines could be collected, Siping
city's prosecutors had intended for the funds to go to the construction of a
new office building. No less audacious was Sun Xiaohong, head of the

<hr />

[30] Ibid., 23.

Supreme Court of Yunnan. During his tenure as head of the intermediate court of Kunming city during 1992–1997, he instructed the court's accounting office to record only 30–40 percent of the court's income from legal fees. The unrecorded income was then deposited in several banks, hidden from auditing, treasury, and tax authorities. By the time Sun left for the provincial Supreme Court in 1998, the intermediate court he headed for five years had accumulated Y77.43 million in slush funds. Against central regulations, decreed in 1989 and again in 1996, the funds were used for employee bonuses and the purchase of more than one hundred vehicles (for a total of 260 employees). Sun even had vehicles smuggled in from border regions so he could upgrade his models three times between 1997 and 1998. After becoming the chief justice of the province's highest court, Sun instructed another expensive round of renovation on his freshly renovated new office.[31] But even Yunnan was outdone by Shenyang. During Mayor Mu Suisin's reign in the 1990s, the city's intermediate court spent Y180 million on a new luxury office building. Each top official had an individual suite that included an office, a lounge room, and a shower/sauna room, all in a city with masses of downsized workers.

Sectarian material interests, in short, have become strong incentives for local agencies to create self-interested policies. As local and departmental protectionism of their administrative prerogatives continues to rise, it has helped to undermine the ability of the central state to have its own directives implemented, its own version of public interests represented, or its own cadre corps controlled at the ground level.

THE DEFEAT OF IDEOLOGICAL AND MORAL DISINCENTIVES

Ideological and moral disincentives concern checking mechanisms "internal" to individuals, as opposed to the "external," structural ones. One traditional mechanism of the party was its ideological and moral exhortation against self-seeking. "Devote yourself whole-heartedly to public interests and rid of selfishness" (*da gong wu si*) and "Serve the people" (*wei renmin fuwu*) were the standard codes of behavior for cadres and party members during the Mao era. But, bypassed by economic considerations and market values, ideological and moral criteria are no longer important in decision making or job performance. Another traditional mechanism, political and ideological

[31] Xin Chao, "The Inside Story of How Yunnan's First Justice Lost his Job," DFLZ 3 (2000): 13–15.

education sessions, all but ceased in workplaces and schools since the 1990s. Political campaigns and criticism/self-criticism sessions, also traditional mechanisms, are no longer used. Although many were dreadful practices that should legitimately have been ended, the lack of substitute mechanisms has served to remove the last defense against self-seeking—or what the Chinese refer to as *bu xiang tan,* not wanting to take graft.

One indication is the legitimization of self-seeking as a value orientation, no longer to be covered up or castigated. Chinese conservatives tend to trace this value shift to ideological sources. While admitting it is human to be selfish, they view the beast as having been enhanced by the rise of money fetishism and self-gratification since market reforms, two decadent values rooted in capitalist influences from abroad and feudal influences from China's past. While conservatives long stopped treating capitalist influences as all bad, they see bad elements sneaking into the door along with the good ones. Typical was the following statement by Jiang Zemin, CCP chairman from 1989 to 2003. Though himself no typical conservative, Jiang cited three ideological causes of corruption out of four major causes at a DIC plenary session in 1993: "feudal and other influences of exploitative systems," "decadent influences from capitalism since reform and opening," "incomplete structures in the transition from the old to the new system," and "insufficient ideological education that gave way to monetary fetishism, hedonism and excessive selfism [*gerenzhuyi*]."[32] By 1997, when capitalist influences already had a stronghold, Jiang criticized cadres for "imitating Western life-styles" and "copying Western values" of self-gratification and self-centeredness (*ziwozhongxin zhuyi*). He cited criticisms of "Western diseases" by American and Japanese writers.[33] (Western visitors, of course, may be just as dismayed by the decadence of corrupt Chinese cadres.)

For sources of ideological and moral decline internal to China, conservatives see a capitulation to a value assault on the ideas of collectivism and public interests, and a failure of the party to assert the latter. In their view, the party's laxity has allowed commercialism and consumerism to prevail over its traditional ethics of diligence and frugality (*jianku fendou*). "Economics in command" has become the party's new ideology.[34] The conservative emphasis here is thus on the strength of cadres' ideological and moral outlook, or the quality of their character. Liberal-minded Chinese, on the other hand,

---

[32] Jiang Zemin, "Speech at the 2nd Plenary Session of the CCPDIC on August 21," *Guangming ribao,* September 15, 1993.

[33] Jiang Zemin, "Excerpts of Speech at the 8th Plenary Session of the CCPCIC, January 29, 1997," RMRB, May 16, 1997.

[34] CCPDIC Office, ed., *Fanfu Changlian,* 131–33, 208–9.

see a different set of ideological and moral factors at work. One is the tradition of rule by man, which induces the Chinese to think about ways of checking power from a moral rather than an institutional angle. Another is the breakdown of the communist ethic and the ideological and moral void this has created. Among more immediate motivations, they acknowledge a discrepancy between officials' salaries and their high expectations stimulated by an awareness of better life-styles. They also recognize the inducements of wealth seeking in a society coming out of scarcity, the pressures for access seeking in a society of weak coordination, and the aspirations for status seeking after achieving both.[35] More specifically, Chinese analysts of all ideological persuasions see the rise of several "internal" driving forces that have disarmed many officials ideologically and morally. These include women, offspring, gambling, and a psychology of an end-of-career scramble.

"Women" as a motivating factor refers to the keeping of mistresses, visiting prostitutes, and the like by officials. As one of the clearest indications of ideological laxity, "life-style" problems (*shenghuo wenti*) are no longer important in cadres' performance and promotion evaluations. Rare before the 1980s and still infrequent before the 1990s, personal lapses such as those are now brushed aside as private matters, or explained away with the claim "officials are also human." Yet reality betrays a shocking story. According to statistics from the draft group for the revision of the Marriage Law (adopted in 2001), more than 95 percent of disciplined officials had mistresses, and 60 percent of corruption cases involving officials had to do with "hoarding concubines."[36] A prosecutor from Nanjing confirms similar ratios from her investigation of corrupt officials.[37] Indeed, as the head of the Marriage Law draft group observes, the need to keep up with the expenses of maintaining mistresses and concubines is often the original driving force that launch officials down a path of graft. Keen on the material side of the exchange, the young and beautiful women usually need to be sheltered privately and expensively. Hence the expression *bao er'nan,* or hoarding a second wife. Multiple mistresses require yet greater "maintenance fees." Along with rich entrepreneurs, especially those from Taiwan and Hong Kong, corrupt officials are among the few groups associated with hoarding mistresses. The practice has become serious enough, especially along the southern coast, that one

---

[35] Wang Huning, *Fanfubai—Zhongguo de Shiyan* (Combating Corruption—the Chinese Experiment) (Beijing: Sanhuan Chubanshe, 1993): 12–15, 81–82.

[36] "Statistics from the "Marriage Law" Draft Group Show that 95 Percent of Corrupt Officials Kept Concubines," DFLZ 8 (2001): 29.

[37] Zhong Wen and Sun Feng, "The Mistresses of Corrupt Officials in the Eyes of a Female Prosecutor," DFLZ 4 (2003): 35–36.

main purpose of the revised Marriage Law was to outlaw it and to protect all women involved.

Yet despite the statistical correlation between mistress keeping and graft taking, no official may be investigated or disciplined for life-style problems per se. The benign neglect is encouraging enough. One is struck not only by the frequency that corrupt officials have mistresses but also by their lack of discreetness about it, even among the highest ranks. Li Jiating, governor of Yunnan, picked out a new lady friend during a public event and openly promised her help if she needed any. She eventually secured business loans with Li's help. Cheng Kejie, governor of Guangxi, had little qualms about letting bribe givers go through his mistress for favors and bribe payments. Deputy governor Meng Qingping of Hubei and deputy governor Hu Changqing of Jiangxi, meanwhile, chased any young beautiful girl in sight and compensated them with help of tax reductions, business loans, and job offers. In the expensive villa built with public funds to house his mistress, Mayor Chen Xitong hung her photos, some nude, including a life-size poster. The brazen manner betrayed the officials' attitude of treating mistresses as a prerogative, rather than a liability, of officialdom. Many fallen officials spoke of their motives as "not wanting to miss the opportunity" while in office, and "not having any regrets" later in life. Given that the phenomenon was almost nonexistent in the prereform days, its rise since then cannot be attributed to human nature alone. Remorseful offenders readily admit to the loss of self-restraint, often blaming the explosion of "hedonism" (*xiangle zhuyi*) and "egoism" (*geren zhuyi*) that has swept aside the society's traditional ethics.

For other officials, the women at home set a different entrapment. Though overall statistics are lacking, the DIC of Zhejiang Province reported "very high" rates of husband-and-wife collaboration in bribe-taking cases between 1994 and 1999 among the nearly one thousand cases involving cadres at the *chu* rank and above. Shandong Province reported a 90 percent rate in the thirty-seven cases closed by the Prosecutors' Office in the outskirts of Tai'an city in the months before 2001.[38] The growing role of the wife is both motivational and tactical. With an encouraging wife, officials often lose their last line of defense against self-seeking impulses. Many a fallen husband would later regret not having a wife who could act as a restraint on him, rather than urging him on. Tactically, both bribe givers and takers find a safety valve in the intermediate role of the wife: easy access and antidetection sensitive. Not surprisingly, wedded collaboration has been on the rise, and the techniques

---

[38] Ibid. and "On the Psychological Factors for the Corrosion of Officials," DFLZ 10 (2000): 20–23.

ever improving. Chinese analyses delineate four types of wifely roles: the be-hind-the-scene interventionist, the cash register, the bully, and the inciter.[39]

The interventionist makes promises to favor seekers, lobbies her husband, or otherwise intervenes in his exercise of power. Such a wife ruined the ca-reer of Xu Yunhong, mayor of Ningbo city, Zhejiang, and a supplementary member of the CCP Central Committee in the late 1990s. The cash register plays the role of a faithful receptionist and bookkeeper. On her busiest day, the wife of Chen Tongqing, mayor of Zhanjiang during the city's reign of smuggling, went to the bank four times to deposit bribe money. The bully takes more initiative by flaunting her powerful connections, usually for pe-cuniary advantages: easy loans, commissions, contracts, among other means. The wife of Lin Guodi, party secretary of the Mechanical Industry De-partment of Hunan, promoted products to reluctant firms under her hus-band's jurisdiction. With her urging, bribe taking became a family enterprise, landing her husband and son in jail for life. The inciter, finally, ridicules the reluctant bribe taker in her husband as "dumb" and "outdated." She urges him to look around at how "everyone is taking it" and to seize the opportu-nity before his power expires. The wife of Qi Huogui, mayor of Dongfang city of Hainan, actively sought out potential bribees for her husband and al-lowed in her home only those visitors who brought along envelopes (with cash or bank certificates). After collecting Y13 million, Qi became the biggest bribe taker in Hainan's history. Except for Xu, all the men cited above re-ceived the death sentence. The role of the wife is increasingly recognized by authorities. Jiangxi, Hebei, and Shenzhen have organized anticorruption training sessions for the spouses of leading officials.

Aiding offspring is another strong motivating force. This is not surprising in a society where parental help is expected and crucial for one to get ahead. But the kind of help has changed in nature and degree over time. During the 1980s, the worst that officials did was to give their (grown) children some convenience in securing goods for speculation and in setting up trading com-panies. The notorious "princeling party" first made their fortunes from these activities. Since the 1990s, the stakes have become higher. For officials with the right positions or connections, their influence is instrumental in the suc-cess of their offspring's business operations, from securing loans and land to developmental rights and construction contracts; and from smuggling to tax evasion. The enormous profitability of their activities makes parental help especially unjust in the eyes of the public. The proliferation of parental help at the highest level has become shocking.

[39] Sheng Xiaoping, "Greedy Domestic Aides behind Corrupt Officials," DFLZ, 4 (2001): 30–31.

The cases of Li Jiating, Xu Yunhong, Chen Tongqing, and Lin Guodi, mentioned above, also involved aiding their offspring. Other high-ranking offenders included Liu Fangren, former party secretary of Guizhou; Liu Zhibing, former deputy governor of Guangxi; Mu Suixin, former mayor of Shenyang; and Wang Zhonglu, former deputy governor of Zhejiang. Even Wu Wenying, model textile worker from the Mao era with an image of simplicity and loyalty to the party, used her position of a national leader to help her son in his business. The latest high-ranking official to fall, former governor Cheng Weigao of Hebei Province, again was guilty of helping his son in this regard.

The other major incentive since the 1990s has been to send offspring to high schools and colleges in Western countries. Unlike the Chinese graduate students who headed overseas in the 1980s and early 1990s, the new wave of younger students are rarely on government or foreign scholarships and depend on family financing. For reasons of language and visa application, the most popular destinations are Britain, Australia, New Zealand, and more recently, Germany. With a monthly salary of a few thousand *yuan,* few average families can afford the annual costs of Y100,000 and more. Yet such students have been on the rise and getting younger. More than 50,000 are in Great Britain, more and more between the ages of fourteen and eighteen. More than 40,000 are in Australia, half of them below the college-entering age. In 2002, overseas-bound students increased by 49 percent from the previous year, thanks largely to the 117,000 youngsters who paid their own way and who made up 94 percent of the total 125,000 students who headed overseas in 2002.[40] Calculated at a rate of Y120,000 ($15,000) per student annually, total costs amount to over U.S. $1.5 billion for the 117,000 students each year.

Where does the money come from? According to Chinese media, it often comes from two types of families: those of officials with "substantive power" and those of businessmen with substantial assets. Among the former, overseas educational expenses can be a way to launder illegally acquired incomes. One cursory piece of evidence is that private-funded students have not only hailed from the more developed regions of major metropolises and coastal cities, but increasingly, relatively underdeveloped provinces of Henan, Shaanxi, Shanxi, Sichuan, and Liaoning. Reported cases confirm these developments. Some of the parents can even be petty officials, such as a village official or village accountant. Chinese newspapers and websites frequently report about the profligate ways of some of the teen students, who make full

---

[40] Chun Fu, "Corruption behind the Wave of Studying Overseas," from *Zhongguo Gongshang Bao,* in DFLZ 10 (2002): 18–19; and Liu Hao, "Overseas Study Causes Enormous Amounts of Domestic Currencies to Flee," from *Beijing Shan Bao,* reprinted in *Qiao Bao,* Aug. 5, 2003; and http://www .networkchinese.com.

payments on expensive houses and drive a Mercedes-Benz or Lincoln. Stacked with cash, such youngsters are otherwise ill prepared for serious studies in a foreign language. Many have bought their way overseas through intermediate organizations, which can arrange dubious programs and schools. Truancy, nightclubs, fast cars, and even crimes have become the main staple of some of these teens thrown in unfamiliar surroundings and without parental guide.[41] Casino gambling is another entrapment that some officials have found irresistible, so much so that the gambling capitals of the East and the West—Macau and Las Vegas—have both targeted mainland officials as the leading source of growth since mid-1990s. The traditional Chinese fascination with gaming was first reignited when visiting officials and CEOs to Hong Kong were treated to nearby Macau excursions. Soon enough officials and CEOs started to reach into their company or official accounts. Shenyang deputy mayor Ma Xiangdong felt the urge so strongly that he frequently flew to Macau for gambling during his one year of training at the Central Party School in Beijing. The visits were unusually bold, as a stint at the party school was often a step toward promotion. Such eager visitors, not surprisingly, have become the darling of Macau's casino houses. As one of them put it, "We like officials from the mainland here. They gamble generously and readily. They don't make trouble for us after losing. With them we have no worry."[42] Chinese gamblers may have lost $259 million in 2001 in Macau, according to a report done for an American casino interested in doing business there.[43]

From reported cases, dozens of city-level officials and CEOs of state firms have fallen at Macau's gambling tables (see appendix 5). They each gambled away between millions of *yuan* to more than a billion *yuan*. At around U.S. $100,000 each shot, the recklessness of the highest rollers says much about the lack of disincentives against misconduct. The most dramatic of the gambling cases involves Jin Jianpei, former CEO of the Hong Kong branch of Yifeng Company, known as the "window to the outside world" for Hunan Province. At the height of his gambling career, he was often staking HK Y7–8 million (U.S. $1 million) in each shot. First sent over to Hong Kong to clean up an investment mess left by his predecessor, Jin took over as CEO in 1990. By 1997, he was a high-rolling regular at Macau's grandest casinos. In forty-four trips he gambled away more than Y133 million (more than U.S. $16 million) of company assets and lost an additional HK Y43 million from

[41] "Corrupt Officials have Secret Passages for Flowing Black Money Overseas, Rich Kids Study Overseas and Buy Expensive Cars and Houses," DFLZ 1 (2003): 16.

[42] Chen Feng, "Casinos in Macau: Graveyards for Corrupt Officials," DFLZ 6 (2001): 39–40.

[43] John Pomfret, "China's High Rollers Find a Seat at Table—in Vegas—Wealthy Aren't Afraid to Blow Millions, Especially When the Money Isn't Theirs," *Washington Post,* March 26, 2002.

securities speculation, which was intended to generate funds to pay his debts. By early 1999, Yifeng Company and its seven subsidiaries had to close down. Bankruptcy reviews showed that the company owed several billions of *yuan* in debts, thanks largely to Jin's gambling.[44]

The drama of the case is matched by deputy mayor Ma Xiangdong of Shenyang, the northern city beset by massive layoffs and industrial decline. Ma and three city officials lost more than Y10 million in three days on a Macau gambling cruise, but were spotted by mainland security agents during an inspection of casinos on the eve of Macau's return to China in mid-1999. Dispatched to check security threats posed by the colony's gangsters, the agents were surprised to spot three Mandarin speakers who frequented prominent casinos and wagered high bets. After video tapings of the trio were sent back home, they were identified as the executive deputy mayor, a head of the treasury department, and a head of the construction commission of Shenyang. Ma lost a total of more than Y30 million in seventeen plus trips to Macau. The investigation of Ma Xiangdong helped to bring down the entire city government in Shenyang.[45] Ma's case taught mainland authorities to be on the outlook for Mandarin-speaking high-rollers in Macau. Plain coats are now said to roam around Macau's casinos to spot fat cats. Partly in response, corrupt officials have turned westward, to Las Vegas.

The westward movement started as early as 1994, shortly after post-1992 reforms relaxed controls over overseas "observation" trips and the financial resources to pay for them. Las Vegas has become a must stop for almost every visiting delegation, many claiming to be here to learn urban planning and the building of a modern city in a poor region. According to one Chinese report, each year 1 million mainlanders visited Las Vegas since then.[46] As the *Washington Post* reports,

> Gambling executives say China's big-time gamblers could become the fastest-growing market among high-stakes Asian players, outstripping those from Hong Kong, Taiwan, and Japan. While the number of Japanese tourists visiting Las Vegas is still 10 times that of Chinese, the increase in high rollers from China and the amount they are willing to gamble have captured the imaginations of Vegas's gambling industry.[47]

Even casino owners worried about negative fallout of the report admitted to

---

[44] Huang He, "The Gambling Career of a Leading Official," DFLZ 2 (2000): 19–21.
[45] Chen Feng, "Casinos in Macau," 39–40.
[46] Xiao Bin, "Overseas Casino Owners Target Mainland Chinese Officials," DFLZ 1 (2003): 14–15.
[47] Pomfret, "China's High Rollers."

"a kernel of truth" in its claims.[48] As in Macau, mainland gamblers to Las Vegas have increasingly come from poorer regions. According to a casino employee who frequently serves Chinese delegations, newcomers from the northeast recently have surpassed old-timers from more developed regions, in numbers as well as in the size of their bets. This seemingly coincided with the trial and execution of Ma Xiangdong, as well as the collapse of the northeast's industrial sector that freed assets for officials and CEOs to plunder. These developments contrast disturbingly with the flocking of northeast-erners to the east coast of America, where these downsized workers from failed SOEs have joined the masses of illegal immigrants.[49] Ironically, taking a cue from their corrupt superiors, many may have applied for their entry visas by showing an invited letter from a Vegas casino.[50]

A final "internal" drive for corruption is the psychology of an end-of-career scramble. This usually involves four situations: before retirement, before the end of one's term limits, before a promotion transfer, or before the fin-ish of a dead-end political career. The first situation is referred to as the "fifty-nine phenomenon" in Chinese, or the rush to take spoils around the retirement age of sixty. Many officials who succumb to this motive have worked conscientiously throughout their career, especially CEOs of state firms who have made great contribution to their firms. Yet the state sector's remunerative system, though far less egalitarian than before, pales with that of the private sector. Many state CEOs, legitimately, feel grossly underpaid in comparison with successful private entrepreneurs. After retirement, all they have left is their monthly pension. Job-related benefits such as company vehicles, medical care, bonuses, aides, or *guanxi* networks will be gone or re-duced. They are also likely to retire to their modest company apartment, rather than the latest home on the market. Such concerns drive them to as-semble some wealth before their power expires. A case in point is Chu Shi-jian, CEO of Yuqi Red Pagoda Tobacco Group, whose case was detailed in chapter 3. Like Chu, other fallen "fifty-niners" tend to be CEOs of state firms, a testimony to their financial and managerial autonomy. Nationally prominent cases include former CEOs of Beijing Electric Power Company, Lanzhou Steel Company, Zhejiang Chemical Plant, Hunan Lianyuan Steel Corporation, and Wuhan Yangtze River Power Company.[51]

---

[48] "Casino Execs Upset Over Chinese Gambler Story," Las Vegas Gaming Wire, March 31, 2002, http://groups.yahoo.com/group/blackjackcardcounterscafe/message/12654.

[49] Based on my firsthand observation.

[50] *Flushing Times,* August 21, 2003 and *Qiao Bao,* August 23, 2003.

[51] Xie Minren, "CEOs of State Firms Fall One after Another," *Dang Feng Tong Xun* 7 (1999); Quan Qiuzhi, "The Causes of *fin-de-siecle* Scramble and Coping Strategies," DFLZ 11 (2000): 15–18; and Ling Mu, "On the Psychological Motives for Corruption," DFLZ 10 (2000): 19–23.

If the preretirement scramble involves ordinarily upright officials, the
other three situations often involve ordinarily more unscrupulous ones, who
are ready to manipulate the cadre system earlier in their career. According to
a study by Yasheng Huang, rotation and promotion are among the mechanisms that the Chinese state uses to effectively manage its bureaucracy. Relocation is often a disincentive against abuse of power, as it is harder to cheat
one's successor than one's superior.[52] However, the many problems of the appointment and promotion system mean that not all officials need to worry
about their track records to survive and thrive, especially if a rotation or relocation is within the jurisdiction of a patron. In fact, it may be an opportunity to engage in a last-chance scramble. On learning about his promotion
to the Changzhi municipal government, Wang Huling, party secretary of
Changzhi county, rushed to make 432 cadre appointments, including 278
promotions, from February to April of 1999. For younger officials who find
their promotion prospects rather dim, two tactics are common. One is to
speed up "snatching money" (*lao qian*) to make up for the failure of "snatching power" (*lao quan*). The other is to "snatch power" through office buying.
Not surprisingly, office buyers are often younger cadres. As revealed by one
investigation, as many as 70 percent of the 246 people who purchased office
from Ding Yangning, party secretary of Zhenghe county, Fujian Province,
were below the age of forty.[53] The growth of young offenders bodes ill for
the CCP's long-term cadre recruitment.

THE DEARTH OF ENFORCEMENT

Institutional lag is a common problem of transitional economies in dire need
of new regulatory infrastructure. But two decades of reform have given China
time to introduce many new institutions and rules for governing the behavior of public officials in a market economy. At the level of institutional building and rule making, indeed, state capacities remain potent. To cite the five
years between 1997 and 2002 alone, a number of corruption-preventing,
market-supporting institutions and rules were established.

In the area of reducing administrative influence, new institutions include
the Law on Contract Bidding (*zhaobiao toubiao fa*), the reform of the administrative approval system (*xingzheng shenpi zhi*), which relieved 789 items from

---

[52] Huang Yasheng. "Managing Chinese Bureaucrats: An Industrial Organization Perspective," *Political Studies* 50:1 (March 2002): 61–79.
[53] Quan Qiuzhi, "The Causes and Remedies for the Phenomenon of 'End-of-Career Explosion
of Greed,'" DFLZ 11 (2000): 15.

the mandatory approval list, and the delinking of revenues (levied from administrative fees and penal fines) from expenditures (*shouzhi liangtiaoxian*). In the area of managing cadres, new institutions include the system of accounting reviews for cadre below the level of the *xian* rank (*jingji shenji zhidu*); the income disclosure system (*shouru shenbao zhidu*); the gifts report system (*lipin dengji zhidu*); the open public affairs system (*gongkai banshi zhidu*); and the system of exchanges, avoidance, and rotation in cadre appointment (*ganbu jiaoliu, huibi, lunhuan zhidu*). In the area of monitoring, new institutions include the Central Inspection Team (*zhongyang xunshi zhu*), which periodically sends down central and provincial inspectors to learn about grass-roots abuse (as a mechanism to complement the bottom-up appeals system), and the hiring of thirty thousand "specially invited monitoring agents" (*teyao jianchayuan*).[54] DIC decrees and bans are yet more voluminous and frequent. A collection of such decrees compiled by the CCPDIC, *Selected Documents of the Chinese Communist Party on Building Party Ethics and Government Integrity*, numbers eight volumes and is 4942 pages in length. Different localities, finally, have their own anticorruption measures, from signing integrity contracts to awarding vigilant spouses.

Yet the actual enforcement of the rules and institutions is often wanting. A few statistics tell much of the story. Although the new law on contract bidding mandates public bidding for projects and purchases that involve dominant state funding, most contracts are still awarded without open bidding. According to inspections by the State Planning Commission, only 63 percent of public construction projects were open to public bidding in 2000. But closer scrutiny, based on seventy-eight state investment projects, showed that a lesser proportion—less than 10 percent—genuinely went through fair and open bidding. The rest simply made a formality of the process. At the construction site of Chengdu's Y120-million Shuangliu International Airport, open bids mandated for all twenty sections of the project were changed to invited bids. Some did not even go through the formality of the bidding process. Problems in one of these sections later delayed the operation of the airport for ten months. Rules on purchase orders, mandated in the same law, fared hardly better. Less than Y10 billion of the actual state purchases in 1999 followed new rules on public purchases, or less than 3 percent of the total spending of the state for the year.[55]

Compliance rates are equally appalling in the implementation of rules on delinking administrative fees, levy incomes, and expenditures. These rules are

---

[54] "1997–2002: Fighting Corruption in China over the Past Five Years," DFLZ 4 (2003): 28–29.
[55] Mao Yongmao, "Prevent Ritualism in the Battle against Corruption," DFLZ 4 (2002): 13–14; Chen Fang, "Problems in the Bidding of Construction Projects," DFLZ 8 (2001): 18–19.

aimed at curbing the excesses and arbitrariness of local levies. Legal, judicial, and regulatory agencies (police, prosecutors' offices, courts, and CIMBs) in particular are required to separate their regular service incomes (fees levied to cover the normal administrative costs of a service) from their penal incomes (fines levied for violations). Penal revenues, in turn, are to be separated from the operational expenditure of an agency. Fines are not to be used to cover the expenditures of an agency, which often end up in vehicle purchases, new constructions, and feasting. But the rules have hardly deterred outrageous levies. The Treasury Department and the State Planning Commission outlawed 238 types of car levies across the country. But the reduction amounted to only one-sixth of the more than fifteen hundred varieties of car levies across the provinces. Beijing residents, for example, only saw one vehicle levy eliminated, a forty-*yuan* "motor vehicle safety fee." Other localities have responded with a classic strategy: "When the above has a policy, the below has a counter-policy," that is, the local governments play "hide and seek" with the central government: when one fee is cut, another is created.[56]

Problems such as these lead Shao Daosheng, researcher at the Chinese Academy of Social Sciences, to argue that it is not the hardware of rules and institutions that China lacks, but the software of humans who take law seriously and who place law above power. The "soft power" of officials, he argues, can overwhelm the "hard power" of the state. This assessment leads him to openly question the prominent Tsinghua scholar, Hu An'gang, who frequently calls for institution building (*zhidu jianshe*) to curb corruption. Even the best institutions and rules would prove meaningless, Shao asserts, if they were treated like a piece of paper. More institution building per se, thus, would not solve the problem of corruption. Specifically he pinpoints officials' "patriarchal style" of high-handedness and rule of man, rooted in the millennium of feudal autocracy and the lack of democratic tradition.[57] In essence, this proposition challenges the conventional wisdom of post-Communist studies on the importance of institution building, emphasizing instead the importance of administrative enforcement and cultural change. It is also a point well grounded in Chinese reality. Almost all fallen officials confessed to not taking anticorruption bans and agencies seriously. And this is fully reciprocated by favor seekers. As Lai Cangxing, head of the Yuanhua smuggling operation, opined, "Institutions, rules, I am not afraid of them no matter how good they are. I am only afraid that leading officials do not have desires."[58]

[56] Cai Engze, "A Power-based Economy," 25.
[57] Shao Daosheng, "Two Problems," 16–18.
[58] Cited in ibid., 16.

As long as they had desires for money, women, or overseas trips, Lai knew, he could buy off every department of the city government. Indeed he did.

Yet the argument is also a circular one: is it the indifference to rules that leads to the lack of enforcement, or the lack of enforcement that encourages the disregard for rules? Evidence points to both structural and attitudinal problems. They can also be intertwined. The presence of DIC and supervising agencies within the work unit, as well as the overlapping of officials who hold administrative and supervisory positions, make colleagues of the supervised and the supervising. As co-workers and often long-term acquaintances, supervisory personnel are often afraid of giving offence, as the following case shows. When the party secretary of a university arranged for relatives and villagers from his hometown to contract several construction projects on campus, the campus DIC agency stayed quite. When the party secretary was suddenly able to buy an apartment beyond his possible legal incomes, whispers about kickbacks circulated on campus. When the finished construction projects turned out to malfunction here and there, a mysterious note about "dirty deeds" was being slipped under the doors of faculty quarters. Yet throughout the process, no one filed a formal complaint and the campus DIC remained silent. Every one continued to greet the party boss and his wife like long-term friends.[59] Even if an official gets disciplined by higher agencies from outside, administrative penalties (e.g., reduction of ranks and salaries, dismissal) may not be actually carried out, since the enforcement is left with the workplace. Some times the disciplinary actions may not even be made known to employees.[60]

The structure and culture of networks also combine to thwart enforcement of anticorruption rules. The structure of networks is often woven by power and pecuniary relations. The culture of networks, on the other hand, is built on a deeply ingrained deference to affective relations. The combined effects can be potent enough to overpower the state. The phenomenon is known as *shuoqing feng,* or the practice of interceding on someone's behalf. Whether it is to win political offices and promotions, bid for public contracts and projects, or dodge disciplinary and law enforcement agencies, interceding can render rules and laws irrelevant. As a bureau head from the Ministry of Rail Transportation revealed from his own experience, during the bidding for a public project there would be interference from many sides, from those in positions of power to those with affective relations with the project officers, bombarding the latter with phone calls, handwritten notes, and all sorts

[59] Based on the author's firsthand observation in the mid-1990s and late 1990s.
[60] Jiang Shaoyong, "How to Deal with the Failure to Enforce Disciplinary Penalties?" DFLZ 6 (2002): 16–17.

of competing pleads for special consideration. Although his own bureau was successful in 70 percent of its bids in 1998, the bureau chief admitted that it was seldom the quality of their designs that won in the end. From his observation, poor designs more often prevailed over high-quality ones, and the stipulations of the law on contract bidding were seldom followed.[61]

Even the discipline of corrupt officials is subject to interceding. And this interceding can prevail over the state, especially at lower levels. As soon as an official learns of an impending investigation or summoning, his first instinct is always to *zhao ren,* or looking for people in the right political position to influence investigators. The latter is often willing to intervene in order to avoid a situation known as "pulling the turnip out with the soil" (*ba luobu dai ni*). That is, the investigation of one offender drags out a whole chain of related cases.[62] At the same time, the offender will exhaust all channels to find people with affective ties to members of the investigating team, from relatives, former teachers, and old classmates to individuals who have done favors for investigators. Their task is to dissuade investigators from carrying on. The formal and informal pressures often combine to delay and dilute investigations, sometimes forever. Meanwhile, whistle-blowers and tipsters frequently face formidable protective networks, complete with well-orchestrated intimidations and revenge. Powerful local networks can decapitate the anticorruption efforts of the state, not just of local disciplinary teams but even of those dispatched from above. As Zeng Jincheng, head of the Transportation Department of Henan Province and Commissioner of Zhoukou District, declared, anticorruption crackdowns "do not reach my rank!" When they finally did in 1997, Zeng shouted furiously at his central and provincial investigators, "You won't be able to bring me down." Typically, he went on to erect formidable barriers for investigators.[63]

The weakness of enforcement at local levels has been shown time and again from its inability to break major cases without the power of the center. The investigation of Guangxi's corruption chains, despite being led by central teams, had to be relocated to Guangdong before it was free from local obstructions. And the investigation of Lai Cangxing's smuggling case had to be led by the deputy head of the CCPDIC herself, Liu Liying, also known as the nation's top corruption buster. From the scale of the Yuanhua case, central authorities realized that such an elaborate operation could not have taken

---

[61] Mao Yongmao, "Prevent Ritualism," 13–14; Chen Fang, "Problems in the Bidding of Construction Projects," DFLZ 8 (2001): 18–19.

[62] Cai Eng'ze, "Interceding Aids Corruption," DFLZ 3 (2003): 21–22.

[63] "Anticorruption Crackdown Usually Does not Reach My Level—the Psychology of Two *Ting*-ranked Officials," DFLZ 7 (2000): 28.

place without significant political backing at local levels. Ms. Liu did not just arrive in Xiamen, but did so with a team of nearly 100 members of the Central Inspection Team on October 22, 1999. But even this was not enough. The scale of local cadre involvement soon called for additional 500 plus inspectors, summoned from across the country. The total number of investigators eventually reached 740, making it the largest investigative team in the history of the PRC.[64] Ms. Liu's direct involvement was also responsible for breaking such major cases as the Wuxi pyramid scheme and Beijing's local corruption chains in 1995.

Finally, globalization and openness to the outside have helped to stall enforcement against corruption. Overseas branches of domestic companies, greater foreign currency autonomy, and the frequency of observation trips have made it easy for officials to stash deposits overseas—appropriated from state firms or agencies—and take flight when the occasion demands. In fact, overseas flight has become the chosen emergency exit for resourceful officials. Before his arrest, Governor Li Jiating of Yunnan had hidden five passports, ready to flee anytime. In 2001 alone, the Prosecutor's Office of Beijing recorded 120 officials as having fled overseas, 70 percent of them SOE officials.[65] Those who fled to Western countries have benefited in particular from differences in the political and legal systems and ideologies between these countries and China. Under what Chinese analysts call the pretexts of "human rights protection and judiciary independence," criminals like Lai Cangxing remain at large and even sheltered as political refugees. Only those not resourceful enough have been extradited back to China, and only from South American, Southeast Asian, and other Asian countries.[66] Overseas flight has become such an acute problem that central decrees were issued in August 2003 to confiscate the passports of high-ranking officials in nine provinces.[67]

CONCLUSION

In this chapter I have documented the decline of a range of disincentives against corrupt behavior in the reform era, especially in the post-1992 period. I have shown that the capacities of the Chinese state have not been suf-

[64] Zhang Xiaoxia, "Liu Liying: A Name that Makes Greedy Officials Tremble with Fear," DFLZ 7 (2001): 15–16.

[65] Wang Yongqian and Zhou Qingyin, "Exposing the Dark Story of Overseas Flight by Corrupt Officials," DFLZ 11 (2002): 34–36.

[66] Ibid. and Tang Nan, "Extraditing Corrupt Officials," DFLZ 1 (2003): 32–33.

[67] Qiao Bao, Sept. 26, 2003.

ficiently adapted or rebuilt to counter that decline. Just as market reforms spurred unprecedented incentives and opportunities for abuse, so have checking mechanisms been weakened against such abuse. At the very least, they have not adequately risen to the challenge.

The sources of this decline are manifold, but include four essential points. Structurally, the core problem of the Chinese checking mechanisms is the irony of how one type of the "overconcentration of power in one person" has been replaced by another. In place of the party secretary in command, power now overconcentrates in the chief executive. Yet the substance of that power has been so enriched by the new economy and by the retreat of the central state from the economy, that the potential and scope for abuse has become exponential. In other words, the "first-in-command" has a whole new meaning in the post-Mao economy. However, the control of the new "first-in-command" has become weaker than ever before: structurally not accountable to the above or the below (in this case, DICs), while concurrently autonomous to make policies, decisions, and many personnel appointments. In a structural improvement, the chief executive is now balanced (though not held accountable) by the party secretary who coexists with him and who oversees personnel matters. But this separation of power is often offset by the prerogatives of the chief executive in economic decisions and in lower-level appointments, and by the overlapping of managerial and party chiefs at public firms. Through budgetary, personnel, and veto power, the new "first-in-command" can also ensure that the local DIC has little independence or muscle in reality.

Administratively, the ability of the state to enforce its rules and checking mechanisms has been weakened, fundamentally, by a similar dynamic. The party hierarchy, once the fierce enforcer of central decrees, has been sidelined by the enhanced autonomy of the executive and managerial apparatus, which is supposed to follow the new regulatory mechanisms and antigraft rules. The party's role, no doubt outdated, has not been replaced by an apparatus powerful and credible enough to ensure routine compliance. The party secretary himself, moreover, has become no less autonomous in areas other than key personnel matters and business decisions. The party's DICs, the state's supervisory system, and the law enforcement agencies deal with abuse only after the fact, while the efforts of the Central Inspection Team and accounting reviewers are sporadic. (Some localities tried using intermediate agencies, such as accounting firms, but many of the latter turn out to be for sale, reminiscent of the Enron Corporation and its accounting firm.) Except when bribes are involved, few penalties await many types of violations, such as excess levies, rigged bidding, cronyism in appointment, disregard for monitoring agencies, or defiance of central decrees. In the absence of credible enforcement, network politics takes over and informality rules. Structures and culture thus reinforce each other: the lack of rule enforcement encourages the disregard for rules, and verse versa.

Ideologically and morally, the state has retreated even more sorrowfully than in the structural and administrative dimensions. Here the state has almost willingly ceded the ground. Despite occasional exhortations to remember the party's tradition of *jianku fendou* (diligence and frugality), the party has not articulated an alternative value platform to balance the onslaught of commercialism and consumerism, the aggrandizement of individual desires and wants, and the legitimization of private "life-styles." By leaving such "life-style" problems out of appointment and promotion considerations, the party in effect lends them some legitimacy. The party's new ideology, advocated by Jiang Zemin in the form of the "Three Represents," provides further rationalization to commercial values, rather than community ones: the party represents the "the requirements in the development of advanced productive forces in China, the orientation of the advanced culture in China, and the fundamental interests of the broadest masses of the people in China." The words "advanced" and "fundamental" here simply refer to economic development. Reluctant to look outside or back at China's own rich tradition, the party has become ideologically and morally barren. It encourages people to "get rich first" but does not exhort civic responsibilities and fair play during and after getting rich. An "anything goes" value orientation can only incite long pent-up desires to run amok.

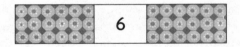

6

CONCLUSION

The Transition to the Market and Post-Socialist Corruption

The complexity of reform experiences across post-Socialist societies has by now cast much doubt on the initial euphoria that liberalization would automatically bring about free markets and open competition. This book is not intended to substantiate the well-known observation that liberalization has resulted in rising corruption in emerging markets. Rather, it aims to document the how and the why, and what the consequences are. By comparing the changing mechanisms and dynamics of corruption in different reform contexts, I have sought to shed light on some important issues in post-Communist transitions. These include the relationship between the transition to the market and corruption, policy mishaps, and systemic irrationalities in post-Communist reform strategies, and more fundamentally, the role of the state in the retreat from socialism and the movement to the market.

THE TRANSITION TO THE MARKET AND CORRUPTION

I have highlighted the interconnection between economic liberalization and corruption by documenting the key characteristics of post-Mao corruption, which not only evolved from the prereform period, but also during China's two periods of reform before and after 1992. These changing characteristics and their relation to market reforms can be seen in a number of areas: the opportunities for corruption, the arenas in which corruption concentrates, the sources of black money, the incentives for corruption, and the regional dynamics of corruption.

Contrary to the conventional wisdom of neoliberal economists and policymakers, progressive liberalization has not reduced corruption but simply created different and even greater expressions of it. And contrary to those who argue that post-Mao corruption has been a continuation of the CCP's organizational and institutional maladies,[1] I find that increased corruption has been largely rooted in the courses of economic liberalization. In the first period, several new policies made the context of corruption different from the prereform era, so that corruption thrived largely in the loopholes of reform policies and institutional lags. The first policy factor, the dual-track system, allowed bureaucrats to interact with the market, yet without added mechanisms against those who cashed power from one track in the other. The results were exactly what rent-seeking theories predict: whenever governmental action interferes to keep prices above or below market levels, it will generate rent-seeking behavior.[2] Another policy factor, decentralization, gave local officials growing autonomy over fiscal and distributive decisions, without added mechanisms from above or below to control how the increased authority was exercised. To the extent that decentralization disperses power among more layers of officials, it involves each official a little more in the decision process where their discretionary power becomes part of spoils available for distribution.[3] A third policy factor, the expansion of government regulation, now over market activities, was instituted without added mechanisms to check how the new regulatory functions were performed. Fourth, SOE reforms, from responsibility to contract experiments, progressively increased managers' autonomy over firm decisions without corresponding requirements of liabilities and transparency. Finally, commercial affiliates of state agencies and other public institutions were allowed to flourish without enforcement of conflict-of-interest rules or fiscal obligations.

In the post-1992 reforms, the end of the plan and a full transition to the market ushered in yet another new context for corruption. This round of transgressions by and large exploited the disintegration of the socialist econ-

[1] Xiaobo Lu, *Cadre and Corruption* (Palo Alto, Calif.: Stanford University Press, 2000).

[2] Anne Krueger, "The Political Economy of a Rent Seeking Society," *American Economic Review* 64 (1974): 291–303; Jadish N. Bhagwati, ed., *Illegal Transactions in International Trade* (New York: North-Holland-American Elsevier, 1974); and J. M. Buchanan, "Rent Seeking and Profit Seeking," in Buchanan et al., eds., *Toward a Theory of the Rent-Seeking Society* (College Station: Texas A & M University Press, 1981): 8–11.

[3] Susan Rose-Ackerman, *Corruption and Government: Causes, Consequences, and Reform* (New York: Cambridge University Press, 1999): 130, 114.

omy and the chaos of the exit. First, while the collapse of the plan reduced irrationalities in production and distribution, the marketization of the factors of production has given cadres control over unprecedented reservoirs of new resources, from land to capital goods and personnel. Second, while the demise of central allocation reduced corruption in administering state funds, capital markets have become sources of new financial abuse for bankers and borrowers alike. Third, while the "stockification" of SOEs aimed to improve incentive mechanisms, shareholding reforms have increased incentives to plunder company assets. Fourth, while the withdrawal of administrative command decreased bureaucratic intervention from above, the new "first-in-command" at local agencies and firms have created new tyrannies at the local level. Finally, the expansion of developmental and infrastructural functions, welfare provisions, and antipoverty programs intended to address the inadequacies of the market have unleashed an explosion of plundering. Through it all, the corresponding decline of checking mechanisms against cadres have given a further boost to the new structural opportunities.

Because of the large number of officials and private parties involved in both periods, the competitive corruption model characterizes the nature of China's reform-era corruption. In this model, according to Rose-Ackerman, rent extraction is shared among multiple officials and private interests in competitive bribery, in contrast to a kleptocracy where a ruler monopolizes rent extraction, and to a bilateral monopoly where rent extraction is shared between the ruler and a few powerful private interests (e.g., mafia-dominated states).[4] The "competitive" nature of China's corruption can be seen in the range of state power affected by it over the two periods. In the first, corrupt officials concentrated in the "three administrative joints" of the state, as it is referred in Chinese. The first "joint" includes the branches of government that exercised economic governance, including industries, agriculture, trade, and transportation. Their functions were changing, but not disappearing. They still administered state control over economic plans and allocation, supply and distribution, business entry and operation, finance and expenditure, domestic and international trade, and construction and transportation. The second "joint" consists of the chief executive branch at each administrative level of the state. Though not directly in charge of economic governance, chief executives had the capacity to place phone calls to subordinate departments, though mainly their family members and lower-level executives pursued such opportunities during the first period. The third "joint" encompasses public-owned industries and businesses, and corporate cadres

[4] Rose-Ackerman, *Corruption and Government*, ch.7.

who controlled managerial, manufacturing, purchase, and marketing aspects of enterprises.

In the second period, the areas of state power affected by corruption have expanded laterally and vertically. The principal culprit is the rise of what Rose-Ackerman terms "high-level corruption," referring to major government projects, programs, concessions, and privatization processes, plus the "upward spiral effects of competitive corruption."[5] In this new phase, rent extraction concentrates in the chief executive offices and offices that exercise macroeconomic and regulatory management of the economy. The "three joints" have remained, but the chief executive branch, especially at local levels, has overtaken economic agencies to become the key source of violations. Moreover, law enforcement and judicial organs have become a new "joint," hence the Chinese phrase "three plus one." Together, these four "joints" have control over decisions affecting properties and property rights, investment and financial resources, SOE properties and property restructuring, construction and infrastructure, commercial regulation and legal/judicial jurisdiction, taxation and other fiscal extraction, developmental and antipoverty assistance, and personnel appointment and promotion. In addition, SOE administrators remain a significant portion of violators despite the declining importance of state manufacturers. Nonmanufacturing SOEs, in the financial, property, and trade sectors, have become powerful new players.

The sources of black money, contrary to the rent literature, have not just come from rents created by government action. They have varied from transaction-based to nontransaction types of corruption, and from one period to the next, depending on whether the plan or the market was the dominant component of the economy. In the first period, the sources of black money were two. One was state distribution, or within-plan and above-plan financial disbursements from the state. The second was income from price differentials of the dual-track system and from issuance of regulatory decisions and advantages. However, state allocation diminished as a major source of black money in the second period, while other sources multiplied. These new sources include state assets and asset shares, bank loans and other capital, state aid funds and tax benefits, developmental and infrastructural investments, levies and fines, and regulatory and judicial fees. In short, the sources of black money stem not only from government action and monopoly, but also from the state's retreat from public ownership, its withdrawal from business management, the devolution of fiscal authority, and the transfer from administra-

[5] Ibid., ch. 3 and p. 124.

tive command to regulatory agencies. The reduction and change of state functions have in themselves created sources of rents and spoils.

The incentives for suppliers of corruption (officials) have shifted from mixed affective and material to mostly material ones over time. This finding helps to explain the discrepancy between those scholars who argue that social networks and the use of them to exchange favors are increasing in importance in China's economic transition,[6] and those who find such practices diminishing in importance as economic transition progresses.[7] As I have shown, during the period before 1992, a combination of affective ties and material incentives tended to motivate officials. The *guanxi* practices had continued from the late Cultural Revolution and the early post-Mao period when they played a central role in the structure of Chinese society, a phenomenon that has been examined by a number of scholars.[8] Their surge since reform was due importantly to the explosion of economic activities and commercial opportunities. Since rent-seeking opportunities largely stemmed from the plan track of the economy before 1992, it was only fitting that officials relied on connections and networks to cash in on the rents, a less blatant and baneful practice than outright bribery. Correspondingly, the types of bribes accepted were usually fairly inexpensive gifts and moderate cash payments. These factors, plus the relative modest size of rents compared with the second period, tempered officials' appetite and the size of bribes. The upsurge of material incentives since then, however, has diminished significantly the importance of social connections and affection-based access in the 1990s.

In this book, I have not as much confirmed the observation that the market imperatives of price and quality are rendering *guanxi* secondary[9] as noted that the basis of connections and access is now commercialized. These connections need to be cultivated primarily through material incentives rather than affective ties. Several factors have contributed to the change since 1992. First, the types, sources, and sizes of official advantages have greatly changed. The demise of the plan and public ownership has unleashed

<hr />

[6] Mayfair Yang, *Gifts, Favors, and Banquets: The Art of Social Relationships in China* (Ithaca: Cornell University Press, 1994); and Yanjie Bian, "Guaxi and the Allocation of Jobs in China," *The China Quarterly* 140 (December 1994): 971–99.

[7] Douglas Guthrie, "The Declining Importance of Guanxi in China's Economic Transition," *The China Quarterly* 154 (June 1998): 254–82. See a rebuttal of his arguments in Yang, "The Resilience of Guanxi and Its New Developments: A Critique of Some New Guanxi Scholarships," *The China Quarterly* 170 (June 2002): 459–76.

[8] Thomas Gold, "After Comradeship: Personal Relations in China since the Cultural Revolution," *The China Quarterly* 104 (December 1985): 657–75; Martin King Whyte and William Parish, *Urban Life in Contemporary China* (Chicago: University of Chicago Press, 1984); Andrew G. Walder, *Communist Neo-Traditionalism: Work and Authority in Chinese Industry* (Berkeley: University of California Press, 1986).

[9] Guthrie, "The Declining Importance of Guanxi," 254–82.

unprecedented opportunities for grand new favors and rents, often chunks of the old or new economy. Second, the nature, value, and basis of social relationships have changed. Deepened commercialization and material stakes have eroded, and sometimes neutralized, the weight of affective ties and rendered routine the exchange of bribes and favors, even in affective relationships. As a result, the post-1992 period has witnessed the decline of noncash bribes and the routinization of cash bribes. Mayfair Yang's insider/outsider dichotomy is no longer meaningful, at least regarding officials' treatment of favor solicitors.[10]

The incentives for the buyers of corruption (bribe givers) have shifted from mixed benign and unscrupulous to mostly malevolent over time. In the early reform period, the revisionist argument that bribes help to overcome structural deficiencies and get around cumbersome bureaucratic regulations was more applicable to nonstate actors who tried to overcome entry barriers the early days. However, the same argument applies poorly to the plethora of speculators, fraudulent investors, and producers, smugglers, and tax cheaters. Instead, the negative effects cited by corruption's critics are on target. Since the early 1990s, bribers' motives have generally corresponded to the characterization of corruption's critics. Instead of structural inequalities, favor seekers are now driven by explicitly self-serving advantages: commercial benefits, monopoly benefits, underhanded competition, property thefts, tax frauds, regulatory oversight, and judiciary partiality.

CORRUPTION AND THE TRANSITION TO THE MARKET

Just as the course of reform has shaped the changing characteristics of corruption, corruption has impacted the course of reform in complex ways. In the first period, the evidence presented in this book lends support to those who argue for the variability of corruption's effects. In the second period, it validates those who emphasize its negative consequences.

Corruption and Models of Post-Socialist Transition

Should corruption's effects be measured against the prereform economy or a well-functioning market? The implicit question here is: is corruption a necessary price to pay for the transition to the market? While the necessity of

---

[10] Mayfair Mei-Hui Yang, "The Gift Economy and State Power in China," *Comparative Studies in Society and History* 31:1 (1989): 25–54.

reform should not be a rationale for tolerating corruption, the answer is somewhat easier in China's earlier reform period. To start from some key questions raised in the Introduction, how did China escape the big bang logic? Was China exceptional and why? I suggest that corruption played a meaningful, if unintended, role in China's initial reform. Unlike Soviet officials under Gorbachev, Chinese officials did not resist reform because China's gradualism allowed them to retain some old functions and acquire new ones. Rather than worrying about losing power, they were able to put their old and new powers to profitable use, and they had a direct and personal interest in ensuring that public policies did not inhibit their market-related activities. Along with legitimate arrangements of profit sharing, corruption helped to act as a solvent for the uncompromisable issues of ideology and interests by turning potential opponents of reform into participants. Rent seeking was the price for institutional stability, but perhaps a necessary price given alternative scenarios.[11] Such institutional stability seemed feasible, as the dominant forms of corruption at the time exploited loopholes of China's largely successful reform policies. By contrast, economic reforms were stalled either by bureaucratic foot-dragging in the Gorbachev era or by bureaucratic plundering after the Soviet collapse.

On the receiving end of corruption, nonstate businesses played a special role in China's reform course. At a time when SOEs were still guaranteed state allocation and distribution, their favor-buying activities helped to level the playing field. Nonstate actors also served as the main constituencies for cadre corruption, providing officials with opportunities to cash in their (old) allocative and (new) regulatory powers in the market. To say that nonstate actors played a major role in the corruption of the early reform period, however, is not to say that corruption played a major role in their spectacular growth. It was one of the contributing factors. The survival and growth of the nonstate sector, especially TVEs, in turn helped to sustain the Chinese sequence of reform. Indeed, one explanation of China's seeming exceptionalism in defying the logic of the interdependence of economic and political reform emphasizes the role of a leading sector, TVEs, which served as the institutional basis of the Chinese sequence of reform.[12] By contrast, in Gorbachev's Soviet Union, where a viable nonstate sector was lacking, it was difficult to introduce new economic institutions.[13] Gorbachev's initial re-

[11] Steven Solnick, "The Breakdown of Hierarchies in the Soviet Union and China," *World Politics* 48:2 (January 1996): esp., 230–38.

[12] Steven Goldstein, "China in Transition: The Political Foundations of Incremental Reform," *The China Quarterly* 144 (December 1995): 1108–21.

[13] Marshall Goldman, "The Chinese Model of Reform: The Solution to Soviet Economic Ills?" *Current History* 92:576 (March 1993): 320–24.

strictions on private business exacerbated the problem. The related failure of
partial reform contributed crucially to the eventual adoption of the big-bang
approach. Once the old economy collapsed, the functional void left by the
retreat of the state and the lack of effective new institutions was filled by a
new economic oligarchy and organized crime. The predatory behavior of
these two groups, in contrast to the productive and dynamic role of Chinese
nonstate actors, has had a strangling impact on the Russian economy. Their
dominance has created a pattern of corruption in Russia that falls under
Rose-Ackerman's model of "bilateral monopoly" or even a "mafia-dominated state."[14]

Why did the Soviet cadre not find economic reform lucrative enough to
embrace it? Judging from their post-Soviet behavior, it is certainly not because it had more moral or ideological commitment than its Chinese counterpart. Three explanations are possible. First, official privileges were greater
in the elitist Soviet Union than in Mao's egalitarian China. Second, a con-
stituency for market-related corruption never developed to China's scale under Gorbachev. Although the Soviet Union had a de facto two-track system
of a sort, created by the black market and enterprise reforms, China's dynamic
nonstate sector presented much greater rent-seeking pressures on officials.
Finally, limited expansion of market activities under Gorbachev failed to
broaden cadres' power into significant new areas of government regulation. In short, Soviet officials had greater incentives to resist economic reform than to utilize it to their advantage. Once the Soviet system collapsed
and shock therapy applied, corruption could not duplicate its effects under
China's gradualism, that is, it could not delay political reform while sustain-
ing economic reform. Rather, systemic disintegration created irresistible opportunities for wholesale plundering of state properties, from Russia's huge
accumulation of fixed assets to her rich deposits of natural resources.

During China's market phase of reform after 1992, however, corruption's
effects can no longer be measured against the prereform economy. Cadre support for reform and compensatory incentives for nonstate actors are no
longer issues. Transgressions and violations no longer serve to loosen up the
rigidities of the planned economy. The level and scope of corruption is no
longer moderate, nor are the affected sectors and official ranks. Systematically
predatory of the old economy and obstructive of the new, corruption in the
second period has had significantly different consequences. Rather than
complimenting ongoing reforms, it has contributed to the key bottlenecks

---

[14] Rose-Ackerman, *Corruption and Government,* 121–24. For a comparison of the Chinese and
Russian case, see Yan Sun, "Reform, State, and Post-Communist Corruption," *Comparative Politics*
32:1 (October 1999): 1–20.

in the post-1992 transition: impasses of SOE reforms, distresses of state financial institutions, discrediting of law enforcement and judicial organs, excessive financial burdens on farmers and businesses, disorganization and deviance of state agencies/agents, misallocation and misdistribution of resources, and fiscal deprivation of the central state. Amid the scrambling for state properties and land assets, post-1992 (and especially post-1997) corruption has shown signs of convergence toward the Russian-type of "spontaneous privatization." Only the lack of systemic disintegration has so far prevented any large-scale, outright plundering. Here, the strength of the Chinese state in the institutional and political dimensions of its capacity, as defined in the Introduction, has served to differentiate the new market economy of China from that of Russia's. The weakness of the Russian state in these dimensions, thanks to sharp intraelite conflicts and strong business pressures, results in a combination of bureaucratic capitalism—where political and administrative elites have the power to control market behavior and rewards—oligarchic capitalism, where an interlocking group of wealthy businessmen monopolize access to policymakers and national resources while restricting domestic and international competition,[15] and mafia-ridden booty capitalism. Indeed, the Russian case exemplifies how the weakness of state institutions can contribute to corruption and organized crime on a pervasive scale.[16] Corruption and organized crime also plague the former Soviet Republics of Central Asia and the Balkan countries of East Central Europe. The domination of legitimate businesses by criminal groups has created serious dangers for economic development, breeding a precarious domestic business environment and driving away foreign competition. Not surprisingly, foreign direct investment from legitimate businesses has been meager in the countries of the former Soviet Union. By contrast, the institutional and political strengths of the Chinese state have helped to avoid possibly the worst combination in a postsocialist context: the amalgamation of bureaucratic capitalism, oligarchic capitalism, and booty capitalism. What emerges in the Chinese case is more consistent with bureaucratic capitalism: one in which political and administrative elites have the power to control market behavior and rewards, and the primary beneficiary of rent extraction is based on the administrative apparatus of the state. In other words, China could have had it even worse.

[15] Cynthia Roberts and Thomas Sherlock, "Bringing the State Back In—Explanations of the Derailed Transition to Democracy," *Comparative Politics* 31:4 (July 1999): 485–86; and Joseph R. Blasi, Maya Kroumova, and Douglas Kruse, *Kremlin Capitalism: Privatizing the Russian Economy* (Ithaca: Cornell University Press, 1997)

[16] Rose-Ackerman, *Corruption and Government,* 23–25.

Efficiency and Obstruction of Competition

Does corruption obstruct or improve efficiency? This is one of the central questions raised in the corruption literature in evaluating corruption's effects, especially transaction-type corruption. According to Rose-Ackerman, bribery may be differentiated between competition for fixed supply of government services and competition for variable supply of government benefits. In the first model, if the corrupt market operates efficiently, the goods and services should go to the seekers with the most willingness to pay. This "market clearing" bribe, as Rose-Ackerman calls it, will be equivalent to the price in an efficient market. The state could have legally sold the goods and services with the same result, except the distribution of revenues—the bribes—go to officials whereas legal payments go to the government coffer. Ideally, although illegal payoffs should act like market prices in this first situation, Rose-Ackerman finds that in reality secrecy and insider deals render a corrupt system less competitive and more uncertain than a legal market. In the second situation, competition for variable supply of government benefits, she finds that corruption is almost certain to lead to inefficiency, as the greater discretion of officials allows them to maximize the manipulation of the quantity and quality of services.[17] In either case, she argues against the revisionist postulation that bribery be regarded as incentive bonuses ("speed money") and as mechanisms to reduce bureaucratic roadblocks. For one cannot rely on bribe payers to judge selectively what constitute inefficient rules and taxes.[18]

Interestingly, each type of corrupt competition, as described by Rose-Ackerman above, respectively characterizes the dominant patterns of transaction-type corruption in China's first and second reform period. During the first, above-quota goods and other extra-plan benefits amounted to fixed supply of benefits that were available for government and enterprise officials to allocate at discretion. Moreover, they were available mainly to those officials who had control over specific goods and services within specific departments and enterprises. Though widespread, the corrupt market for above-quota allocation did not really act like a legal market. Bribe payers were usually insiders, so that neither bribe prices nor supply information were available to the public. Bribe payers were able to hike prices when reselling the favors in the market. If the above-plan track was intended to reward the more efficient producers and increase market supply, illegal payoffs added a

[17] Ibid., 12–14.
[18] Ibid., 21–22.

costly and arbitrary "middle man," or many middle men, thus distorting the original intent of government program. In short, monopoly benefits and speculative profiteering were the major negative consequences of corrupt competition in the first period.

However, corruption's worst effects were also mitigated in this period because of the presence of three conditions. One is when the ties among the transaction parties were more affective. Affective ties ensured lower transaction costs (size of bribes) and more favorable outcomes—guaranteed favors, cheaper goods, or adequately finished projects. The second is when corruption transactions enabled less-privileged groups to gain access to the economy and government services. To the extent that some less-privileged actors were able to get around formal discriminatory policies, their survival and thriving through the "cracks" of the economy did indeed increase competition. But the process also created a different set of market barriers and corroded the overall business climate. In particular, the thriving of TVEs, based in part on corrupt competition, had been at the expense of SOEs in this regard. Finally, in this period, corruption was concentrated in the *allocating process*, where "who gets what at what prices" was determined, rather than in the *decision-making process* where "what policies and projects" were determined. In the former, arguably, corruption's effects were more tempered than they were in the latter, an occurrence more common in the second period.

During the second period, officials' discretion over the quantity, quality, and recipients of services has greatly expanded, contributing to what Rose-Ackerman calls variable supply of benefits and beneficiaries. As a result, the corrupt market has worsened and inefficiency aggravated for several reasons. Foremost, every local government, state agency, and public enterprise now has a great deal of sectarian discretion over how much benefit to supply to the public and how much to extract from it. This discretion is often embodied in the personal discretion of the chief executive. Compounded by policy ambiguities, local protectionism, absent supervision, and weak rule of law, each organization or its chief can try to maximize personal benefits from its strategic position for supplies and services they administer. The result is an inefficient and unfair market for almost everything that affects the general public or the private sector. Second, for services where standards are required—such as qualification for a contract, a project, a loan, land development, import authorization, or tax privileges—unqualified individuals and firms are likely to be the most willing to pay and pay handsomely. The result is either the undermining of the qualification process and violation of regulations, or "corruption with theft," such as exemption from legal payments like customs duties or taxes.[19]

[19] Andrei Shleifer and Robert Vishny, "Corruption," *Quarterly Journal of Economics* 108 (1993): 601.

If corruption has indeed been more negative on economic transition, how is one then to understand the fact that China's growth rates have been even more impressive in the second period? Distributional inequities may be a key answer. While market transition and economic performance may have been more impressive than in the first period, the higher growth of the second period has not meant a better economy or larger economic pie for all social groups, thanks importantly to corruption. In fact many groups have had it worse in the second period.

Distributional Inequalities and Social Stability

With its emphasis on economic costs and efficiency issues, the corruption literature in the English language often neglects distributional consequences of corruption. Yet in the Chinese context, distributional considerations often outweigh other factors. They also crucially affect public reactions to reform and regime legitimacy. Both analysts and the public in China tend to see corruption as a main reason for social polarization since reform. The injustice of this polarization, perceived to be rooted in corruption, has been a constant source of public indignation from Tiananmen protests to periodic peasant and labor unrest. In this book, I have confirmed that two groups have benefited most from corruption: perpetrators inside the officialdom and recipients of official favors outside it. Have these groups got "rich first" mainly by illegal means, as the Chinese public generally perceives? This book does not provide direct answers to that. What the book does show is the various arenas of corruption that have contributed to the sense of relative and absolute deprivation among social groups. As studies of modernization and revolution have shown, relative deprivation can be a potent impetus for social mobilization and protest movements.[20]

Above all, there is uneven distribution of profit-seeking opportunities among public officeholders and those without such office, as well as among public officeholders from more "lucrative" agencies and those without such "substantive" powers. Strategically located officials have been able to dispense marketable favors, appropriate public funds, extract public levies, and extort fines. This "easy" and quick path to wealth is not only unavailable to nonoffice holders but is a detriment to the latter. The socioeconomic consequence here is especially visible in the second period. State-owned-enterprise workers have seldom benefited from the privatization or "stockfication" of their firms. The general public has not benefited from the massive concession of

---

[20] E.g., Samuel Huntington, *Political Order in Changing Societies* (New Haven: Yale University Press, 1968).

public land and properties to new private owners, nor from the overpriced
land developments that result from repeated speculation of land and building contracts, nor from the wide range of fees and charges levied by local
agencies, nor from the shady constructions and failed infrastructural projects
caused by abuse and negligence, nor from the type of "law enforcement by
fines" practiced by some police agencies and courts. Poor farmers and citizens of underdeveloped regions have not benefited much from the state's developmental assistance and programs. And to those officeholders with only
fixed salary incomes, the excessive wealth of other officials must certainly
have come from the multitude of strategically endowed venues for self-enrichment. This is the very pressure that has driven the purchase of office, especially in underdeveloped regions.

Second, there is an uneven distribution of interest allocation and profiteering opportunities, which generates real and perceived distributional inequities across regions and sectors. Favorably located localities such as coastal
regions and urban centers have been able to enjoy developmental opportunities, commercial activities, preferential policies, and geographical advantages not found in less geographically and structurally endowed regions,
affording the former many more avenues for the exchange of power and
money. Interior, northern, and underdeveloped regions have lagged behind,
not because they have greater and graver corruption to begin with, as some
have claimed.[21] Rather, their lack of development has contributed to peculiar types of corruption that particularly impede development.

Third and importantly, there is uneven distribution of benefit sharing between managers and employees of public enterprises at SOEs. Managers endowed with autonomous powers have been able to make self-interested
decisions at the expense of enterprises and workers. Despite the increase of
offenders in government agencies, SOE managers remain the largest group of
violators, especially among the nontransaction types of corruption. Though
not all SOE failures in recent years can be blamed on managerial corruption,
the latter is often a major cause for the bankruptcy of smaller SOEs and those
whose operations are not seriously affected by globalization. The failure of
Beijing's once mighty Capital Steel Company, of Shenyang's once dominant
industrial economy, of Zhanjiang's sugar industries, of Chongqing's imported
LCD and CCD manufacturing line, and of the Yifeng Trading Company of
Hunan, to cite just a few dramatic examples from this book, can be directly
and exclusively attributed to top-level corruption among city and company

---

[21] S. N. S. Cheung, "Simplistic General Equilibrium Theory of Corruption," *Contemporary Economic Policy* 14 (1996): 1–5.

officials. At least partly due to corruption, SOE workers have been the major victims of market transition in the second period. Laid off en masse, often owned years of back pay and benefits, and sometimes deprived of minimal levels of unemployment payments, jobless workers have become a routine sight in industrial cities and urban centers. They have become the leading source of social instability.

At the other end, this book confirms that the bulk of the buyers of official favors come from several key groups: entrepreneurs, contractors, traders, TVEs, and other nonstate firms in the first reform period, joined by SOEs in the second reform period. Several distributional consequences follow. Unfair competition from nonstate actors has disadvantaged SOEs, which are subject to state accounting procedures, as well as those nonstate businesses unable to buy official access. Poor products and substandard constructions have enriched contractors, suppliers, and builders, but undermined public interests and investments. Influence-peddled project awarding and property allocation have favored less scrupulous state firms and managers, as have bribe-based bank lending and investment financing. Unprofitable ventures, in turn, have contributed to wasteful undertakings, nonperforming loans, and insolvent banks. Defaulted and nonperforming loans have troubled banks and undermined the health of the country's financial system. Evasion and cheating of taxes and tariffs have reduced state revenues, forced localities to resort to levies, passed fiscal burdens onto the public, and shortchanged both the immediate pressing needs of society and long-term developmental goals of the country.

All of these have also greatly skewed income distribution, as unscrupulous players have been more likely and quickly to profiteer and prosper. And distributional inequities, fostered by corrupt activities, have done the most to inflame the public's sense of injustice, undermine public confidence in reforms, and pose serious threats to social and political stability. As Chen Feng's study of labor protests has shown, workers' motivation to protest increases and their militancy intensifies if they believe that their economic plight is exacerbated by managerial corruption at the workplace, that is, if managers are perceived as enriching themselves at the expense of firms and workers.[22] And as this author has observed on the role of corruption in the 1989 Tiananmen movement, members of those government agencies, public organizations, and socioeconomic sectors kept out of *guan dao* activities (official profiteering) were most likely to participate in the protest movement.[23]

[22] Feng Chen, "Subsistence Crises, Managerial Corruption, and Labor Protests in China," *The China Journal* (July 2000): 41–63.
[23] Yan Sun, "The Chinese Protests of 1989: the Issue of Corruption," *Asian Survey* 31:8 (1991): 762–82.

Nontransaction Corruption and Dissipation of Public Resources

Students of corruption in the West, accustomed to market economies, often neglect nontransaction types of corruption. But in an economy with significant public investments and a lingering public sector, nontransaction types remain significant. In the absence of patron–client exchange, access to the public coffer is the key feature of this one-way corruption. Embezzlement, misappropriation, accounting violation, squandering, and negligence (as treated in this book) have all been made possibly by the presence of the public coffer. Organized smuggling and tax frauds are essentially nontransaction corruption, since the net result is the depletion of the public coffer by defrauded taxes, tariffs, and refunds. Nontransaction types can be more detrimental and cause greater social waste in both relative and absolute terms. However, their consequences have been scantily noted by students of corruption, as corruption has almost become synonymous with two-way exchanges in the corruption literature.

In the Chinese context, several economic consequences result from nontransaction types of corruption, depending on what officials do with the looted public funds. Absolute financial losses result for society when hoarding, consumption, capital flight, defrauding (of loans, contracts, rebates, etc.), and market losses (i.e., funds lost in speculative activities) occur. The likelihood of hoarding, consumption, and capital flight, in particular, is increased by the criminal nature of embezzlement. Second, serious financial losses are incurred when firm assets are diverted or plundered, custom duties and industrial taxes evaded, profits underreported or unreported, losses written off and costs inflated. Only the diversion of SOE assets to private businesses or outside-run firms presents less than clear-cut scenarios. Does such illicit transfer of ownership result in economic efficiency, since the de facto privatization entails changes in incentive structures? The reality does not seem so sanguine. While increased profits go to the new owners, the losses are surely passed back to the original SOEs. Moreover, improved profitability will likely come less from innovation and efficiency than the displacement of the SOE workforce by migrant labor, dependence on the resources and markets already built by SOEs, and reliance on SOEs as a fallback mechanism. Any efficiency improvements are more than likely to be balanced by the distributional consequences and social stability costs.

Interestingly, as China's marketization has deepened in the second reform period, nontransaction corruption has not shrunk. Instead it has grown in size and scale. The main reason is the drastic expansion of the sources and sizes of the public coffer and public investments, as well as of the opportunities and temptations for appropriation: from nibbling away at state assets from within the state economy in the first reform period to snatching chunks of the state economy in the second period.

THE NATURE OF THE STATE AND POST-SOCIALIST CORRUPTION

I have demonstrated that a progressive worsening of corruption has been re-inforced by a progressive weakening of the state, contrary to neoliberal con-tentions in China and popular discourses in the West that blame an excessive state.

Before the early 1990s, the erosion of the state was tempered by the lin-gering plan track. This contradictory feature spurred opportunistic trans-gression, which was largely contained in the irrational joints of the mixed system. Thus, while plan commands no longer dominated decision making at state agencies and firms, the erosion of the state applied mainly to the above-plan portions. Moreover, while routine decision powers were devolved to firms or local governments, the latter still largely depended on higher state agencies for material, financial, personnel, and institutional support. Further-more, while SOE reforms during this phase (responsibility, contract, and lease systems) progressively weakened the state by separating ownership from man-agement, the state did not relinquish ownership as a matter of principle or practice, thus closing doors to wholesale plundering. In addition, while the separation of the party and the state at local levels proceeded at the expense of the party, routine appointments and promotions still required the formal approval of superior agencies. Grass-roots offices of the DIC, moreover, sur-vived in most public institutions—in part because these institutions still ex-isted intact. If mechanisms and a reputation for discipline were crucial for maintaining links of hierarchical authority, they largely existed and persisted only in the first reform phase.

In terms of its influence over the economy and its capacity against abuse, the state has become progressively weakened since radical reforms in 1992. The state has lost much control over local agencies, agents, and firms by virtue of its deprecated power over local economies, factors of production, and per-sonnel matters. This weakening can be seen in various ways. By handing over discretionary power to the chief executive, the state has opened the way for arbitrary exercise of power. By removing its claims on ownership of public properties and resources, the state has given license to diversion and dilution of state assets. While local chiefs still need the approval of higher state agen-cies to be appointed and promoted, personnel matters at lower ranks have become their independent prerogatives, allowing them to assign partners in crime to key posts. The ability to make sectarian policies, aided by expanded autonomy and commercialization of state agencies, leads to misuse of levy rights over legitimate or illegitimate services by local agencies. This not only usurps the state's extractive power, but also misrepresents and distorts the state at local levels.

Higher state agencies, moreover, can no longer police where the levies and expenses go. Strong sectarian benefits to local agencies, in contrast to depleted state fiscal capabilities, have played an important role in preventing the state from building a strong, loyal cadre corps at local levels or an effective checking and enforcement mechanism. The growing independence of localities—especially local chiefs—has also weakened disciplinary and supervisory agencies, which are dependent on and accountable to local governments and party committees. The reduction of party branches to nominal existence, or even their virtual decapitation at the grass-roots, has undermined yet another traditional mechanism of control. The deemphasis of ideological and moral criteria and the inattention to viable substitutes have disarmed the state on the normative front. Finally, the difficulty of actual enforcement has frequently made a formality of the state's anticorruption rules and mechanisms.

The crux of the change in the strength of the state, in short, is the declining ability of the center to control its agencies and agents in light of their expanding power.

Missing Links in the Transition to the Market

Fundamentally, the weakening of the state stems from the difficulties of transforming an economy based on command mechanisms to one based on regulatory mechanisms. In many areas of the new market economy, regulatory mechanisms are ostensibly missing or deficient. And in areas where many new mechanisms have been put into place, enforcement is equally missing or deficient. Both problems have led to open loopholes and easy abuse. These are the missing links in the building of state capacity during the transition to the market.

Foremost among these are the missing links in the accounting system. Under central planning, budgetary and fiscal matters were relatively simple for public organizations and outside reviewers. But they have been complicated by the multiplication of financial sources, expansion of expenditure, and enhancement of local autonomy. How can the independence of in-house accountants be ensured while agencies and firms have become so autonomous? How can outside reviewers keep track and monitor the flow of revenues and expenses, levies and fines, slush funds and investment earnings on a routine basis? How can shareholders and workers monitor the expense accounts and reimbursements of key executives? Missing links are also apparent in the enforcement of contract bidding laws. How should the credentials for bidders and standards for bidding be determined, and by whom? How should the integrity of the appraisal and verification processes be ensured? What about the standards and procedures of quality inspection? What agencies and agents should enforce the relevant rules and mechanisms?

Equally evident are missing mechanisms in the appraisal process and management of state assets. Amid the onslaught of shareholding reforms, standards, procedures, and regulations for appraising SOE properties remain either muddled or weakly enforced. Some assets may be inherently impossible to appraise, but others are not—for instance, revenues, expenses, loans, credits, and leases. The management of rearranged state assets requires not only new rules but even more importantly, enforcers of rules. Much emphasis has been placed on granting firms more autonomy and decision power, but little on penalties for mismanagement, bad decision making, and operational losses. Much acclaim has been given to the "stockification" of public firms, yet scant attention has been paid to enforcing rules about dividing and buying IPOs and other shares. Missing mechanisms are also apparent in the supervision of purchase and marketing procedures at firms and retail businesses. How can transparency about price and quality competition be assured? What mechanisms will protect against the use of commissions in exchange for poor and fake products? How can the government safeguard against frauds in invoicing, payments, and deliveries?

State monitoring is particularly weak over the ability of agencies and firms to creatively raise revenues, extract levies, operate affiliate businesses, and spend illegal incomes on their own, all without being accountable to any other source of authority. Some local governments openly set up numerical targets for levies (*chuangshou zhibiao*) for subordinate agencies. The targets must be fulfilled before full allocation of local state funding will be made. If public organizations are permitted to spend the money they raise, they have obvious incentives to raise them arbitrarily and illicitly. Should they get approval for charging and raising services fees? Can nonprofit public agencies operate for-profit businesses? If so, how can these earnings be monitored? Additionally, the traditional practice of material perks for ranked cadre remains a reservoir of unchecked and unregulated abuse. The practice is a legacy of wartime communism when supplies were limited. But the expansion of extra-budget resources, coupled with weakened state supervision, has led to elaborate use of public funds that is no longer confined to work-related ne-

cessities or to key officials. Should the old perks of a bygone era be eliminated? If not, how should their responsible usage be monitored?

Finally, the existing system of disciplinary control is functionally ill equipped
to deal with abuse arising out of the transitional economy and does not address new issues of conflicts of interests. Despite the tripartite monitoring
structures—party discipline, state supervision, and law enforcement—the
checking system lacks the political and financial independence to control errant officials, especially at local levels. Disciplinary agencies can seldom bring
down key officials at its equivalent administrative level, that is, the level it is
supposed to supervise. It is almost always done with the involvement of party
committees and disciplinary agencies at the next higher level. Most nationally known cases have been exposed and investigated because of the involvement of the central DIC. How to address the contradictions and ineffectiveness
of anticorruption mechanisms will be a long-term daunting challenge for the
Chinese system.

State Building and the Transition to the Market

Students of post-Communist transition have identified the failure of state
building as the central reason for derailed transition to market democracy, especially in post-Soviet Russia.[24] Some attribute the failure to the political
strategy of the reform elite.[25] Others blame their neoliberal ideology, which
led the government to neglect state building while placing undue faith in the
"invisible hand."[26] Still others find the Russian leaders to have lost control
over much of the process after launching economic reform without building basic institutions in the postcollapse context.[27] The result is pervasive
lawlessness, corruption, and rent seeking in post-Soviet Russia.[28] The problem also persists in other former Soviet Republics and to a lesser extent in
Central European economies.[29]

[24] See a review of recent studies on the Russian transition by Roberts and Sherlock, "Bringing
the State Back In," 477–97.

[25] Adam Przworski, *Democracy and Market: Political and Economic Reformers in Eastern Europe and
Latin America* (Cambridge: Cambridge University Press, 1991): 165ff; Peter Rutland, "Has Democracy Failed Russia?" *National Interest* (winter 1994–95): 3–12.

[26] Peter Stavraski, *State Building in Post-Soviet Russia: The Chicago Boys and the Decline of Administrative Capacity* (Washington, D.C.: Kennan Institute, 1993).

[27] Roberts and Sherlock, "Bringing the State Back in," 478.

[28] CSIS Task Force, ed., *Russian Organized Crime and Corruption—Putin's Challenge* (Washington,
D.C.: Center for Strategic and International Studies Press, 2000); Victor Sergeyev, *The Wild East:
Crime and Lawlessness in Post-Communist Russia* (Armonk, N.Y.: M. E. Sharpe, 1998).

[29] William L. Miller, Abe Grodeland, and Tatyana Koshechkina, eds., *A Culture of Corruption: Coping with Governance in post-Communist Europe* (Budapest: Central Europe Press, 2001); Daniel Kaufmann, "Diminishing Returns to Administrative Controls and the Emergence of the Unofficial
Economy: A Framework of Analysis and Applications to Ukraine," *Economic Policy* (supplement, December 1994): 52–69.

In comparison with some other transitional economies, especially Russia and other former Soviet republics, state capacity has not deteriorated to the worst possible levels nor weakened in all dimensions in the Chinese case. In the institutional dimension, intraelite conflict is less polarized in China than in the transitional democracies, not least Russia. The political and economic rules of the game remain fairly well defined and legitimated among political elites, and occasional deviants such as Zhao Ziyang are easily contained. Politicians have sufficient autonomy to attempt state building, because minimized intraelite polarization mitigates the need to allocate state resources to attract and cement political allies. In fact the post-Mao elite has been overwhelmingly supportive of efforts to combat corruption. In the political/social dimension, state autonomy from society and sufficient societal compliance—akin to that enjoyed by East Asian regimes during their authoritarian reigns—allay pressures for political exchange. However, bureaucratic self-interests and increased local autonomy have acted as societal constraints on the enhancement of state capacity, including the state's resolve and capabilities to fight corruption. The potential allies of the state for the task of state building, meanwhile, happen to be among the most removed from state/society links and the most alienated from the state: the aggravated victims of cadre corruption, especially those downsized from state firms that have been bankrupted by corrupt CEOs and those overburdened by arbitrary extractions from village bullies.

It is in the administrative dimension, however, that the Chinese state suffers the most deficiencies. The ability of the central state to provide essential public goods—especially the infrastructure for a market economy, and law and order—and to ensure policy implementation have been seriously weakened by its growing loss of control over fiscal resources, extractive mechanisms, state agencies, and state agents. As shown in chapter 5, while the mechanisms of the party/state to control its agents have been on the decline, the power of state agencies and agents has been rapidly on the rise. The dynamics of this dual development have been the twin processes of decentralization and transformation of state functions in the course of reform. As Lu notes, "Equipped with regulatory power but without effective institutional constraints, state agencies have tapped into the new opportunities to seek profits from the rapidly growing numbers of businesses and other profit or nonprofit organizations. This process takes place at two levels: the department level and the individual level."[30] If the emphasis here is on the tensions of horizontal decentralization (between the state and staff), other analyses emphasizing the tensions of vertical decentralization (between the central and

---

[30] Lu, *Cadre and Corruption,* 252.

local states) are equally compelling. In the juxtaposition between the two loci of power, decentralizing reforms have allowed local officials to tap into their entrenched power base to thwart or distort central policies in both rural and urban sectors.[31] At the very least, long-term conflicts between the central and local states have persisted under reform, especially at the policy implementation level.[32] The reach of the state, at the same time, has been significantly curtailed by the tripartite simultaneous expansion of demands on state capacity, of the power of state agencies and agents, and of the autonomy of local agencies and officials.

Indeed, it is safe to assert that weak administrative capacity is a serious obstacle to the consolidation of markets or democracies in any transitional regime. It is not an easy task even for advanced democracies, all under challenge to modernize capacity amid pressures of globalization. And it is here, in the administrative dimension, that we find what is perhaps the central issue in the study of post-Communist transition: the interaction of transitional sequencing with the problem of the state. Should political transition precede the economic one to found institutions of effectiveness and accountability? Or should economic transition precede the political one to build economic society, property rights, and market infrastructure first? Or should the dual transitions be tackled simultaneously? If China's rampant corruption is often attributed by China's liberal right to the lag of political reform, Russia's pervasive lawlessness is usually blamed by China's liberal left on its radical political reforms that precipitated a dramatic weakening of the state. Yet given national conditions and contexts, neither side can feasibly demonstrate that each country could have tamed its corruption problem had it adopted the other sequence of transition.

Would the total elimination of the public sector have removed incentives for corruption, as China's neoliberals argue? Would democratization have injected transparency and accountability into the Chinese political system, as many Western and Chinese analysts would agree? Or would China have deteriorated to the state of post-Soviet republics, as many Chinese fear? A definitive answer is implausible given diverse national contexts. True to the premise of Chinese neoliberals, the demise of the state in the case of the dual-track system did reduce the type of rent seeking and profiteering dominant

[31] Helen Siu, *Agents and Victims in South China: Accomplices in Rural Revolution* (New Haven: Yale University Press, 1989); Jean Oi, *State and Peasant in Contemporary China* (Berkeley: University of California Press, 1989); and Margaret Pearson, *Joint Ventures in the People's Republic of China* (Berkeley: University of California Press, 1989).

[32] David Lampton, ed., *Policy Implementation in Post-Mao China* (Berkeley: University of California Press, 1987); Wang Shaoguang, "From Revolution to Involution: State Capacity, Local Power, and (Un)governability in China," Unpublished manuscript, 1991.

in the first period. But other state actions that have caused corruption, especially in the second period, are more difficult to remove on philosophical or practical grounds, as they have either been part of national developmental strategies or the transitional process, or simply implausible to hand to the market. Land privatization and distribution, SOE stockification, and bank financing are part and parcel of the state's efforts to withdraw from the economy. Developmental aid, infrastructure building, tax incentives, and import controls are integral to the state's new developmental strategies. Business regulation, awarding of public projects and contracts, law enforcement, and judiciary adjudication are universal across political systems and not usually handled by the market. Even if nonstate agencies are to handle many of the tasks here, there will always remain the question of how to supervise human agents and arbitrary decision processes.

The democratic alternative offers promising anticorruption potential, especially in two areas: media exposure and periodic removal of corrupt officials through democratic processes. Prime Minister Zhu Rongji himself reportedly used media exposure to threaten unruly and corrupt officials. If bad publicity and popular pressure are not welcome in an authoritarian system, they will be even less so in a democratic one. Elections and open media, while unable to guarantee the selection of honest officials, will more easily expose and remove dishonest ones. However, even democracy—especially at its fledging stage—may not be sufficient to constrain corruption, if the experiences of post-Soviet republics and of Chinese villages serve as guides. Both the media and the electoral process have been influenced by monetary contributions, corrupt operators, intimidation, and even the mafia. Already in China, vote buying has emerged as a new form of corruption in township and county-level elections, as has mafia-backed politics.[33] Ma Xiangdong, deputy mayor of Shenyang, ranked among the most corrupt but was elected by Shenyang's NPC over another candidate, who later died fighting a flood on his new post as party secretary of a lesser city. Chinese reporters who expose corruption often encounter dissuasions from the *guanxi* networks of featured offenders, intimidation phone calls, personal slander, and physical violence. Even before its actual publication, the medium of a corruption story may receive warning calls, threats of libel suits, and nasty visitors.[34]

[33] Che Xiaohui, "Defeating the Effort to Buy the County's Magistrate's Election," DFLZ 12 (2001): 25–27; Li Shuangquan, "Buying Votes to Become Deputy County Magistrate, Going to Prison before Official Cap is Warm," DFLZ 2 (2002): 20–22; Liu Hai-yi, "Alert: China's Mafia Groups Are Penetrating into Politics," DFLZ 4 (2001): 14–16.

[34] Ye Hualong and Zheng Ruoru, "Strengthen Supervision by the Media and Public Opinions, Promote the Building of Party Ethics and Government Integrity," DFLZ 5 (2001): 24–26.

And as transitional democracies have shown, it takes time for a democratic culture to take root, for democratic procedures and practices to be taken seriously, and for rule of law to become habitual. Not surprisingly, while Chinese anticorruption agencies and agents make frequent visits to Western countries for new ideas and practices, it is the laws and practices of Singapore and Hong Kong—with their strong apparatus and impressive track records—that interest Chinese legal and disciplinary professionals most. Chinese scholars also like to point out that established democracies in China's neighborhood have proven to be no guarantees against rampant and chronic corruption: India, Philippines, and even Japan.[35] At the same time, a democratizing system also entails structural vulnerabilities. Contrasting the process of corruption in Communist and post-Communist states, Shleifer and Vishny differentiate between the efficiency effects of different structures of corruption. Centralized structures, such as that of the Communist era, tend to produce joint monopoly, which usually induce a more limited degree of rent seeking. Decentralized structures, on the other hand, tend to produce independent monopoly in the corruption process. This in turn usually encourages fragmented rent seeking and a greater degree of dissipation of rents. Joint monopoly, thus, entails relatively less dissipation and potentially less detrimental outcomes from the standpoint of development.[36] In other words, more decision makers, more discretionary powers, and more decision processes are involved in decentralized structures, leading to more bribes required to get things done. Moreover, outcomes of bribes are also more uncertain in more decentralized structures.[37]

From the Chinese experience, one thing is clear: since the type of corruption has been "path dependent" on the type of opportunities, incentives, and disincentives spurred by the reform process, it would have been difficult to foresee the type of state capacities necessary to safeguard the transition to the market and a regulatory state. Policy correctives and institutional mechanisms against corruption, as it turns out, are also path dependent on learning, situational responses, and then, long-term remedies. In between, the existing state should be well utilized, reformed, and even strengthened, as the main—if not the sole—available fallback mechanism. After all, "most institutional history moves slowly," as Robert Putnam observes, "where institu-

---

[35] Selected speakers at the Second Chinese Political Scientists Forum, at Hong Kong University, August 25–27, 2001.
[36] Shleifer and Vishny, "Corruption," 599. See also Paul Hutchcroft, "The Politics of Privilege: Assessing the Impact of Rents, Corruption, and Clientelism on Third World Development," *Political Studies* 45 (1997): esp. 648–49.
[37] Rose-Ackerman, *Corruption and Government*, 130, 114.

tion building (and not mere constitution writing) is concerned, time is measured in decades."[38] And most relevant for China's path of transition, the state
capacity of its cultural affiliates Singapore and Hong Kong during their developmental stage, especially in the administrative dimension, provide useful
lessons.

[38] Robert Putnam with Robert Leonardi and Raffaella Y. Nanetti, *Making Democracy Work: Civic Traditions in Modern Italy* (Princeton, N.J.: Princeton University Press, 1993): 184.

APPENDIX 1

CASEBOOKS USED

1. Chongqing Branch of the Discipline Inspection Commission of the Central Party Committee, *Dangfeng Lianzheng Wenzhai* (Digest of Party Ethics and Administrative Integrity). Chongqing: Chong Branch of CCPDIC. 1996–2003. A digest of corruption-related reports from periodicals around the country.

2. Discipline Inspection Work Committee of the Central State Organs, *Zhongyang Guojia Jiguan Dangnei Weiji Anli Xuanbian* (Selected Cases of Discipline Violations among Party Members in Central State Organs). Beijing: the People's Publishing House, 1994. A collection of disciplined officials from central state agencies.

3. Luo Jingxuan and Lin Jusheng, eds., *Lianzheng Jiaoyu Anli* (Cases for Education in Honest Administration). Beijing: The Public Security Press of China, 1992. A collection of prosecuted and disciplined officials from the shipping sector.

4. Ying Songnian et al., eds., *Lianzheng, Qinzheng, Suzheng* (Honest Administration, Diligent Administration, and Cleansed Administration). Beijing: The Chinese University of Politics and Law Press, 1992. A collection of prosecuted and disciplined cases from across the country.

5. Wang Lian and Zheng Jie, eds., *Fanfubai Anli Xuanbian* (Selected Corruption Cases). Beijing: The Chinese Financial and Economic Press, 1989. A collection of major corruption cases from 1978 to 1989.

6. Lin Chuduan et al., *Tanwuzui yu Luoyonggongkuanzui Ge'an Yanjiu* (A Study of Embezzlement and Misappropriation Cases) Chengdu: Sichuan University Press, 1992. A collection of disputed, ambiguous cases representative of the reform period.

7. Zhao Changqin et al., *Huiluzui Ge'an Yanjiu* (A Study of Bribery Cases). Chengdu: Sichuan University Press, 1991. Bribery cases representative of the reform period.

8. Zhu Jintao et al, *Jingji Fanzui Bianhu Anli Xuanbian* (Selected Collection of Defended Economic Crime Cases). Changsha: Hunan University Press, 1989. A collection of successfully defended cases involving economic crimes.

9. Editorial Board of the Criminal Case Series of the Supreme People's Procuratorial Office, *Xingshi Fanzui Anli Congshu: Toujidaobazui* (Criminal Case Series: Illegal Profiteering). Beijing: The Chinese Procuratorial Press, 1992. A collection of prosecuted profiteering cases.

10. Editorial Board for the Series on Combating Economic Violations, ed., *Dangqian Jingji Weifa Weiji Fanzui Anli Rending Chuli Pingxi* (The Identification and Treatment of Economic Violations at Present). Beijing: The Chinese Foursquare Press, 1996. A collection of cases representative of the reform period.

SUPPLEMENTARY CASEBOOKS

11. The Chinese Institute of Applied Legal Studies of the Supreme People's Court, ed., *Renmin Fayuan Anlixuan* (Selected Collection of Criminal Cases of the People's Court). Beijing: Renmin Fayuan Chubanshe, 1992–96.

12. Editorial Board of the "Current Crimes and Violations Book Series," *Danqian Tanwu Huilu, Feifa Suode Weifa Weiji Fanzui de Zhengce Falu Jiexian yu Rending Chuli* (The Policy and Legal Definitions, and the Identification and Treatment of Current Crimes and Violations Including Embezzlement, Bribery, and Illegal Earnings). Beijing: the Chinese Foursquare Press, 1995.

13. Editorial Group of the Supreme People's Procuratorate, *Zhongda Tanwu Shouhui Duzhi Zuian Anli Xuanbian* (Selected Collection of Major Embezzlement, Bribery, Malfeasance Crime Cases). Beijing: the Chinese University of Politics and Law Press, 1989.

APPENDIX 2

LIST OF PERIODICALS DIGESTED

Selected periodicals digested in *Dangfeng Lianzheng Wenzhai,* 1990–1998; and in *Dangfeng Lianzheng,* 1998–2003 (Chongqing: Chongqing Branch of CCPCID).

PERIODICALS ON MONITORING AND DISCIPLINARY MATTERS

Bintuan Jijian Jiancha (Discipline Inspection and Administrative Monitoring in the Production Corps)

Changlian Yuekan (Integrity Promotion Monthly)

Changchun Jijian Jiancha (Changchun Discipline Inspection and Administrative Monitoring), Jiling

Changsha Dangfeng Zhengji (Changsha Party Ethics and Administrative Discipline), Hunan

Chenzhong (Bells of Dawn)

Chutian Fengji (Chutian Party Ethics and Discipline), Hubei

Dangfeng (Party Ethics)

Daqing Dangfeng Lianzheng (Daqing Journal of Party Ethics and Administrative Integrity)

Dangfeng Jianshe (Building of Party Ethics)

Dangfeng Lianzheng Yuekan (Monthly Journal of Party Ethics and Administrative Integrity), Jianxi

Dangfeng Tongxun (Communications on Party Ethics), Gansu

Dangfeng yu Dangji (Party Ethics and Party Discipline)

Dangfeng yu Lianzheng (Party Ethics and Administrative Integrity), Ningxia

Dangfeng Yuebao (Party Ethics Monthly), Changzhou, Jiansu

Dangfeng Yuebao (Party Ethics Monthly), Liaoning

Dangji (Party Discipline), Guangxi

Datequ Dangfeng (Party Ethics in the Big Economic Zone)

Fanfu Daokan (Anticorruption Herald)

Fangyuan (Foursquare)

Fangyuan Yuekan (Foursquare Monthly)
Fengji chuang (Windows on Party Ethics and Discipline)
Guizhou Dangfeng Lianzheng (Guizhou Party Ethics and Administrative Integrity)
Jianghuai Fengji (Jianghuai Party Ethics and Discipline), Jiangsu
Jijian Jiancha (Discipline Inspection and Administrative Monitoring), Heilongjiang
Jijian Jiancha (Discipline Inspection and Administrative Monitoring), Yunnan
Jijian yu Jiancha (Discipline Inspection and Administrative Monitoring)
Jiancha Shao (Watchtower)
Jiangsu Jijian (Jiangsu Discipline Inspection)
Jilu Jiancha Xinxi (News on Discipline Inspection)
Jingjian (Mirror Lessons)
Jing Zhong (Alarm Bells)
Ji yu Fa (Discipline and Law)
Lianzheng zhi Sheng (Voice of Honest Government)
Linyi Jijian Jiancha (Linyi Discipline Inspection and Administrative Monitoring), Shandong
Minxing Jijian Jiancha (Minxing Discipline Inspection and Administrative Monitoring), Shanghai
Ming Jian (Clear Warnings or Clear Lessons), Heilongjiang
Nanjing Jijian (Nanjing Discipline Inspection), Nanjing
Qianjiang Lian Chao (Qianjiang Tide of Honesty), Hubei
Qing Feng (Honest Style), Zhenjiang, Jiangsu
Shidai Fengji (Party Ethics and Discipline of the Times)
Shi yu Fei (Right and Wrong), Beijing
Yunnan Jiancha (Yunnan Administrative Monitoring)
Zhengqi (Uprightness), Shanxi
Zhongguo Jilu Jijian Bao (Chinese Discipline and Discipline Inspection Times)
Zhongguo Jiancha (Administrative Monitoring in China)
Zhongguo Jijian Jiancha Bao (Chinese Discipline Inspection and Monitoring Times)

PERIODICALS ON PARTY ORGANIZATION AND PERSONNEL

Dang de Shenghuo (Party Life)
Dangiian Yanjiu (Studies in Party Building)
Dangiian Wenhui (Collected Writings on Party Building)
Dangyuan Te Kan (Special Journal for Party Members)
Dangyuan zhi You (Friends of Party Members)
Dangzheng Fangyuan (The Party and State Corner)
Dangzheng Ganbu Luntan (Forum of Party and State Officials)
Dangzheng Ganbu Xuekan (Studies of Party and State Officials)
Gongchandangyuan (Communist)
Jiguan dongtai (Developments in Government Agencies)
Lingdao Kexue (Leadership Science)
Zhongcheng Weishi (Loyal Guard)
Zhibu Shenghuo (Life in the Party Branch), Shandong

Zhongguo Dangzheng Ganbu Luntan (Forum for Party and State Cadres in China)
Zhuzhi Renshi Bao (Organization and Personnel Times)

PERIODICALS ON RULE OF LAW

An'hui Fazhi Bao (An'hui Legal Times)
Beijing Fazhi Bao (Beijing Legal Times)
Falu yu Xinwen (Law and the Media)
Fazhi Daobao (Legal Herald)
Fazhi Jianbao (Legal Bulletin)
Fazhi Ribao (Legal Daily)
Fazhi Shijie (Legal World)
Fazhi Tiandi (Legal World)
Fazhi yu Jingji (Law and Economics)
Fazhi yu Shehui (Law and Society)
Fazhi Yuekan (Legal Monthly)
Fazhi yu Zhengzhi (Law and Politics)
Fazhi Zhoubao (Legal Weekly)
Guangxi Zhengfa Bao (Guangxi Law and Politics Times)
Hubei Fazhi Bao (Hubei Legal Times), Hubei
Huaibei Dangfeng Lianzheng (Huaibei Party Ethics and Discipline), An'hui
Jiancha Ribao (Prosecutorial Daily)
Jiangxi Fanzhi Bao (Jiangxi Legal Times)
Jingwei Xian (Longitudes and Latitudes), Tianjin
Liaoning Fazhi Bao (Liaoning Legal Times), Liaoning
Mingzhu yu Fazhi (Democracy and Rule of Law)
Renminfayuan Bao (People's Court Times)
Sanxiang Fengji (Sanxiang Party Ethics and Inspection), Hunan
Shandong Fazhi Bao (Shandong Legal Times), Shandong
Shanghai Fazhi Bao (Shanghai Legal Times), Shanghai
Shenzhen Fazhi Bao (Shenzhen Legal Times), Shenzhen, Guangzhou
Tianjin Fazhi Bao (Tianjin Legal Times), Tianjin
Xuzhou Fengji (Xuzhou Party Ethics and Discipline), Xuzhou, Jiangsu
Zhejiang Fazhi Bao (Zhejiang Legal Times)
Zhengfa Xuekan (Studies of Law and Politics)
Zhongguo Jiancha Bao (Chinese Prosecutorial Times)

OTHER PERIODICALS USED IN THIS STUDY

Beifang Shichang Bao (Northern Market Times)
Beijing Ribao (Beijing Daily)
Beijing Shang Bao (Beijing Business Times)
Beijing Shehui Kexue (Beijing Social Sciences)
Fazhi Liaowang (Legal Outlook)

Fa Xue (Legal Studies)
Jiefang Ribao (Liberation Times)
Jingji yu Fa (Economics and Law)
Liao Wang (Outlook Weekly)
Lilun Xuexi Yuekan (Theory Research Monthly)
Makesizhuyi yu Xianshi (Marxism and Reality)
Qiao Bao (Overseas Chinese Times)
Renmin Ribao (People's Daily)
Shehuizhuyi Yanqiu (Studies of Socialism)
She Hui (Society)
Shidai Chao (Tide of the Times)
Xinhua Yuebao (Xinhua Monthly)
Xinhua Wenzhai (Xinhua Digest)
Xueshu Yuekan (Monthly Journal of Research)
Zhengzhi yu Falu (Politics and Law)
Zhongguo Gongshang Bao (Chinese Industry and Commerce Times)
Zhongguo Jingji Shibao (China Economic Times)

LIST OF WORST CONSTRUCTION FAILURES

Selected list of reported worst construction failures in the 1990s due to graft and substandard construction.

COLLAPSE OF RESIDENTIAL BUILDINGS

March 1997   Collapse of an employee apartment building in Jiangkou Township of Putian County, Fujian.

July 1997   Collapse of a five-story residential building in the Southern Development Zone of Changshan County, Zhejiang.

1997   Four residential buildings rendered hazardous by substandard materials and shady workmanship, resulting in a loss of Y1.53 million; in Wangchuan Township, Hui'an County, Fujian.

March 1998   Collapse of two separate buildings on the same day, resulting in more than a dozen deaths and Y7 million lost in construction costs; Nanjing, Jiangsu.

Jan. 1999   Collapse of a brand-new four-story house, killing three construction workers and injuring seven in the Xinsha Development Zone of Changsha County, Hunan.

CRACKING OR COLLAPSE OF BRIDGES AND DRY BRIDGES

Dec. 1998   Sudden collapse of parts of a dry bridge on the Shenyang-Siping Highway, Liaoning Province, causing deadly accidents.

1998   Cracking in fourteen of the seventeen dry bridges on the Foshan-Kaiping Highway, Guangdong Province, several months after their completion at a cost of Y3.278 million.

Dec. 1998   Collapse of a sixty-meter sky bridge, over the main road that passed through Yunyang County in the heart of the Three Gorges project, with a loss of several lives and Y1 million in construction costs; Chongqing.

Dec. 1998   Massive collapse of a dry bridge over the Longquan road during construc-
               tion, in Shapingba borough, Chongqing.

Jan. 1999   Collapse of the Qijiang Rainbow Bridge, completed just a year earlier for
               Y6 million, killing forty people; Chongqing.

SINKING OF HIGHWAYS AND ROADS

Oct. 1998   Sporadic sinking in the Kunming-Luquan Road, Yunnan Province, sixteen
               days after its completion. The road, lying between the provincial capital to
               the Yi and Miao Autonomous Region, was one of the province's major "an-
               tipoverty" projects and cost Y380 million to construct.

1998   Visible wearing and tearing of Interstate 209 at the Tuliu section of Yun
               County, Hubei Province, merely two months after its opening.

CRUMBLING OF DYKES AND EMBANKMENTS

1998   Crumbling of the embankments at the Jiujiang River, Jiangxi Province, de-
               spite (or because of) recent reinforcements in 1994–1996. Steel rods stick-
               ing out of the cracks were only the size of chopsticks.

1998   Failure of all 470 open caissons to meet standards in the construction of the
               Qiantangjiang Dyke, Hangzhou, Zhejiang Province. Designed as major ob-
               stacle structures to block floods, each caisson required at least 3.5 meters of
               concrete filling in the ground. But none was found to be over 1.6 meters.
               The new dyke, five hundred meters in length, cost Y5 million to build and
               was supposed to be Hangzhou's major antiflood project.

POOR CONSTRUCTION OF AIRPORTS AND TRAIN STATIONS

1995   Visible structural flaws in the Beijing West Railway Station shortly after its
               completion in Sept. 1995: mortars falling, rods sticking out, walls and floors
               leaking. Promoted as "Asia's number one train station," the station was one
               of the major infrastructure projects of the central government's "Eighth
               Five-year Plan" and cost Y4.3 million to construct.

Mid-1990s   Runways rendered unusable by low-grade concrete at the Jinan Airport and
               Weifang Airport, both in Shandong Province. They were constructed only
               a few years earlier in 1984 and 1989.

1990s   Two-thirds of rail stands worn-out at the Shanghai Railway Station, merely
               eight years after their installation.

Source: *Yao Zenhua, "Severely Punish Corruption in the Construction Sector,"* DFLZ *5 (May 1999): 16–17.*

APPENDIX 4

LIST OF WORST OFFICE SELLERS

Selected list of reported worst sellers of public office.

He Jianling   Party secretary of Hepu County and later mayor of Beihai city, both in Guangxi, collected Y240,000 for arranging twenty-four job placements and promotions in the late 1990s. The posts included directorships and deputy directorships of the bureaus of construction, trade, foreign trade, customs, treasury, state assets, land, taxes, labor, industrial and commercial regulation, civilian affairs, special economic zones, personnel and organization, legal affairs, etc.

Hu Xuejian   Mayor of Tai'an city of Shandong from 1990–1992 and party secretary from 1992–1995, accepted Y610,000 from forty officials and more than one hundred bribes, including individuals who were to become deputy party secretary of the city, secretary general of the city government, (two) deputy mayors, head of the communications department, and chief of the city police.

Ji Changfu   Director of the organization and personnel bureau for Yangxian County, Shaanxi, promoted four relatives to key county offices in 1996: his wife as deputy director of the statistics bureau, her older brother as director of the auditing bureau, her sister-in-law as director of the construction sector unions, and the latter's brother as deputy head of the economic section of the county court. These posts completed a family dominance over the county's economic life.

Li Chenglong   Party secretary of Yuling County and later mayor of Guigang city of Guangxi during the 1990s, had the highest loot in Guangxi before Cheng Kejie, at Y16 million in bribe taking and other illegal income. Some of the funds came from the sale of offices to leading local private entrepreneurs.

Li Tiecheng   During his tenure as party secretary of Jingyu County of Liaoning from
                   1992–2000, acceptedY1.42 million from 162 individuals for favors re-
                   lating to cadre nomination, appointment, promotion, and transfer. The
                   bribers included almost all officials above the *ke* and *ju* ranks in the
                   county.

Liu Xinnian   Governor of Julu County, Hebei, pocketedY17,000 for selling just two
                   lucrative offices: a deputy head of the county's land administration bu-
                   reau and a deputy head of the supply bureau.

Wang Huling   Party secretary of Changzhi County, Shanxi, in the two months (Feb.–
                   April 1999) before moving to another job, transferred 432 officials and
                   promoted 278 individuals to the *ke* and deputy *ke* rank. The feat earned
                   him the distinction of a "wholeseller of offices."

Wang Xinkang   Governor of Huaxian County of Henan from 1993–1998, made 865
                   cadre transfers, among them 445 promotions. He harvestedY360,000.

Yang Sanxiu   Deputy mayor of Anyang city, Henan, put price tags on office place-
                   ments. For Y6000, he worked hard to promote a factory chief, dis-
                   missed for misconduct, to be a deputy mayor. Yang acceptedY139,620
                   for eighteen promotions.

Zeng Jincheng   Head of the construction bureau of Henan Province and later com-
                   missioner of Zhoukou District, also Henan, accepted Y332,000 for
                   promoting fifteen people.

Zhang Xinlu   Deputy party secretary, party secretary and then governor of Boxin
                   County, Shandong, collected overY80,000 from more than forty peo-
                   ple, mostly for offices.

Zheng Zesheng   Party secretary and later governor of Fengxi County, Shanxi, over the
                   objections of colleagues tried to appoint a convicted embezzler to head
                   the anticorruption section of the prosecutors' office. ForY40,000, the
                   briber wanted to hold the office so there would be no further expo-
                   sure of his problems. Despite two anonymous tips to provincial au-
                   thorities, Zheng managed to appoint him the head of the county's
                   planning bureau.

ZhengYuansheng Party secretary for Guangfeng County, Jiangxi Province, accepted a
                   total of Y140,000 for fifty-three promotions and placements.

Source: *DFLZ, various issues, 1995–2003.*

APPENDIX 5

LIST OF FALLEN GAMBLERS

Selected list of reported officials who have fallen at Macau's casino tables, 1999–2001.

Cen Huanreng   Head of Jiangzhou Township, En'ping city, Guangdong.

Guo Gangling   Head of the Economic TV Station of Xiantao city, Hubei.

Jin Jianpei   CEO of the Hong Kong station of Hubei Yifeng Company, Hubei, the province's "window to the world." Y133 million.

Li Jingfang   Head of the Treasury Department of Shenyang city, Liaoning.

Ma Xiangdong   Executive deputy mayor and member of the Standing Committee of Shenyang city government, Liaoning.

Ning Xianjie   Head of the Construction Commission of Shenyang, Liaoning.

Wei Guangqian   Head of the Liancheng Aluminum Plant of Lanzhou, Gansu.

Wei Huai   CEO of Macau Xinji Trading Company, Ltd., of Foshan city, Guangdong; the city's "window to the world." Y100 million.

Wu Biao   CEO of Ningbo Development and Trust Investment Company; chairmen, board of directors, and CEO of Jinying Group, Ltd., Zhejiang.

Wu Xuezhi   Head of a Vehicle Trading Company (SOE), Shi Yan city, Hebei.

Xie Heting   Guangdong Food Enterprise Group, Guangdong.

Xie Jianzuo   Deputy head of the government office of the Chengqu Borough, Jiangmen city; and CEO of Chengqu E'xiong Enterprise and Development Company, Guangdong.

Ye Defan   Deputy mayor of Hangzhou city, Zhejiang.

Zhang Junfu   Head of the Wuling Vehicle Sales Corporation Ltd., Yunnan.

Zhou   CEO of Xi'an Mechanical and Electric Equipment Corporation, Ltd.,
  Changqing   Shaanxi. Y48 million.

Zhu Chengling   Head of the supplies and marketing bureau of Zhejiang.

Source: DFLZ *6 (2001): 40.*

CHINESE LANGUAGE BIBLIOGRAPHY

CCPDIC Office of Public Promulgation and Education, ed. *Fanfu Changlian Jianghua* (Topics on Fighting Corruption and Promoting Honest Administration). Beijing: Zhonggong Zhongyang Dangxiao Chubanshe, 1994.

The Central Party School. *Tanzhuang Huaifazhe Jie* (Lessons for Violators of Law). Beijing: Zhonggong Zhongyang Dangxiao Chubanshe, 1993.

Chen Bo. *Zhongguo Fanfubai Er'shinian* (Twenty Years of Fighting Corruption in China). Beijing: Renmin Chubanshe, 2000.

Chen Jian. *Liushi de Zhongguo* (The Loss of State Properties in China). Beijing: Chengshi Chbanshe, 1998.

Chen Zhengyun, ed. *Jinrong Fanzui Toushi* (Analyzing Crimes in the Financial Sector). Beijing: Zhongguo Fazhi Chubanshe, 1995.

Cheng Hu and Zhang Lu, eds. *Zhongguo Fangchan Da Texie* (A Report on the Hot Spots in the Property Market). Beijing: Zhongguo Shenji Chubanshe, 1993.

The Chinese Association of Prosecutorial Studies, ed. *Fan Tanwu Shouhui Lunji* (Collected Papers on Controlling Embezzlement and Bribery). Beijing: Zhongguo Jiancha Chubanshe, 1990.

The DIC Office and the Supervisory Office of the Supreme People's Court, eds. *Jijian Jiancha Gongzuo Shouce* (Manual of Disciplinary and Supervisory Work). Beijing: Renmin Fayuan Chubanshe, 1994.

The DIC Office, Supervisory Office, and Marxism-Leninism Research Office of Beijing University, eds. *Fanfubai Zongheng Tan* (Essays on Combating Corruption). Beijing: Beijing Daxue Chubanshe, 1994.

Editorial Board of the Law Yearbook of China. *Zhongguo Falu Nianjian* (Law Yearbook of China). Beijing: Zhongguo Zhengfa Daxue, 1991–2003.

Editorial Board of the Prosecutorial Yearbook of China. *Zhongguo Jiancha Nianjian* (The Prosecutorial Yearbook of China). Beijing: Zhongguo Jiancha Chubanshe, 1991–1999.

Editorial Board of the Supreme People's Procuratorate, ed. *Baochi Lianjie Fandui Fubai Wenxian Xuanbian* (Selected Documents on Upholding Integrity and Fighting Corruption). Beijing: Zhongguo Zhengfa Daxue Chubanshe, 1989.

Gu Xiaorong, ed. *Zhengquan Weifa Fanzui* (Transgressions and Crimes in the Stock Exchange). Shanghai: Shanghai Renmin Chubanshe, 1994.

He Qinglian. *Xiandaihua de Xianjing* (Traps of Modernization). Beijing: Xiandai Zhongguo Chubanshe, 1998.

Hong Wei. *Fanfu da Jucuo* (Major Measures against Corruption). Beijing: Zhongguo Chengshi Chubanshe, 1998.

Hou Shaowen and Zhang Xinbin. *Lianzheng Jianshe Sixiang Baoku* (Reference Materials for Building Honest Government). Shandong: Jinan Chubanshe, 1995.

Hu An'gang. *Zhongguo:Tiaozhan Fubai* (China: Challenging Corruption). Zhejiang: Zhejiang Renmin Chubanshe, 2001.

Jun Ye. *Jieceng de Fubai* (Corruption among Social Strata). Guangdong: Zhuhai Chubanshe 1998.

Lan Bo. *Zai Zousi Kuangchao de Beihou* (Behind the Maddening Wave of Smuggling). Beijing: Gaige Chubanshe, 1999.

Lang Sheng, ed. *"Guanyu Chengzhi Pohuai Jinrong Zhixu Fanzui de Jueding" Shiyi* (Notes on "The Decree on Punishing Crimes of Impairing the Financial Order"). Beijing: Zhongguo Jihua Chubanshe, 1995.

Leadership Group for Fighting Corruption in the Financial Sector, ed. *Fanfubai Gongzuo Wenjian Huibian* (Collected Documents on Anti-Corruption Work). Beijing: Zhongguo Jinrong Chubanshe, 1995.

Li Xiao and Zhao Yan, eds. *Gongheguo Sutan Neimo Jishi* (Inside Report on Fighting Corruption in the People's Republic). Beijing:Tuanjie Chubanshe, 1993.

Liu Guoguang, ed. *Zhongguo zai Yijiujiusannian: Jingji Fazhan de Fenxi yu Yuce* (China in 1993:Analysis and Predictions of Economic Development). Beijing: Zhongguo Sheke Chubanshe, 1992.

Liu Hainian, Li Ling, and Zhang Guangxing. *Yifa Zhiguo yu Lianzheng Jianshe* (Rule of Law and Building Honest Government). Beijing: Fazhi Chubanshe, 1999.

Liu Mingbo, ed. *Lianzheng Sixiang yu Lilun* (Theories of and Reflections on Honest Administration). Beijing: Renmin Chubanshe, 1994.

Liu Ning and Tian Huming, eds. *Zhongguo zhi Tong* (The Agony of China). Beijing:Wenhua Yishu Chubanshe, 2001.

Ma Zhixin. *Quanli Heidong* (The Black Hole of Power). Bejing: Gaige Chubanshe, 1999.

Pan Duola. *Zhongguo de Panduola* (China's Pandora Box).Tianjin:Tianjin Renmin Chubanshe, 2000.

Quan Yanchi. *Deng Pufang yu "Kanghua"* (Deng Pufang and the Kanghua Company).Yunnan:Yunnan Chubanshe, 1994.

Research Department of the DIC Office of Chongqing, ed. *Fanfu Changlian Lu* (Collected Articles on Fighting Corruption and Promoting Integrity). Chongqing: DIC Office of Chongqing, 1991.

Shao Daosheng. *Zhongguo Shehui de Kunhuai* (China's Perplexities). Beijing: Shehui Kexue Chubanshe, 1996.

Wang Huning. *Fanfubai—Zhongguo de Shiyan* (Combating Corruption—the Chinese Experiment). Beijing: Sanhuan Chubanshe, 1993.

Wang Zhifang, Lin Lujian, and Zhang Zhiwei. *Fanfubai Lun* (On Combating Corruption). Hangzhou: Zhejiang Renmin Chubanshe, 1991.

Wei Pingxiong and Wang Ranji. *Tanwu yu Shouhui de Rending he Chuli* (Identifying and Handling Embezzlement and Bribery Cases). Beijing: Qunzhong Chubanshe, 1992.

Wen Ming. *Zhongguo Youchanzhe Baogao* (A Report on the Propertied Class in China). Beijing: Zhongguo Gongshang Lianhe Chubanshe 1999.

Wu Haimin. *Gongheguo Fachu "Zuihou Tongdie"* (The People's Republic Issues the "Ultimatum"). Beijing: Xueyuan Chubanshe, 1990.

Xiao Yang, ed. *Huiluo Fanzui Yanjiu* (A Study of Bribery). Beijing: Falu Chubanshe, 1994.

Ye Sheng and Wang Haijun, eds. *Jingji Tizhi Zhuanbian de Guoji Bijiao* (International Comparison of Economic Restructuring). Beijing: Gaige Chubanshe, 1993.

Yu Min. *Gongheguo Fanfubai Shilu* (Report on Fighting Corruption in the People's Republic). Beijing: Tuanjie Chubanshe, 1993.

Zhao Fengxiang and Qiao Biyang, eds. *Jinrong Jiancha Lilun yu Shijian* (The Theory and Practice of Monitoring Financial Institutions). (Beijing: Zhongguo Jinrong Chubanshe, 1991.

Zhong Shi. *Nie Hai Chen Zhou* (Buried by the Evil Sea). Beijing: Sifang Chubanshe, 1998.

Zhou Changkang, ed. *Shichang Jingji yu Fanzui Kongzhi* (The Market Economy and Control of Crimes). Beijing: Fazhan Chubanshe, 1994.

Zhu Lixin. *Chaban Tanwu Shouhui Anjian Zhifa Shouce* (Manual for the Investigation of Embezzlement and Bribery). Beijing: Zhongguo Jiancha Chubanshe, 2001.

ENGLISH LANGUAGE BIBLIOGRAPHY

Aoki, Masahiko, and Hyung-Ki Kim. *Corporate Governance in Transitional Economies: Insider Control and the Role of Banks.* Washington D.C.: World Bank, 1995.

Aslund, Anders. *Gorbachev's Struggle for Economic Reform.* London: Pinter, 1989.

———, ed. *Economic Transformation in Russia.* New York: St. Martin's Press, 1994.

———. *How Russia Became a Market Economy.* Washington, D.C.: The Brookings Institute, 1995.

Bardhan, Pranab. "Corruption and Growth: A Review of Issues." *Journal of Economic Literature* 35 (September 1997): 1320–46.

Bayley, David H. "The Effects of Corruption in a Developing Nation." *Western Political Quarterly* 19 (1966): 719–23.

Ben-Dor, Gabriel. "Corruption, Institutionalization, and Political Development: the Revisionist Theses Revisited." *Comparative Political Studies* 7:1 (1974): 63–83.

Bernstein, Thomas, and Lu Xiaobo. *Taxation without Representation in Rural China.* London: Cambridge University Press, 2003.

Bhagwati, Jadish N., ed. *Illegal Transactions in International Trade.* New York: North-Holland–American Elsevier, 1974.

Bian Yanjie. "Guanxi and the Allocation of Jobs in China," *China Quarterly,* 140 (Dec. 1994): 971–99.

Blasi, Joseph R., Maya Kroumova, and Douglas Kruse. *Kremlin Capitalism: Privatizing the Russian Economy.* Ithaca: Cornell University Press, 1997.

Brada, Josef C. "The Transformation from Communism to Capitalism: How Far? How Fast?" *Post-Soviet Affairs* 9:2 (April–June 1993): 87–110.

Brus, Wlodzimierz. "Marketization and Democratization: The Sino-Soviet Divergence." *Cambridge Journal of Economics* 17 (1993): 433–44.

Buchanan, James M., R. D. Tollison, and G. Tullock, eds. *Toward a Theory of the Rent-Seeking Society.* College Station: Texas A & M University Press, 1981.

Chen Feng. "Subsistence Crisis, Managerial Corruption and Labor Protests in China." *China Journal* (July 2000), 41–63.

Chen Kang, Gary H. Jefferson, and Inderjit Singh. "Lessons from China's Economic Reform." *Journal of Comparative Economics* 16 (1992): 201–25.

Chibber, Pradeep, and Samuel Eldersveld. "Local Elites and Popular Support for Economic Reform in China and India." *Comparative Political Studies* 33:3 (April 2000): 350–73.

Cohen, Ariel. "Crime without Punishment." *Journal of Democracy,* 6:2 (April 1995): 34–45.

Commission on Security and Cooperation in Europe. *Briefing on Crime and Corruption in Russia.* Washington, D.C.: The Commission, 1994.

CSIS Task Force Report. *Russian Organized Crime and Corruption: Putin's Challenge.* Washington D.C.: Center for Strategic Studies, 2000.

deLeon, Peter. *Thinking about Political Corruption.* Armonk, N.Y.: M. E. Sharpe, 1993.

Ding Xueliang. "Who Gets What, How? When Chinese State-Owned Enterprises Become Shareholding Companies." *Problems of Post-Communism* 46:3 (May–June 1999): 32–41.

———. "The Illicit Asset Stripping of Chinese State Firms." *China Journal* 43 (January 2000): 1–28.

———. "Informal Privatization through Internationalization: The Rise of Nomenklature Capitalism in China's Offshore Business." *British Journal of Political Science* 30 (Part 1) (January 2000): 121–46.

———. "Systemic Irregularity and Spontaneous Property Transformation in the Chinese Financial System." *China Quarterly* 163 (September 2000), 655–76.

Ericson, Richard E. "The Classical Soviet-type Economy: Nature of the System and Implications for Reform." *Journal of Economic Perspectives* 5:4 (Fall 1991).

Evans, Peter. *Embedded Autonomy: State and Industrial Transformation.* Princeton, N.J.: Princeton University Press, 1995.

Evans, Peter, Dietrich Rueschemeyer, and Theda Skocpol, eds. *Bringing the State Back In.* New York: Cambridge University Press, 1985.

Fewsmith, Joseph. *China since Tiananmen.* New York: Cambridge University Press, 2001.

Frydman, Roman, Cheryle W. Gray, and Andrzej Rapaczynski, eds. *Corporate Governance in Central Europe and Russia,* vols. 1 and 2. Budapest: Central European University Press, 1996.

Gill, Graeme. "Sources of Political Reform in the Soviet Union." *Studies in Comparative Communism* 24:3 (September 1991): 235–57.

Gold, Thomas. "After Comradeship: Personal Relations in China since the Cultural Revolution." *China Quarterly* 104 (December 1985): 657–75.

Goldman, Marshall. "The Chinese Model of Reform: The Solution to Soviet Economic Ills?" *Current History* 92:576 (March 1993): 320–24.

Goldstein, Steven. "China in Transition: The Political Foundations of Incremental Reform." *China Quarterly* 144 (December 1995): 1105–31.

Gomulka, Stanislaw, Yong-Chool Ha, and Cae-One Kim. *Economic Reform in the Socialist World.* London: Macmillan, 1989.

Gong Ting. *The Politics of Corruption in Contemporary China: An Analysis of Policy Outcomes.* New York: Praeger, 1994.

———. "Jumping into the Sea: Cadre Entrepreneurs in China." *Problems of Post-Communism* (July–August 1996): 26–33.

——. "Forms and Characteristics of Corruption in the 1990s: Change with Continuity." *Communist and Post-Communist Studies* 30:3 (1997): 277–88.

——. "Dangerous Collusion: Corruption as Collective Venture in Contemporary China." *Communist and Post-Communist Studies* 35:1 (2002): 85–105.

Gregory, Paul. *Restructuring the Soviet Bureaucracy.* London: Cambridge University Press, 1990.

Grindle, Merilee. *Challenging the State: Crisis and Innovation in Latin America and Africa.* London: Cambridge University Press, 1996.

Guthrie, Douglas. "The Declining Importance of Guanxi in China's Economic Transition." *China Quarterly* 154 (June 1998): 254–82.

Heidenheimer, A. J., and Michael Johnston. *Political Corruption: Concepts and Contexts.* 3d ed. New Brunswick, N.J.: Transaction Publishers, 2002.

Heidenheimer, A. J., M. Johnston, and V. Le Vine. *Political Corruption: A Handbook.* New Brunswick, N.J.: Transaction Publishers, 1989.

Hellman, Joel. "Winners Take All: The Politics of Partial Reform in Post-Communist Transitions." *World Politics* 50 (January 1998): 203–34.

Hodder-Williams, Richard. *An Introduction to the Politics of Tropical Africa.* London: Allen & Unwin, 1985.

Huang Yasheng. "Managing Chinese Bureaucrats: An Industrial Organization Perspective." *Political Studies* 50:1 (March 2002): 61–79.

Huntington, Samuel. *Political Order in Changing Societies.* Yale University, 1967.

——. "Modernization and Corruption." In A. J. Heidenheimer, ed., *Political Corruption: Readings in Comparative Analysis.* New York: Holt, Rinehart and Winston, 1970: 479–86.

Hutchcroft, Paul. "The Politics of Privilege: Assessing the Impact of Rents, Corruption, and Clientelism on Third World Development." *Political Studies* 45 (1997): 639–58.

——. *Booty Capitalism: the Politics of Banking in the Philippines.* Ithaca: Cornell University Press, 1998.

Johnston, Michael. "The Search for Definitions: The Vitality of Politics and the Issue of Corruption." *International Social Science Journal* 149 (Summer 1996): 321–35.

Johnston, Michael, and Yufan Hao. "China's Surge of Corruption." *Journal of Democracy* 6:4 (October 1995): 80–94.

Kaufmann, Daniel. "Diminishing Returns to Administrative Controls and the Emergence of the Unofficial Economy: A Framework of Analysis and Applications to Ukraine." *Economic Policy* 19 (supplement, December 1994): 52–69.

——. "Corruption: the Facts." *Foreign Policy* 107 (Summer 1997): 114–31.

Kennedy, Scott. "Comrade's Dilemma: Corruption and Growth in Transitional Economies." *Problems of Post-Communism* 44:2 (March–April 1997): 28–36.

Khan, Mushtaq H., and K. S. Jomo, eds. *Rents, Rent-Seeking, and Economic Development: Theory and Evidence from Asia.* London: Cambridge University Press, 2000.

——. "Patron-Client Networks and the Economic Effects of Corruption in Asia." In Heidenheimer and Johnston, eds., *Political Corruption: Concept and Context.* New Brunswick, N.J.: Transaction Publishers, 2002: 467–88.

Klitgaard, Robert. *Controlling Corruption.* Berkeley: University of California Press, 1988.

Knight, Peter T. *Economic Reform in Socialist Countries.* Washington, D.C.: The World Bank, 1983.

Krueger, Anne. "The Political Economy of a Rent Seeking Society." *American Economic Review* 64 (1974): 291–303.

Kwong, Julia. *The Political Economy of Corruption in China.* Armonk, N.Y.: M. E. Sharpe, 1997.

Lampton, David, ed. *Policy Implementation in Post-Mao China.* Berkeley: University of California Press, 1987.

Lane, David, and Cameron Ross. "Limitations of Party Control: the Government Bureaucracy in the USSR." *Communist and Post-Communist Studies* 27:1 (1994): 19–38.

LaPalombara, Joseph. "Structural and Institutional Aspects of Corruption." *Social Research* 61:2 (1994): 328.

Leff, N. H. "Economic Development through Bureaucratic Corruption." *The American Behavioral Scientist* 8:3 (1964): 8–14.

Levi, M. *Of Rule and Revenue.* Berkeley: University of California Press, 1988.

Linz, Juan, and Alfred Stepan. *Problems of Democratic Transition and Consolidation.* Baltimore: The Johns Hopkins University Press, 1996.

Liu, Alan. "The Politics of Corruption in the People's Republic of China." *American Political Science Review* 77:2 (1983): 602–21.

Lu Xiaobo. "From Rank-Seeking to Rent-Seeking: Changing Administrative Ethos and Corruption in Reform China." *Crime, Law, and Social Change* 32:4 (1999): 347–70.

———. "Booty Socialism, Bureau-preneurs, and the State in Transition: Organizational Corruption in China." *Comparative Politics* 32:3 (2000): 273–94.

———. *Cadre and Corruption: The Organizational Involution of the Chinese Communist Party.* Stanford, Calif.: Stanford University Press, 2000.

MacIntyre, Andrew, ed. *Business and Government in Industrializing Asia.* St. Leonards, Australia: Allen and Unwin, 1994.

Manion, Melanie. "Corruption by Design: Bribery in Chinese Enterprise Licensing." *Journal of Law, Economics, and Organization* 12:1 (April 1996): 167–95.

Mauro, Paolo. "Corruption and Growth." *Quarterly Journal of Economics* 109 (August 1995): 681–712.

McFaul, Michael. "State Power, Institutional Change, and the Politics of Privatization in Russia." *World Politics* 47:2 (January 1995): 210–43.

———. "The Allocation of Property Rights in Russia." *Communist and Post-Communist Studies* 29:3 (1996): 287–308.

Miller, William L., Abe Grodeland, and Tatyana Koshechkina, eds. *A Culture of Corruption: Coping with Governance in Post-Communist Europe.* Budapest: Central Europe Press, 2001.

Montinola, Gabriella, Q. Yinqyi, and B. Weingast. "Federalism Chinese Style: The Political Basis for Economic Success in China." *World Politics* 48:1 (1995): 50–81.

Murphy, Kevin, Andrei Shleifer, and Robert Vishny. "The Transition to a Market Economy: The Pitfalls of Partial Reform." *Quarterly Journal of Economics* 107 (August 1992): 889–906.

———. "Why Is Rent-Seeking So Costly to Growth?" *American Economic Review* 83:2 (May 1993): 409–14.

Myrdal, Gunnar. "Corruption: Its Causes and Effects." In Gunnar Myrdal, *Asian Drama: An Inquiry into the Poverty of Nations,* vol. 2. New York: Twentieth Century Fund, 1968: 937–58.

Nas, Tevfik F., Albert C. Price, and Charles T. Weber. "A Policy-Oriented Theory of Corruption." *American Political Science Review* 80:1 (March 1986): 107–19.

Naughton, Barry. *Growing out of the Plan: Chinese Economic Reform, 1978–1993.* London: Cambridge University Press, 1996.

Nolan, Peter. *State and Market in the Chinese Economy: Essays on Controversial Issues.* London: Macmillan, 1992.

——. *China's Rise, Russia's Fall.* New York: St. Martin's Press, 1995.

North, Douglas. *Structure and Change in Economic History.* New York: W. W. Norton, 1981.

——. *Institutions, International Change, and Economic Performance.* London: Cambridge University Press, 1990.

Nye, Joseph S. "Corruption and Political Development: A Cost-Benefit Analysis." *American Political Science Review* 61 (1967): 417–27.

O'Brien, Kevin. "Implementing Political Reform in China's Villages." *Australian Journal of Chinese Affairs* 32 (July 1994): 33–59

Oi, Jean C. *State and Peasant in Contemporary China.* Berkeley: University of California Press, 1989.

——. "Fiscal Reform and the Economic Foundations of Local State Corporatism in China." *World Politics* 45:10 (1992): 99–126

——. "The Role of Local State in China's Transitional Economy." *China Quarterly* 144 (1995): 1132–49.

Ostergaard, Clemens S., and Christina Petersen. "Official Profiteering and the Tiananmen Square Demonstrations in China." *Corruption and Reform* 6 (1991): 81–107.

Pearson, Margaret. *Joint Ventures in the People's Republic of China.* Berkeley: University of California Press, 1989.

——. *China's New Business Elite: The Political Consequences of Economic Reform.* Berkeley: University of California Press, 1997.

Poznanski, Kazimierz. "Political Economy of Privatization in Eastern Europe." In Beverly Crawford, ed., *Markets, States, and Democracy.* Boulder, Colo.: Westview, 1995: 204–26.

Prybyla, Jan. *Reform in China and Other Socialist Economies.* Washington, D.C.: AEI Press, 1990.

——. "The Road from Socialism: Why, Where, What, and How." *Problems of Communism* 40:1–2 (January–April 1991): 1–17.

Przworski, Adam. *Democracy and Market: Political and Economic Reformers in Eastern Europe and Latin America.* New York: Cambridge University Press, 1991.

Putnam, Robert, with Robert Leonardi and Raffaella Y. Nanetti. *Making Democracy Work: Civic Traditions in Modern Italy.* Princeton, N.J.: Princeton University Press, 1993.

Putterman, Louis. "On the Past and Future of China's Township and Village-Owned Enterprises." *World Development* 25:10 (1997): 1639–55.

Rapaczynski, Andrzej. "The Roles of the State and the Market in Establishing Property Rights." *Journal of Economic Perspectives* 10:2 (1996): 87–103.

Riding, A. *Mexico: Inside the Volcano.* London: I. B. Tauris, 1987.

Roberts, Cynthia, and Thomas Sherlock. "Bringing the State Back In—Explanations of the Derailed Transition to Democracy." *Comparative Politics* 31:4 (July 1999): 477–97.

Roeder, Philip G. *Red Sunset: The Failure of Soviet Politics.* Princeton, N.J.: Princeton University Press, 1993.

Rose-Ackerman, Susan. *Corruption: A Study in Political Economy.* New York: Academic Press, 1978.

———. "The Political Economy of Corruption." In Kimberly Elliot, *Corruption and the Global Economy.* Washington, D.C.: Institute of Economic Studies, 1997: 31–60

———. *Government and Corruption: Causes, Consequences, and Reform.* New York: Cambridge University Press, 1999.

Rowley, Charles K., Robert D. Tollison, and Gordon Tullock, eds. *The Political Economy of Rent Seeking.* Boston: Kluwer Academic, 1988.

Rutland, Peter. "Has Democracy Failed Russia?" *National Interest* (Winter 1994–95): 3–12.

Sands, Barbara N. "Decentralizing an Economy: The Role of Bureaucratic Corruption in China's Economic Reforms." *Public Choice* 65 (1990): 85–91.

Sargeson, Sally, and Zhang Jian. "Reassessing the Role of the Local State: A Case Study of Local Government Intervention in Property Rights Reform in a Hangzhou District." *China Journal* 42 (July 1999): 77–99.

Scott, James. "An Essay on the Political Functions of Corruption." *Asian Studies* 5 (1967): 501–23.

Sergeyev, Victor. *The Wild East: Crime and Lawlessness in Post-Communist Russia.* Armonk, N.Y.: M. E. Sharpe, 1998.

Shleifer, Andrei, and Robert W. Vishny. "Corruption." *Quarterly Journal of Economics* 108:3 (August 1993) 599–617.

Siu, Helen. *Agents and Victims in South China: Accomplices in Rural Revolution.* New Haven: Yale University Press, 1989.

Solnick, Steven. "The Breakdown of Hierarchies in the Soviet Union and China." *World Politics* 48:2 (January 1996): 209–38.

Stark, David. "Recombinant Property in East European Capitalism." *American Journal of Sociology* 101:4 (January 1996): 993–1027.

Stavraski, Peter. *State Building in Post-Soviet Russia: The Chicago Boys and the Decline of Administrative Capacity.* Washington, D.C.: Kennan Institute, 1993.

Stinchcombe, Arthur L. *Constructing Social Theories.* New York: Harcourt, Brace, 1968.

Sun Yan. "The Chinese Protests of 1989: The Issue of Corruption." *Asian Survey* 3:8 (1991): 762–82.

———. "Reform, State, and Post-Communist Corruption: Is Corruption Less Destructive in China than in Russia?" *Comparative Politics* 32:1 (October 1999): 1–20.

———. "The Politics of Conceptualizing Corruption in Reform China." *Crime, Law, and Social Change* 35:1 (April 2001): 245–70.

Theobald, Robin. *Corruption, Development, and Underdevelopment.* Durham, N.C.: Duke University Press, 1990.

Tollison, Robert D. "Rent Seeking: A Survey." *KYKLOS* 35 (1982): 575–602.

Tsai, Kellee. *Back-Alley Banking: Private Entrepreneurs in China.* Ithaca: Cornell University Press, 2002.

Unger, Jon. *The Rural Transformation of China.* Armonk, N.Y.: M. E. Sharpe, 2002.

Varese, Federico. "The Transition to the Market and Corruption in Post-socialist Russia." *Political Studies* 45 (1997): 579–96.

Wade, Robert. *Governing the Market.* Princeton, N.J.: Princeton University Press, 1990.

Walder, Andrew G. *Communist Neo-Traditionalism: Work and Authority in Chinese Industry.* Berkeley: University of California Press, 1986.

Wang Shaoguang. "From Revolution to Involution: State Capacity, Local Power, and (Un)governability in China." Unpublished manuscript, 1991.

Wang Shaoguang and Hu Angang. *Report on the State of the Nation: Strengthening the Leading Role of the Central Government during the Transition to the Market Economy.* New Haven: Yale University Press, 1993.

Ward, Peter. ed. *Corruption, Development and Inequality.* London: Routledge, 1989.

Waterbury, John. "Endemic and Planned Corruption in a Monarchial Regime." *World Politics* 25 (July 1973): 533–55.

———. "Corruption, Political Stability, and Development: Comparative Evidence from Egypt and Morocco." *Government and Opposition* 11 (Autumn 1976): 426–45.

Wedeman, Andrew. "Looters, Rent-Scrappers, and Dividend-Collectors: Corruption and Growth in Zaire, South Korea, and the Philippines." *Journal of Developing Areas* 31:4 (Summer 1997): 457–78.

———. "Stealing from the Farmers: Institutional Corruption and the 1992 IOU crisis." *China Quarterly* 152 (December 1997): 81–109.

———. "Budgets, Extra-Budgets and Small Treasuries." *Journal of Contemporary China* 9:25 (November 2000): 489–512.

Weder, Beatrice. *Model, Myth, or Miracle: Reassessing the Role of Governments in the East Asian Experience.* New York: United Nations University Press, 1999.

Weichhardt, Reiner, ed. *Soviet Economic Reform: Implementation under Way?* Brussels: NATO Colloquium, 1989.

Whiting, Susan. "The Regional Evolution of Ownership Forms: Shareholding Cooperatives and Rural Industries in Shanghai and Wenzhou." In Jean Oi and Andrew Walder eds., *Property Rights and Economic Reform in China.* Stanford, Calif.: Stanford University Press, 1999: 171–202.

———. *Power and Wealth in Rural China.* London: Cambridge University Press, 2001.

Whyte, Martin King, and William Parish. *Urban Life in Contemporary China.* Chicago: University of Chicago Press, 1984.

Yang, Mayfair Mei-Hui. "The Gift Economy and State Power in China." *Comparative Studies in Society and History* 31:1 (1989): 25–54.

———. *Gifts, Favors, and Banquets: The Art of Social Relationships in China.* Ithaca: Cornell University Press, 1994.

———. "The Resilience of Guanxi and its New Developments: A Critique of Some New Guanxi Scholarships," *China Quarterly,* 170 (June 2002): 459–76.

Young, Christopher. "The Strategy of Political Liberalization: A Comparative View of Gorbachev's Reforms." *World Politics* 45:1 (October 1992): 47–65.

INDEX

absolute power thesis, 10

accounting reviews, 185, 190, 208–9

accounting violations (*weifan caijing jilu*), 27, 32, 35, 96–99; extraction of funds from public, 97, 111; first reform period, 40, 96–97; second reform period, 40, 97

administrative approval system, reform of (*xingzheng shenpi zhi*), 184–85

administrative intervention, 82, 113

administrative joints, 194–95

Agricultural Bank of China, 91

allocation: of regulated services, 43, 55–56, 60, 96, 195, 198, 202; of rents, 14–15

An'hui Province, 163, 165

anticorruption offensives, 37, 68, 72, 131, 134, 188

antipoverty funds, 61, 75, 141–45

Antismuggling Offices, 136, 138

Bank of China, 84

banks, 44, 61–62, 78, 91; access to funds, 88, 90–91, 98; negligence, 109–10. *See also* Loans

Beijing, 84, 116, 126, 204; top-down interactive model, 129–31. *See also* Chen Xiaotong; Chen Xitong; Wang Baosheng

Bernstein, Thomas, 122

big-bang approach, 4, 198–99

bilateral monopoly, 194, 199

black money, 28, *36*

booty capitalism, 14, 16, 200

bottom-up model, 24, 124–26, 153–54, 156; smuggling, 131, 136

bribe taking (*shouhui*), 2, 12, 19, 28–29, 33, *43*, 48, 60, *89,* 116, 194; citizen tips, 38, 74; collective, 81–82; difficulty in detecting, 38, 81–82; family and, 58, 79; fear of exposure, 72–73; incentives, 54, 56–57, 84–85, 197; land-related, 82–83; loan-related, 82, 84; public offices and, 67–68; purchase agents and, 56–57, 73; quality improvement and, 57–58; reform periods, 41, 53–54; speed money, 12, 59, 72, 201; trends, 38, *39;* TVEs and, 57–58, 75–78; uncertain outcomes, 73–74; unsolicited, 125–26, 139. *See also* Transaction types of corruption

bureaucratic capitalism, 7, 16, 200

Business International index, 12–13

business networks, 17–18, 71–72

Cadre and Corruption (Lu), 9

cadre recruitment system, 163–68, 185; economics in command, 165, 169; medium-level cadres, 167–68; promotion while engaging in corruption, 166–67; traditional methods, 163–64. *See also* Rank (*ji*) system

capital flight, 12, 15, 35, 115. *See also* Overseas flight

capitalism, 7, 16, 176, 200

Capital Steel Company, 129, 155, 204

casebooks, 20–23, 217–18; categories of corruption, 26–27

cell phones, 66, 103–4

Central European economies, 6, 210–11

Central Inspection Team (*zhongyang xunshi zhu*), 185, 188–90